D0229766 2/03

Organization of Multimedia Resources

Organization of Multimedia Resources

Principles and Practice of Information Retrieval

Mary A. Burke

© Mary A. Burke 1999

All rights reserved. No part of this publication may be reproduced, stored in a retrieval system, or transmitted in any form or by any means, electronic, mechanical, photocopying, recording or otherwise without the permission of the publisher.

Published by
Gower Publishing Limited
Gower House
Croft Road
Aldershot
Hampshire GU11 3HR
England

Gower
Old Post Road
Brookfield
Vermont 05036
USA

Mary A. Burke has asserted her right under the Copyright, Designs and Patents Act 1988 to be identified as the author of this work.

British Library Cataloguing in Publication Data
Burke, Mary
   Organization of multimedia information
   1. Collection management (Libraries)
   I. Title
   025.2'1

ISBN 0 566 08171 7

Library of Congress Cataloging-in-Publication Data
Burke, Mary A., 1949–
   Organization of multimedia resources : principles and practice of information retrieval / Mary A. Burke.
      p.   cm
   ISBN 0 566-08171-7 (hardback)
   1. Information retrieval. 2. Interactive multimedia. 3. Nonbook materials.
4. Digital libraries.   I. Title.
   Z695.9 .B93 1999
   025.5'24—dc21

                                                                98–36866
                                                                CIP

Typeset in 11/12 Times by Wearset, Boldon, Tyne and Wear and printed in Great Britain by M.P.G. Ltd, Bodmin.

Contents

List of figures

List of tables

Acknowledgements

This book is the culmination of contributions and support from a large number of people and organizations, both personal and professional.

It certainly would not exist without the willingness of the representatives of numerous information agencies who gave generously of their time to discuss their retrieval systems frankly with me. I would like to express my particular gratitude to those who agreed to have samples of their data or systems included; these are acknowledged individually as they occur.

Three key people who encouraged me at significant points in my career deserve special recognition: Barry Mahon, Michael Lynch and John Dean. Several loyal friends helped in various practical ways, including Jessica Bates, Noreen Hayes, Emma Keogh and Ann O'Brien.

Colleagues and students in the Department of Library and Information Studies, University College Dublin have enriched my exploration of the topic of organization of information over the last twenty-one years. I hope this book provides the key to the door for a wider readership.

This publication is dedicated with love and thanks to my mother, Mary Theresa, who always put 'the book' ahead of her own interests with characteristic unselfishness. As a superb spiritual and academic role model, who also showed me how to be a patient and perserverant teacher, she provided the encouragement and inspiration which made it all possible.

M.A.B.

Abbreviations

AACR2	Anglo-American Cataloguing Rules
AAT	*Getty Art & Architecture Thesaurus*
ALA	American Library Association
ANSCR	Alpha-Numeric System for Classification of Recordings
ANSI	American National Standards Institute
A-REV	*Advanced Revelation*
ASCII	American Standard Code for Information Interchange: a standard digital data system for representing alphanumeric characters; also known as 'plain text'
ASLIB	Association of Special Libraries and Information Bureaux
BC	Bliss Bibliographic Classification
BCM	British Classification of Music
BLOB	Binary Large Object
BSI	British Standards Institution
BT	Broader Term (in a thesaurus)
CD	Compact Disk: a laserdisk which can carry digital audio and visual information
CD-I	Compact Disk-Interactive: a type of CD-ROM which stores analogue data
CD-ROM	Compact Disk Read-Only Memory: a CD specifically designed for use with a computer
CD-TV	Commodore Dynamic Total Vision
CHIN	Canadian Heritage Information Network
CIDOC	Comité International pour la Documentation du Conseil International des Musées/International Committee for Documentation of the International Council of Museums
CMN	Common-Practice Music Notation
CPU	Central Processing Unit
DAT	Digital Audio Tape

DBMS	Database Management System
DPI	Dots Per Inch: a measure of the resolution of a computer-produced image
DVI	Digital Video Interactive
ERIC	Educational Resources Information Center (USA)
FID	Fédération Internationale de Documentation/International Federation for Information and Documentation
GMD	General Material Designations
HARMONICA	Harmonised Access and Retrieval for Music-Oriented Networked Information – Concerted Action
HTML	Hypertext Mark-up Language
IAFA	Internet Anonymous FTP Archives
IEE	Institute of Electrical Engineers (UK)
IETF	Internet Engineering Task Force
IFLA	International Federation of Library Associations
INSPEC	Information Service in Physics, Electrotechnology, Computers and Control
ISBD	International Standard for Bibliographic Description
ISBD (G)	International Standard for Bibliographic Description (General)
ISBD (NBM)	International Standard for Bibliographic Description (Non-Book Materials)
ISBD (PM)	International Standard for Bibliographic Description (Printed Music)
ISDN	Integrated Services Digital Network
ISO	International Organization for Standardization
KWAC	Key Word And Context
KWIC	Key Word In Context
KWOC	Key Word Out of Context
LAN	Local Area Network
LC	Library of Congress
LCSH	Library of Congress Subject Headings
LP	Long Play: a 12 inch vinyl record carrying an audio programme of 30 minutes or more
MARC	Machine-Readable Cataloguing
Mb	Megabyte
MDA	Museum Documentation Association (UK)
MeSH	*Medical Subject Headings*
MIDI	Musical Instrument Digital Interface
MLA	Music Library Association (USA)
MPC	Multimedia Personal Computer
MPEG	Motion Picture Expert Group: a compression standard for moving images
MRL	Music Representation Language

NLM	National Library of Medicine (USA)
NSA	National Sound Archive, British Library
NT	Narrower Term (in a thesaurus)
OCLC	Online Computer Library Center (USA)
OPAC	Online Public Access Catalogue
PMEST	Personality, Matter, Energy, Space and Time: Ranganathan's (1963) system of information facets for documentation
PURL	Persistent Uniform Resource Locator
QBIC	Query By Image Content
RAM	Random-Access Memory
RAMEAU	Répertoire d'Autorité Matière Encyclopédique et Alphabétique Unifié: French equivalent to LCSH
RLIN	Research Library Information Network (USA)
RT	Related Term (in a thesaurus)
SMDL	Standard Music Description Language
SOAP	Seal Of Approval
SQL	Standard Query Language
SVGA	Super Video Graphic Adapter: a computer graphic card or monitor capable of relatively high resolution
TEI	Text Encoding Initiative
TGM I	*Thesaurus for Graphic Materials I: Subject Terms* (Library of Congress, 1995)
TGM II	*Thesaurus for Graphic Materials II: Genre and Physical Characteristic Terms* (Library of Congress, 1995)
TGN	Getty Thesaurus of Geographic Names
UBCIM	Universal Bibliographic Control International MARC
UDC	Universal Decimal Classification
UF	Used For (in a thesaurus)
UKMARC	UK-specific variant of MARC
ULAN	Union List of Artists' Names
UNIMARC	International standardized variant of MARC
URC	Uniform Resource Characteristic
URI	Uniform Resource Identifier
URL	Uniform Resource Locator
URN	Uniform Resource Name
WORM	Write Once, Read Many: a type of disk used to store large amounts of data

Chapter 1

Introduction

1.1   Aims and scope

In a society where audio and visual stimuli are required to catch people's attention, multimedia plays an important role in many areas of information, education, business and entertainment.

This book examines the problems and challenges these multimedia resources pose for information retrieval, and develops appropriate principles and practical methods for their organization. The ultimate goal is the management of these items in a multimedia system, but in order to do this, it is necessary to investigate the retrieval issues created by the individual media.

The term 'multimedia' has different meanings in different contexts. Traditionally, it has meant the use of more than one medium: for example, a tape/slide programme or a motion picture with sound. The more modern definition used in this book identifies multimedia as:

> the integrated storage, retrieval and display of words, numbers, images and sounds by a computer system.

The component media, which may include text, graphics, animation, speech, music and video, are referred to as 'items' or 'objects'. These items are managed in a multimedia database, where the ability to retrieve an individual item, or groups of items with specific characteristics, is a key function.

The development of mass-storage systems using CD-ROMs, video disks and other multimedia formats has made it possible to input, store and display vast amounts of information, including digitized visual and audio information. The dramatic rate of development of Internet services and access tools has brought a world-wide range of information sources within reach of most computer users. A wide variety of methods may be applied to the organization of, and retrieval from, these collections. These range from the traditional tools of librarianship, such as cataloguing, classification and indexing, to the tools of artificial intelligence, such as pattern recognition and speech analysis. The study of various specialized forms of material is also relevant: for example, the principles of iconography and pictorial comprehension can be applied to most visual material, and those of musicology to other types of audio material.

Some of the issues involved in creating multimedia databases also arise for text. For example, decisions must be made about who is responsible for creating an item, about the identification and description of its subject matter, and about the use of standards to describe its physical characteristics. Additional challenges arise for multimedia items: for example, consistent subject analysis is even more difficult to achieve for the themes of a visual or audio item than for a textual one. It becomes important to recognize the variety of perceptions which different people, including the compilers and the users of an information service, may have of the message conveyed by a particular visual or audio item. In many cases, the multimedia item may be a manifestation of a work which was produced originally in another medium, so that it is necessary to distinguish between the original and the manifestation in a retrieval system.

1.2   Multimedia information

Multimedia systems use computers for the integrated storage, retrieval and display of information in the form of words, numbers, images and sounds. Storage in electronic form is significant because it enables control and access via a computer interface. This definition allows for a system with components on different physical media (e.g. floppy disk and CD-ROM) as well as on a single physical medium. Thus multimedia blends multiple technologies in order to communicate information by presenting text, sound and pictures all from a single source. Full multimedia systems are dependent on digital technology, and this will be the trend in systems of the future. In the interim, it is possible to develop adequate multimedia systems which have some components stored on analogue media such as videotape, analogue video disks or non-digital cassette tape. The definition used here excludes traditional audio-visual presentations (tape/slide programmes, for example) which do not exist in electronic form.

It is useful to examine some contrasting definitions of the term 'multimedia' as used in different contexts:

- Multimedia refers to the delivery of information in intuitive, multi-sensory ways through the integration of hitherto distinct media – text, graphics, computer animation, motion video and sound – in a single presentation under the control of the computer (Raskin, 1990).

- Buckland (1991) considers multimedia to be the combination of text and still images, which can also include sound and moving images. He identifies the irony of using the term 'multimedia' to describe what is essentially a monomedium, where all of the data is stored digitally, and converted into the various media only when retrieved.

- Bailey (1990) defines a multimedia computer system as one that can create, import, integrate, store, retrieve, edit and delete two or more different media in digital form, such as audio, image, full-motion video and text information.

- Chen (1990) emphasizes that multimedia and hypermedia refer to a synthesis of text, data, graphics, animation, optical storage, image processing and sound, which epitomizes technology integration.

- Feldman (1991) identifies multimedia databases as searchable electronic databases – information structures which offer a potentially networked service to users.

- Luther (1992) describes a multimedia computer system as being capable of all the usual presentation types (text, animation, graphics, etc.) plus recorded real audio, full-screen motion video of real scenes, and photographic-quality still images. This definition recognizes that a computer is inherently a digital device, and that multimedia peripherals should be digital. As a result, the ingredients of multimedia as defined by Luther are a computer with all its usual capabilities, recorded digital audio capability, recorded digital video capability, digital still image capability, and interactivity.

- The glossary of Cawkell's (1996) handbook defines multimedia as 'a computer-controlled system embodying at least two of the following media: text, images, pictures, sound, video, motion video, or graphics.'

Analysis of these varied definitions indicates three main causes for the differences in meaning:

- the extent to which the components of multimedia exist in electronic form;

- the extent to which the components are integrated to give monomedia as opposed to multimedia;

- the extent to which multimedia is an interactive system which enables the user to retrieve material selectively, as opposed to a presentation system which guides the user along pre-programmed paths and does not allow for selective retrieval; interactivity means that the users are in control, as what they see and hear are the result of choices they have made.

Table 1.1   *Categorization of multimedia systems*

Components	Integration possible?	Selective retrieval?
Non-electronic:		
Text	No	From surrogates only
Audio	No	From surrogates only
Image	No	From surrogates only
Moving image	No	From surrogates only
Electronic:		
Analogue	Partial	Possible
Digital	Full	Possible
Mixed analogue and digital	Partial	Possible

These variations, and their implications for retrieval, are summarized in Table 1.1. The nature of these components, the extent of their integration into a single medium and the level of interactivity are major issues for the development of multimedia systems. At least four possible levels of computerization result:

1. The items, which may correspond to a variety of physical media (audio, visual and textual) are available in a digitized form which allows them to be stored on computer back-up storage media, transferred to the central processing unit (CPU), and then displayed on a screen, or printed on paper, or heard on a speaker system, as appropriate. It is possible to analyse and manipulate the computerized data for retrieval and display. This is a fully integrated multimedia system.
2. The second level is broadly similar, but some of the items, or some parts of them, may exist in analogue form. The physical devices on which they are recorded and played are controllable by a computer, for example video tape and a video recorder. This is intermediate multimedia technology, and has scope for the creation of sophisticated retrieval facilities if the necessary level of human analysis and description is carried out on the items. Appropriate technological interfaces, such as soundcards, are required to convert data from analogue to digital and vice versa. This is a partially integrated multimedia system.
3. We may have genuine multimedia products which exist as separate, isolated entities. The retrieval system may be based on surrogates which identify the existence of these items, for example an encyclopaedia on CD-ROM, or an educational programme on the handling of medical emergencies in the home, or a collection of sound effects on tape.
4. The items may exist in many different physical forms, none of which are computerized. (We are concerned only with the management of the surrogates which may be computerized.)

Definition 1 is the preferred definition, and the one which will be significant in the future. Definition 2 still has a role to play, as much audio and visual data is only available in analogue form. Definitions 3 and 4 are of peripheral interest only, in that they are not considered to be 'multimedia' for the purposes of this book, but we can learn from how issues such as creatorship, subject description and surrogates are handled for these items.

1.3   Multimedia hardware and software

There are many different configurations of multimedia hardware and software. Hardware includes the computer, mass-storage and other peripheral devices needed to create and use a multimedia product. Software includes the authoring software used to create multimedia, the operating system software which manages the computer system and its connected peripheral devices, and the access software necessary to browse or search the multimedia system.

The continuous evolution in processing speeds, storage capacities and costs for multimedia hardware makes it virtually impossible to define multimedia in terms of current or future technology. Cawkell (1996) describes the useful concept of a Multimedia Personal Computer (MPC) which was developed by the MPC's marketing council as: 'a personal computer which includes a CD-ROM drive, an audio adapter, *Microsoft Windows* with multimedia extensions and speakers or headphones'. The minimum configuration for an MPC level 3 machine for playback of multimedia is as follows:

- 32Mb RAM
- 3Gb hard disk
- 233MHz Pentium processor
- 4 × CD-ROM drive
- 24 bit MIDI soundcard
- SVGA and MPEG video standard support.

The current MPC standards, which are certain to evolve during the lifetime of this book, are available on the Internet.[1]

Mass-storage devices (optical storage media) are essential for multimedia. The most significant digital media are CD-ROM, CD-I and CD-TV. CD-ROM (Compact Disk Read-Only Memory) is the equivalent of an audio CD, which stores many types of digital information in the same way that music is stored on a digital music CD. CD-I (Compact Disk-Interactive) is a compact disk that can store not only text but also video and audio. It differs from CD-ROM only in the way the information is encoded. This publishing platform, which is primarily aimed at the consumer market, defines standards for the information stored on compact disk, as well as the hardware and operating system necessary to access titles. CD-TV stands for Commodore Dynamic Total Vision, a self-contained compact disk player that connects to a television.

1.4   Conceptual approaches to the organization of information

Traditional methods of information retrieval are based on two fundamentally different approaches to the organization of items. The first of these approaches concentrates on arranging the items in a linear sequence. It facilitates browsing, and enables limited retrieval of specific items by the characteristic which has been used to arrange them. Examples include:

- the use of a scheme such as the Dewey Decimal Classification to arrange books on shelves in libraries;
- a listing of entries in a printed directory or index;
- a menu of choices on a computer system.

The second approach recognizes the multi-faceted nature of many items, and does not attempt to pigeonhole them in a linear sequence. The methods which result do not allow for browsing, but facilitate precise retrieval of specific items from a number of different perspectives. The most significant example is the combination of search terms when using a computer database in order to limit retrieval to items which contain all of the specified search terms.

More flexible approaches, such as hypertext, offer a compromise between these methods, and are particularly appropriate to multimedia. Hypertext – non-linear text – provides multiple, connected pathways through a body of information, allowing users to jump easily from one topic to a related one. This allows for retrieval from different perspectives, at the expense of the effort required to create and update the links, and with a danger that users will become lost in the meanderings which result. The concept of publishing hypertext 'books' and 'libraries' requires logical organization of the contents in order to allow varied approaches to the material, and to prevent users becoming disorientated. The associative processes of human memory and Web-based navigation on the Internet, provide rather different examples of hypertext systems.

Hypermedia extends the hypertext approach to a range of media which may be in text, graphics, audio or video form. It combines multimedia and hypertext to facilitate many different ways of retrieving the information. Examples include the many encyclopaedias and other reference works which are now published on CD-ROM.

1.5   Surrogates

A surrogate is a replacement for, or an alternative to, an original item. It contains details of the original item which enable its potential usefulness to be assessed and the item itself to be located. Surrogates also allow for the arrangement of original items by one method (e.g. a linear arrangement) and the surrogates by another (e.g. in a computer database). They facilitate alternative ways of identifying useful items, such as by creator and subject.

Establishing a standard surrogate structure for multimedia information presents difficulties, as although standards may exist for specific media, formats and institutions, there is no single generally recognized standard. Bibliographic agencies such as libraries and abstracting services have been at the forefront of the development of detailed standards for surrogates. While these detailed standards are theoretically desirable, their implementation poses difficulties in a rapidly evolving multimedia environment such as the Internet.

1.6 Subject content

Regardless of the retrieval mechanism which is adopted, there are challenges in identifying and representing the subject content of items.

'Aboutness', which may be defined as the overall subject theme of an item, is normally heavily influenced by the words contained in a text item. These words may be used directly as the basis for information retrieval in a full-text system, or they may subconsciously influence the assignment of descriptive words or phrases by a human indexer. Even so, there are many problems in determining subject content, which are exacerbated by the variety of perspectives which users with different backgrounds will bring to a subject area, and by the influences of different cultural attitudes.

These problems are magnified for visual and audio information, as the degree of control imposed by the relatively standard meaning of words is lost, with no immediate replacement. One difficulty is the variation in interpretation of different items, where background and culture have even more influence than for text. Thus an audio tape of an interview with a released hostage may be seen as being about totally different topics by a sociologist, a psychologist, a historian, a politician, a speech therapist and a linguist. Similarly, a photograph or a painting of a white priest chatting with a group of black children outside a church in rural Africa will have a multitude of different meanings for different viewers – male dominance, Church influence, missionary work, famine, developing countries, church architecture, clothing fashions, etc. – in addition to the more technical concepts which an artist or photographer may identify.

In the two examples above, words and phrases have been assigned in a rather arbitrary fashion, without considering whether they are the most appropriate ones or not. Standardization of subject terms may be necessary in order to allow for accurate retrieval. This can be achieved with the use of subject heading lists or thesauri. Classification schemes such as the Dewey Decimal Classification or the Library of Congress Classification also enable logical arrangement by subject.

1.7   Electronic data structures

If the original items exist in computerized form, the way they are organized in computer storage will effect their retrieval and use. Various alternatives exist for their logical and physical organization in computer storage. These data structures enable the objectives of browsing and specific retrieval described above to be implemented, using the appropriate surrogate structure and subject content analysis.

1.8   The challenge: A broadcast news agency

The theory in this book will be linked directly to a range of multimedia information retrieval systems, and will be applicable at three levels:

1. the organization of the items in their original formats;
2. the creation of a database of surrogates of the items;
3. the creation of a full multimedia database for all or part of the collection.

An active and archival collection of multimedia sources in a broadcast news agency could be considered as a sample collection to which various theories of organization of information will be linked. These are the details of the hypothetical collection:

- It consists of approximately 100 000 items in a variety of different formats, and is growing at a rate of 5000 items per year.
- The items include full-text articles, photographs, drawings, prints, slides, films, videos and sound recordings.
- Some items are mixed media, for example an article accompanied by a photograph, a map and a statistical table, a video sequence with notes, etc.
- There is a requirement for a helpful physical arrangement of the items, and also for the retrieval of specific items.
- The main users are staff of the information service, but journalists and the general public also have access.
- Microcomputers and database management software are widely available within the organization, and there is a budgetary commitment to expenditure on hardware and software.

- Many of the information items are now produced on digital media, which may be stored on, and retrieved by, a computer.
- The gradual development of an integrated multimedia system is an essential objective.
- There is a commercial market for various subsets of the multimedia product, for example a section of the collection dealing with a specific subject, or in a specific medium, or created by a significant individual.

When designing a multimedia database system for this type of collection, one has to answer a number of questions, which are presented below, with references to the chapters in this book where the answers are developed:

- What are the original information items? (See Chapter 2.)
- Which objective is more important: browsing or precise retrieval? (See Chapter 3.)
- Is the arrangement of the original items themselves an issue?
  - If so, how should these be organized? (See Chapter 3.)
- Is it necessary to create surrogates of the items (see Chapter 4)? If so:
  - What type(s) of surrogate, if any, are appropriate?
  - How should the surrogates be organized?
  - How detailed should the surrogates be?
  - What access points should the surrogates have?
- Who is the creator? (See Chapter 4.)
  - Did additional people or groups make additional contributions?
  - What form of the creator's name should be used?
- What are the individual items about? (See Chapter 5.)
  - What words, phrases, codes or labels describe this subject content?
- Do the items exist in hard copy or electronic form, or both? (See Chapter 6.)
- What additional issues and problems arise when dealing with visual and audio information? (See Chapters 7 and 8.)
- How are the information items, the users and the system likely to change in the future? (See Chapter 9.)

1.9 Wider applications of the principles developed

Although a specific application of multimedia storage and retrieval has been selected as an example above, the principles and practice developed in this book have far wider relevance. The range of applications, which is covered thoroughly by many other sources, such as Cawkell (1996), includes the following:

- archival storage in a business environment;
- audio-visual collection (photographs, slides, audio and video tapes);
- authoring a multimedia publication;

- computer data files;
- display of goods at a sales point;
- language laboratory resources;
- market researchers' work files;
- membership files of an organization;
- music or general audio collections (LPs, singles, cassette tapes, CDs);
- newspaper archives/libraries;
- students' lecture notes and background reading;
- television or film companies' video archives;
- books and other resources in libraries;
- education;
- electronic publishing, mail and video-conferencing;
- museums and art galleries;
- office files.

The last five items will be discussed in more detail below.

1.9.1   Libraries

There are a number of significant developments for multimedia in libraries, including:

- incorporation of multimedia resources with books and other media;
- addition of images to Online Public Access Catalogue (OPAC) records;
- digitization of collections – for example, the American Memory project at Library of Congress aims to make a significant part of its Americana collections available online by the year 2000;
- a paradigm shift from ownership to access, especially in academic libraries;
- electronic journals – for example, the ELINOR project at De Montfort University;
- Internet and networking – for example, remote access to OPACs via the Internet.

1.9.2   Education

Current trends in education in many parts of the world require changing models of academic participation and interaction by students and staff which depend on remote electronic access to lecture content, reference sources and multimedia learning tools. Developments in multimedia educational technology and remote access to resources support the following educational policies:

- greater emphasis on individual learning programmes;
- provision of courses by distance learning;
- commitment to supporting lifelong learning.

1.9.3   Electronic publishing

We are moving rapidly towards a scenario where information is published as multimedia, intended for use in a number of ways:

- personal – locally on an individual's workstation;
- institutional – networked access within an organization or closed group;
- public – as a service accessible over remote networks by the general public.

The electronic media may include reference material on local CD-ROMs, constantly changing numeric and video files on a shared computer, and myriad remote resources.

1.9.4   Museums and art galleries

Museums have requirements to manage collections efficiently and securely, while allowing for their display and use by a varied user population. They also deal with a variety of different physical formats, and have significant preservation and security challenges. Their items are usually unique, or available only in very limited numbers compared with library holdings, so the same potential for shared record-creation does not exist. Thus museum automation in general and museum development of multimedia systems in particular have evolved independently in each institution. Two strong influences have been the Museum Documentation Association in the UK,[2] and Archives & Museum Informatics in the USA.[3]

Automated collection management systems which incorporate digital representations of the museum items are now widespread. In some cases, they may not include digital images; they may consist of surrogates only. An added bonus of digitized representations is that these can form the basis for various electronic user guides and tours. There has also been much international development in registers of works of art in order to prevent theft and to trace stolen items.

Some of the earlier work on applications in galleries and museums is synthesized in specific chapters of the conference proceedings edited by Stone and Buckland (1992). The applications in museums and art galleries fall into the following general categories:

- hypertext tours, which are basically linear, with some scope for branching;

- broad, classified (hierarchical) approaches, corresponding to rooms or areas within the museums or galleries;
- database search facilities for specific artefacts.

It is interesting that most of these approaches are implemented in parallel, and appear to be targeted at different levels of users. For example, the first two approaches are suited to general users who are unfamiliar with the details of the collection; the third is geared to more knowledgeable researchers. David Bearman identifies three significant levels of museum data:

- the repository as a whole;
- any aggregation of items (collections or groups);
- items, including parts and pieces of objects, specimens, records or artefacts.[4]

1.9.5   Office files

Existing general-purpose office retrieval systems are based on the storage and retrieval of textual and numeric information, either as hard copy or computer data files. In specialized applications, still or moving images may be stored: for example, architectural drawings or advertisement clips. In other specialized areas, audio recordings may be important: for example, a sound effects recording company, a college of music, or a radio company.

One can visualize how the storage and retrieval of office records could be transformed by replacing the cumbersome procedures of typing memos, minutes of meetings and procedures with appropriate digital audio-visual representations, supported by sophisticated access and retrieval facilities. Voice-mail systems are the first step in this type of development. The office database would consist of a collection of interlinked multimedia data files. Speech recognition and output would be important features of this system.

1.10   Organization of this book

The organization of this book is determined by the problem-solving approach described above for the sample collection.

Chapter 1 introduces the scope and contents of the book.

Chapters 2, 3 and 4 present the basic principles of information retrieval. Chapter 2 examines multimedia information items and the relationships between them. Chapter 3 deals with conceptual approaches to the organization of information, under the headings of pre-, post- and multi-coordinate retrieval mechanisms, in relation to browsing and the retrieval of specific items. Chapter 4 discusses surrogates, focusing on description, access points and location indicators. Chapter 5 deals with subject content, including subject analysis, representation, codes and standards. The material in these chapters is not specific to multimedia items, but provides an essential basis for handling these items.

Chapter 6 outlines the alternative electronic data structures which are applicable to multimedia items, including sequential and direct-access files, hypertext, database management systems and multimedia authoring systems. This chapter requires some knowledge of relevant areas of computer technology, or a willingness to explore them.

Chapters 7 and 8 identify the specific problems associated with visual and audio information respectively, and make recommendations for their organization and retrieval. These chapters are included because we need to understand the characteristics of these types of information items if they are to be included as components of a multimedia system.

Chapter 9 discusses the likely future development of multimedia information systems.

It is envisaged that some readers will use this book in a sequential fashion, by using the first five chapters to gain a broad-based introduction to information retrieval principles which are applicable in, but not restricted to, a multimedia environment. Others may already have this background, and may be in a position to move directly to the more advanced chapters which deal with electronic data structures and specific types of medium, with occasional references back to the earlier chapters.

Many of the examples used in this book are Web pages, with references to their addresses given as notes or as part of a source statement. While these addresses are accurate just before publication, some may change with time. If a Web address does not work, the best approach is to find the Web page of the parent institution and navigate from there.

1.11   Practical assignments

In Chapters 3–5, readers are encouraged to relate theoretical concepts to real-world examples of information retrieval systems. The range of systems to which the principles may be applied includes:

- the OPAC of a specific library, and the items in the same library – for example, either a library you use, or the Library of Congress, whose OPAC can be accessed with a Web browser at the URL ⟨http://lcweb.loc.gov/catalog/⟩, or with Telnet at ⟨locis.loc.gov⟩;
- the printed telephone directories (name and classified) for your country or region (the classified directory is known as the *Golden Pages* or *Yellow Pages* in many countries);
- Internet resources in general, but in particular a search engine such as AltaVista, at the URL ⟨http://www.altavista.com/⟩;

- Printed bibliographic service, e.g. Library and Information Science Abstracts (LISA);
- Encyclopaedia (printed or CD-ROM);
- Electronic bibliographic service, e.g. database on CD-ROM;
- Manual catalogue of a specific library and items in the same library;
- Catalogue or index to a local studies collection and the collection itself;
- Catalogue/listing of an art/museum/photographic collection exhibition and the items themselves;
- Booksellers' listings/directories and books in a bookshop;
- Stock list for a shop, retailers or manufacturers and the items themselves;
- Office files;
- Articles and items of various types in a specific newspaper;
- Film/CD/video/audio tapes guide/directory and a collection of the items themselves (personal collection or in a shop);
- Language laboratory catalogue and resources (books, tapes, videos, etc.);
- Videotext-based information service, e.g. CEEFAX, ORACLE, MINITEL;
- Organization of computer files in *MS-DOS* or *Windows* or Macintosh format, or in a specific application, e.g. *Microsoft Word*.

Sample answers to the practical assignments for the first three of these systems are presented at the ends of the relevant chapters.

1.12 Notes

[1] Kolterjahn – multimedia – mpc: ⟨http://www.hgs.se/~kp95ckn/mpc.html⟩.
[2] Museum Documentation Association On-line ⟨http://www.open.gov.uk/mdocassn⟩.
[3] Archives & Museum Informatics: ⟨http://www.archimuse.com/⟩.
[4] Bearman, David (1994) 'Towards a reference model':
     ⟨http://www.lis.pitt.edu/~nhprc/prog6-5.html⟩.

1.13 References and further reading

Bailey, Charles W. Jr (1990) 'Intelligent multimedia computer systems: Emerging information resources in the network environment', *Library Hi Tech*, **29** (1), 29–41.

Bordogna, G. et al. (1990a) 'Pictorial indexing for an integrated pictorial and textual IR environment', *Journal of Information Science*, **16**, 165–73.

Bordogna, G. et al. (1990b) 'A system architecture for multimedia information retrieval', *Journal of Information Science*, **16**, 229–38.

Buckland, Michael K. (1991) 'Information retrieval of more than text',
Journal of the American Society for Information Science, **42** (8), 586–8.

Bulick, Stephen (1990) 'Future prospects for network-based multimedia
information retrieval', *The Electronic Library*, **8** (2), 88–99.

Cawkell, A.E. (1996) *The Multimedia Handbook*, London: Routledge.

Chen, Ching-chih (1988) 'Hypermedia information delivery: The
experience of PROJECT EMPEROR-I', *Proceedings of the 12th
International Online Meeting* (6–8 December 1988, London, England),
Oxford: Learned Information, 9–13.

Chen, Ching-chih, Miranda, S. and Seidel, S. (1988) 'The new concept of
HYPERBASE and its experimentation on the "First Emperor of
China" videodisc', *Microcomputers for Information Management*, **5**
(4), 217–46.

Chen, Ching-chih (1990) 'The challenge to library and information professionals in the visual information age', *Microcomputers for Information
Management*, **7** (4), 255–72.

Chen, Ching-chih (1991) 'Analog, digital and multimedia: Implications for
information access', *Online Information '91* (10–12 December 1991,
London, England), 283–91.

Fairhead, Harry (1991) 'Down to Earth', *Computer Shopper*, April, 177–84.

Feldman, Tony (1991) *Multimedia in the 1990s*, BNB Research Fund
Report, **54**, Boston Spa: British Library.

Flanders, Bruce (1992) 'Multimedia programs to reach an MTV generation', *American Libraries*, **23** (2), 135–7.

Gaines, Brian R. and Vickers, Joan N. (1988) 'Design considerations for
hypermedia systems', *Microcomputers for Information Management*, **5**
(1), 1–27.

Halin, Gilles and Harmon, Catherine (1989) 'A hypermedia structure for
an interactive and progressive image retrieval system', *Proceedings of
the 13th International Online Information Meeting* (12–14 December
1989, London, England), Oxford: Learned Information, 477–81.

Luther, Arch C. (1992) *Designing Interactive Multimedia*, New York:
Bantam Books.

Nelson, Theodor Holm (1988) 'Unifying tomorrow's hypermedia', *Proceedings of the 12th International Online Meeting* (6–8 December 1988,
London, England), Oxford: Learned Information, 1–7.

Pring, Isobel (1990) 'Can DVI and CDI both become successful?', *Information World Review*, September, 20–1.

Raskin, Robin (1990) 'Multimedia: The next frontier for business?', *PC
Magazine*, July, 151–92.

Stone, Susan and Buckland, Michael (eds) (1992) *Solutions in Multimedia:
State-of-the-art Solutions in Multimedia and Hypertext*, Proceedings of
the 1991 Mid-Year Meeting of the American Society for Information

Science, San Jose, CA, April 1991, Medford, NJ: Learned Information.

Worthington, Bill and Robinson, Brian (1991) *The Medium is not the Message: Mixed Mode Document Technology*, Hatfield: Electronics Research and Development Centre, Hatfield Polytechnic.

Chapter 2

Information items

2.1 Introduction

At first, it may appear that the definition of an information item is self-evident: it is some definite chunk of information which may exist in one or more types of media. But even this definition contains some ambiguity, as it is not clear whether we mean a physical or a logical item. The more philosophical question of whether one is retrieving data, information or knowledge is outside the scope of this book, as is the issue of whether an item is an information item only if its purpose is to convey information: for example, a sample of a piece of rock exists independently of its function as a source of information for archaeologists or geologists.

In theory, every phenomenon in a day-to-day situation may be considered an information resource, even if it is a very transitory circumstance such as a cloud formation or the pattern formed by a colony of ants exiting from an ant-hill. In practice, a phenomenon will only become relevant for inclusion in a retrieval system if it is identified as conveying some information relevant to the purpose of the system. This may involve taking the object from its natural habitat and creating a surrogate which documents its features and purposes, for example by extracting a fossil from the earth and displaying it with descriptive commentary in a museum. (A theoretical discussion of this area is presented in other sources, e.g. Buckland 1991a, 1991b, 1997; Otlet 1990.)

2.2 Logical and physical items

In creating an information retrieval system, our primary concern may be the management of either the physical items or the information contained in these items. This distinction may be illustrated by taking the example of a collection of video tapes which contain recordings of different events. Some events may be spread over more than one video tape. The event corresponds to a logical unit, the tape to a physical unit. From the perspective of an information service, we want to store, retrieve and manipulate discrete units of knowledge which are capable of satisfying specific information needs. From the perspective of a records management or archival system, we are primarily concerned with the storage, retrieval and manipulation of the physical items or objects. Ideally, we should be able to work with both logical and physical items, and to show the relationships between them. So if a particular physical item contains a number of distinct information items, or if a particular information item is spread over a number of physical items, the information retrieval system should reflect these relationships.

2.3   Collection–series–item–part

The structure of the information item may be even more complex: there may be a collection of items with distinct parts, for example a multi-part document or a recording of a concert in which a number of distinct musical items were performed. A sculpture which is composed of a number of individual pieces, or a collection of ancient coins found at a particular site also provide examples of this structure. In some situations, it may be more appropriate to deal at the collection level; at others, item or part level may be more suitable. Archival services place a strong emphasis on the integrity of a collection of papers, and facilitate the perusal of this material in chronological sequence. Libraries deal primarily with the physical item – the book, journal, video tape or computer disk – while showing series links through the catalogue. They may exploit component parts of some materials, for example by providing analytical entries in the catalogue for chapters or sections of works. Abstracting and indexing services, such as Library and Information Science Abstracts, deal with parts of works, as they provide entries for individual articles in journals and papers in conference proceedings, but they generally treat a book as an item, even though it may have many sections. A multimedia database could be defined as a collection, with the individual media items as the parts.

The Internet Web structure provides a complex illustration of collection–series–item–part relationships. One could identify the Web pages about one organization as a collection, a group of related pages on the same topic as an item, and each individual page as a part. Alternatively, one could argue that each individual Web page is an item. The American Memory Collections of the Library of Congress provide a good example of these levels.[1] The collections include historical materials in various formats, including documents, maps, motion pictures, prints, photographs and sound

Table 2.1   *American Memory Collections by library division*

Overall collections

Library divisions	No. of sub-collections
American Folklife Center	1
General Collections	2
Geography & Map Division	1
Hebraic Section of the African and Middle Eastern Division	1
Law Library	1
Manuscript Division	5
Motion Picture, Broadcasting and Recorded Sound Division	3
Music Division	1
Prints and Photographs Division	14
Rare Books and Special Collections Division	6

Divisions and sub-collections

The American Folklife Center, which consists of one sub-collection, is described as: 'a multiformat ethnographic field collection that includes sound recordings, still photos, drawings and written documents from a variety of European ethnic and English and Spanish speaking communities in Northern California'.

The 14 sub-collections in the Prints and Photographs Division range from 'approximately 29 000 photographs of buildings, interiors, and gardens of renowned architects and interior designers' to '880 views of foreign countries and their native forms of transportation by William Henry Jackson'.

Items

Each of these sub-collections consists of a large number of individual items, e.g. the 29 000 or 880 visual images in the two examples above.

Source: American Memory Collections by library division: ⟨http://lcweb2.loc.gov/ammem/amdiv.html⟩.

recordings. These are divided into ten main divisions, as shown in Table 2.1. Each of these divisions consists of one or more smaller collections: for example, the American Folklife Center contains material in a range of formats about California in the 1930s, while the Manuscript Division houses five sub-collections on topics such as 'The Evolution of the Conservation Movement'. Each of these sub-collections consists of many individual items in different formats. The American Memory collections, or any of the divisions, or any of the sub-collections, could be seen as a collection. There are no hard and fast rules regarding the scale of a collection, but one needs to be clear about the levels involved, and how they are to be portrayed in a retrieval system.

2.4   Concept of manifestations of an item

A further level of complexity arises when one considers that an item may be a manifestation of another item: for example, a book may be a revised version of an original by another author; a photograph may be taken by one individual, developed and printed creatively by another, and may manifest an item which was created by another, such as the architect of a bridge. A sculpture may involve input from different people at various stages of the creative process: for instance, the routine work may be done by a junior under the supervision of a renowned sculptor who puts the finishing touches on the object. We may have a sound recording of an item of choral music written by a particular composer, in a particular rendition by a specific orchestra, choir and soloist, as part of a specific festival. It becomes difficult to resolve the question of which item is being handled, from the point of view of description and access points. The problems become exacerbated when one deals with multimedia items which may involve conversion of items from one medium to another – for example, a film or play based on a book.

Many of these problems come down to questions of an original work and a manifestation of this, with four different types of manifestation:

1. facsimile of original item (mechanical reproduction in the same medium);
2. distinct facsimile (facsimile with individual annotations or mistakes);
3. adaptation/interpretation of item in same medium;
4. adaptation/interpretation of item in new medium.

Type 1 corresponds to mass-produced and distributed identical objects, where there is no need to distinguish one copy from another. Type 2 is very similar to a type 1 relationship, with an additional need to distinguish individual copies, perhaps for location and loan purposes, or because they have been annotated or personalized in some way, or because they have suffered damage. Type 3 corresponds to a revision, a new edition or a modification of an original item in the same medium. Type 4 corresponds to a translation, an adaptation of an original work in a different medium. Examples of original and manifested works of each type are presented in Table 2.2. Different aspects of the item will change from the original to the manifestation of each of the four types. The pattern of changes is shown in Table 2.3.

The distinction between each of the four types of manifestation is helpful in indicating the differences which will arise when the manifested items are managed in a retrieval system. In general, for types 1 and 2, the characteristics of the original item are more important than those of the manifestation; as one moves to types 3 and 4, the manifestation becomes more important than the original item.

Conflicting views exist regarding the extent to which we should be concerned with the minor variations between type 2 information items, depending on the relative importance attached to theoretical objectives as opposed to practical realities. On the one hand, one could argue that if there are any substantial differences in the description, the creator or the subject between the two items, separate entries should be made in a

Table 2.2   *Examples of original items and manifestations*

Type of manifestation	Original work	Manifestation
1	Master copy of book, disk, tape, film, photograph	Multiple identical copies of book, disk, tape, film, photograph
2	Master copy of book, disk, tape, film, photograph	Multiple distinguishable copies of book, disk, tape, film, photograph
3	Original book, disk, tape, film, photograph	Revision or translation of book, disk, tape, film, photograph
4	Music score	Execution of musical work
4	Book	Play or film based on book
4	Oil painting	Photograph of painting
4	Photograph of painting	Print of photograph of painting
4	Encyclopaedia	CD-ROM version of encyclopaedia
4	Printed newspaper	Modified version of a newspaper on the Internet

retrieval system; on the other hand, financial and human constraints may result in the items being treated as virtually identical, only one entry being made, with annotations to indicate the variations.

If there are significant differences between any features of the two items – creator or subject, or physical description – then they merit individual treatment. It must be emphasized that this is a highly subjective decision, as differences which are very significant in one context will be irrelevant in another. Also, the scale of operation is likely to affect the amount of attention given to individual items. A photograph of a scene at different times of the year is a good example. The differences may be minor for some users, but could be very significant to a botanist or a detective looking for clues. The attention which can be given to a specialized collection of photographs in a research centre will be considerably greater than for the same collection as part of a general resource in a multi-purpose library or accessible on the Internet. The time available for describing the items, and the speed with which they become obsolete are also significant factors.

These issues have been considered in detail by Weihs (1979) for non-

Table 2.3   *Changes from an original item to its four types of manifestation*

Type	Creator	Subject	Description	Medium
		Changes in:		
1	No	No	No	No
2	No	No	Yes (minor)	No
3	Yes/No	Yes/No	Yes	No
4	Yes/No	Yes/No	Yes	Yes

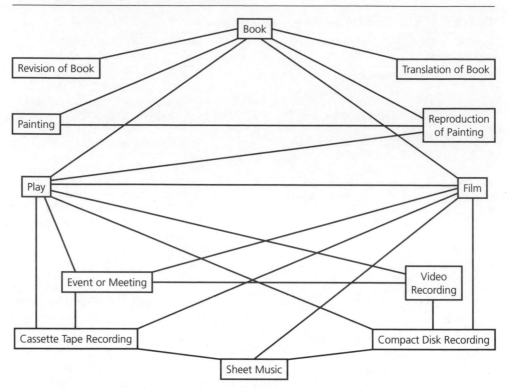

Figure 2.1   Relationships between original items and their manifestations

book materials, by Shatford (1984) for pictures, and by Thomas (1992) for sound recordings. Weihs discusses whether materials composed of more than one part should be catalogued as individual items, or as sets. She recommends that if 'each item in a set [would] have a significantly different class number and subject headings', then each part should be catalogued separately. The findings of Shatford and Thomas will be discussed in Chapters 7 and 8, respectively. The complex network of relationships which can result for multimedia items is shown in Figures 2.1 and 2.2.

2.5   Other types of relationship

More complex relationships than those identified above may exist for multimedia items. These can usually be broken down into a combination of two or more of the relationships already identified, for example:

- a recording of a piece of music, and a film which includes a different version of this as a component of a backing track;

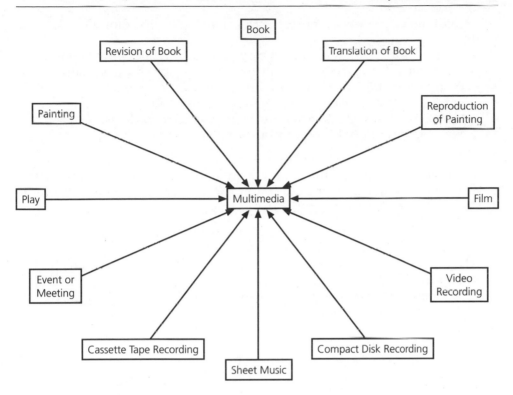

Figure 2.2   **Relationships between original and manifested multimedia items**

- a quotation in a play, and a book which contains this original quotation;
- a printed version of a newspaper, and extracts of that newspaper on the Internet, with video clips added.

These relationships can be analysed into a combination of a whole–part relationship and a manifested item.

2.6   Categorization of multimedia

The range of original items which may be part of a multimedia database includes one or more of the following:

- cartographic materials, such as globes, maps, relief models;
- works of art, such as originals and reproductions of paintings and sculptures;
- educational materials, such as charts, filmstrips, flash cards, pictures,

photographs, postcards, posters, transparencies, kits, dioramas, games, realia;
- technical resources, such as reproductions of architectural renderings, study prints, slides, technical drawings, microscope slides, models;
- moving-image materials, such as films and video recordings;
- computer software, including programs and data files;
- audio resources, such as music and other sound recordings;
- text resources in books, periodicals, newspapers, manuscripts or micro-forms.

It is helpful to categorize these multimedia components according to the criteria which influence their description and retrieval, which are shown in Table 2.4. This is the categorization which results:

- **Audio CDs of ... played by ... one of a series** – Sounds and text / Manifestation / Continuous / Abstract / Content / CD player / Both;
- **Original oil paintings by Matisse** – Image / Original / Discrete / Abstract / Both / None / Both;
- **Electronic text with hypertext software** – Words and software / Original / Concrete / Both / Computer / Both;

Table 2.4   *Criteria for the categorization of multimedia items*

Criterion	Explanation	Chief implications
Channel	Is the information conveyed as words, numbers, images, sounds, computer software, or a combination of more than one of these channels?	Physical description, and format-specific features (see Chapters 7 and 8).
Original/manifestation	Is the item original, or a manifestation of an original?	Responsibility for creatorship, subject analysis and physical description (see Chapters 4 and 5).
Discrete/continuous	Is it a discrete, self-contained image, or one which is continuous and contains a succession of images?	Subject content and physical description of item (see Chapters 4 and 5).
Concrete/abstract subject	Is the subject matter of the item mainly concrete (an image of something) or mainly abstract (does not represent anything)?	Subject content (see Chapter 5).
Medium/content	Is the content of the item of interest, or is it the medium through which it is conveyed that is important?	Conceptual approaches, physical description and subject content (see Chapters 3, 4 and 5).
Equipment	Is special equipment required to access the information (e.g. microform viewer, cassette recorder, film projector, computer, Internet browser)?	Physical description and instructions for use (see Chapter 4).
Generalists/specialists	Do the users of the items have any specialist knowledge of the medium or the content?	Main retrieval mechanism and subject content (see Chapters 3 and 5).

- **Encyclopaedia on CD-ROM** – Words, numbers, images and sounds / Original / Discrete / Concrete / Content / Computer / Generalists;
- **Film documentaries** – Images and sounds / Manifestation / Continuous / Concrete / Content / Projector / Both;
- **Multimedia database** – All / Original / Discrete / Concrete / Content / Computer / Both;
- **Internet information resource** – All / Manifestation / Continuous / Concrete / Content / Internet browser / Both.

2.7   Summary

The concept of an information item is complex and open to many interpretations. The ability to combine various components into an overall multimedia system adds to the complexity. For the broadcast news agency described in Section 1.8, all the concepts of information items, and of relationships between them, exist. The physical items correspond to the video and audio tapes and equivalent formats; the logical items correspond to a programme or show; collection–series–item–part corresponds to a series of programmes, the programme on a specific day, items within that programme, and sections of these items. From a legal perspective, it is often essential to distinguish between various different manifestations of an information item: different takes or versions of a television programme become important, in addition to the final broadcast version.

The concept of an original item and its manifestations broadens to the creation of 'audit trails' to monitor individual contributions. In debates about responsibility for creation of electronic documents, the various manifestations which lead to a final item become significant. The designer of an information retrieval system must balance the desirability, and possible legal necessity, of distinguishing between related items against the implications of greater technical complexity and demands on costs and time which would be needed. The Internet is a minefield of multiple, uncontrolled manifestations of information items which cause considerable frustration for the user.

2.8   Notes

1   American Memory Collections by library division: ⟨http://lcweb2.loc.gov/ammem/amdiv.html⟩.

2.9   References

Buckland, Michael K. (1991a) 'Information as thing', *Journal of the American Society for Information Science*, **42** (5), 351–60.

Buckland, Michael K. (1991b) 'Information retrieval of more than text', *Journal of the American Society for Information Science*, **42** (8), 586–8.

Buckland, Michael K. (1997) 'What is a "document"?', *Journal of the American Society for Information Science*, **48** (9), 804–9.

Otlet, Paul (1990) *International Organisation and Dissemination of Knowledge: Selected Essays of Paul Otlet*, FID **684**, Amsterdam: Elsevier.

Shatford, Sara (1984) 'Describing a picture: A thousand words are seldom cost effective', *Cataloguing and Classification Quarterly*, **4** (4), 13–30.

Thomas, David H. (1992) *Archival Information Processing for Sound Recordings: The Design of a Database for the Rodgers and Hammerstein Archives of Recorded Sound*, Technical Report 21, Canton, MA: Music Library Association.

Weihs, Jean et al. (1979) *Nonbook Materials* (2nd edn), Ottawa, Ontario: Canadian Library Association.

Chapter 3

Conceptual approaches

3.1 Introduction

The intention of this chapter is to give a general appreciation of the issues involved in the organization of information in manual and computerized environments which can then be used as a basis for the discussion of storage and retrieval systems for specific media, including textual, audio, visual and multimedia.

There are three key issues which must be resolved:

1. Which objective is more important: browsing or precise retrieval? The two fundamentally different approaches to the organization of information which were identified in Section 1.4 form the basis of this chapter. More flexible approaches, such as hypertext, are also discussed.
2. What is being organized: information items only, or surrogates only, or both? Having both allows for a greater number of complementary solutions under item 1; this topic is covered briefly in this chapter, with a fuller discussion of surrogates in Chapter 4.
3. What aspects of the items are important: subject, creator, other? This decision will affect the access points by which users can retrieve items. The role of access points is introduced in this chapter, and the more detailed issues of creator and subject access are explored in Chapters 4 and 5 respectively.

Two basic approaches exist for the physical arrangement of information items and their surrogates – *pre-coordinate* and *post-coordinate* – and they facilitate the objectives of browsing and retrieval of specific items respectively. They may be applied both to information items and their surrogates; in the discussion which follows, the emphasis is placed on information items rather than surrogates.

3.2   Pre-coordinate approach

The pre-coordinate approach arranges items in a logical order, on the assumption that there is one preferred sequence which is appropriate for arranging the items or surrogates. There is little or no attempt to cater for users who want to retrieve an item from different perspectives, as these different perspectives are combined – or coordinated – within the retrieval system. For example, complex topics such as 'songs by Elvis Presley dealing with teenage love' or 'reports on the use of computers in universities' would be filed under one primary concept: 'popular music' or 'third-level education'. This concept would be identified as the predominant one, and the item would not be retrievable by the other concepts, such as 'teenagers' or 'computers'. The juxtaposition of items is significant: users should be able to browse and find that adjacent items are related in some way. This process is equivalent to pigeon-holing, with the intention of putting each item in one, and only one, place in the sequence. This may be difficult to implement in practice, where several conflicting sequences may be appropriate for any collection, and an item may belong in more than one place in a sequence. The logical order is linear and mono-dimensional, as exemplified by the arrangement of goods on supermarket shelves, correspondence files in filing cabinets, most catalogue or index card files, library classification schemes and scientific taxonomy.

Printed information sources, because of their linear nature, are usually pre-coordinate. This approach may also be implemented in an electronic environment, for example as a menu of choices presented by a computer system which asks users to make selections on a hierarchical basis. This method is particularly dominant in videotext systems such as CEEFAX, ORACLE and MINITEL. It may also be observed in OPACs, other database systems, gophers and Internet search engines such as Yahoo! and Excite. Pre-coordinate retrieval is particularly appropriate for general users, who may be rather vague about their information needs and who are looking for 'something' on a topic, rather than comprehensive answers to complex questions.

A pre-coordinate arrangement may be applied to both the original items and their surrogates. Different pre-coordinate arrangements may also be used within one collection. For example, entries in a printed directory may be presented in one sequence (alphabetical by title), with additional indexes giving different sequences (author, subject, place). Pre-coordinate arrangements are usually implemented in some linear sequence, for example:

- by name of principal creator;
- by some logical classified approach, such as by subject or by title;
- by date of creation or accession;

- by physical medium, including by size;
- by frequency of use;
- by administrative criteria.

The most widely used arrangement is by subject, as evidenced by applications as diverse as library shelf arrangement and subject hierarchies on computer systems. Examples of the latter, for the AERTEL Irish teletext service[1] and the Yahoo! Internet search engine[2] are presented in Figure 3.1 and Figure 3.2, respectively.

3.3 Post-coordinate approach

A post-coordinate approach does not attempt to place information items in any logical sequence. There is an independent retrieval mechanism which allows for the combination – or coordination – of multiple search terms at the time of retrieval, so that specific items may be identified and their location established. Browsing is not catered for by this approach, unless some complementary retrieval tool is provided. The location of the item is irrelevant, as it is retrieved by linking various descriptive components together. Access points or retrieval keys provide the basis for retrieval. These may be creator, subject, date or other characteristics. The items themselves may be arranged in some order which is convenient from an administrative perspective, but does not claim to be logical for the users. This arrangement may be by date of accession or creation, size, physical format, storage requirements, etc. Post-coordinate retrieval may be applied to both the original items and their surrogates. For example, searching a library OPAC using a combination of search terms retrieves surrogates in the form of entries in the catalogue. Carrying out a similar search on a collection of audio recordings stored in digitized form will retrieve original items.

Examples of this mechanism include punched card systems with a variety of names (peek-a-boo, optical coincidence, feature cards) and database systems which allow for the use of Boolean AND logic. Computers provide a very efficient means of carrying out coordination, as database structures allow concepts to be linked. Post-coordinate systems may be implemented in any of the following ways:

- manual;
- mechanized;
- computerized.

Manual systems are implemented using index cards on which a simple search term is recorded at the top of each card, and the identification numbers of the items which deal with this search term are listed systematically on the card. A complex search involving two or more search terms is

RTÉ ONLINE   *Teletext*

TELEVISION   RADIO   TELETEXT   MUSIC   ABOUT RTE
Programme Index   Email   Contacting Us   RTE Stations   Special Events   Audio and Video   Schedules   Help

RTE'S TELETEXT SERVICE
PRESS TEXT NOW

Phone: (01) 2082284 **Fax:** (01) 2083094 **Email:** aertel@rte.ie

Aertel - RTÉ's Teletext Service

Aertel, RTÉ's teletext service celebrated its tenth birthday last year.

From a humble installed base of 6,000 teletext televisions and an on-air time of 4 hours a day, 5 days a week in 1987, Aertel's growth has been remarkable.

The service is now updated 14 hours a day seven days a week and contains thousands of pages of information.

Aertel is a free service provided by RTÉ. No licence fee money is used to fund the service, in fact Aertel has become so successful that it is completely self financing.

With over half a million teletext television sets now in Ireland, Aertel has become one of the primary sources for up to the minute information on a wide range of topics.

Whether its news or cinema listings, football scores or flight times, they're all on Aertel and available at the press of a button (or the click of a mouse).

Aertel teletext is now available 24 hours a day in many places and, 7 days a week. Aertel has continued to develop its service with a World Wide Web facility and the development of Aertel Interactive.

NEWS	103
Main Headlines	103
FINANCE	130
WEATHER	160
A-Z INDEX	595
LOTTO	150
TV TODAY	170
RTÉ 1	171
N 2	172
T na G (N2)	470
What's On Now	180
RADIO TODAY	184
Radio One	185
2 FM	186
FM 3	187
R na G	482
SPORT	200
Sport Headlines	201
Main Soccer	220
Local Soccer (N2)	540
Main GAA	240
Local GAA (N2)	560
Horse Racing	250
ENTERTAINMENT	300
Cinema	310
Music	320
Sound Check	327/328
Theatre	330
Books	340
TV Extra	350
Radio Extra	380
TRAVEL	500
Aer Lingus	400
Ferries	590/591
Holidays	510
Bus Éireann	520
Airports	570
GAELTEXT (N2)	480
Nuacht	481
FÁS JOBS	680

Figure 3.1   AERTEL teletext system: Pre-coordinate approach
Source: AERTEL page 101: ⟨http://www.rte.ie/aertel/index.html⟩.

 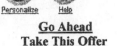

What's New   Check Email   Personalize   Help

Yahoo! Pager   GO DUTCH BID.COM   **Go Ahead**
instant stock alerts   win a $10k trip! Click Here **Take This Offer**

options

Yahoo! Travel - book airline tickets, cruises, hotel rooms, rental cars

Shopping - Yellow Pages - People Search - Maps - Classifieds - Personals - Message Boards - **Chat**
Email - **Pager** - My Yahoo! - Today's News - Sports - Weather - TV - Stock Quotes - **more...**

Arts & Humanities   **News & Media**   **In the News**
Literature, Photography...   Current Events, Newspapers, TV...
                                                               · Tanzania detains
                                                                 bombing suspects
Business & Economy   **Recreation & Sports**
Companies, Finance, Jobs...   Sports, Travel, Autos, Outdoors... · Starr Clinton
                                                                 investigation

Computers & Internet   **Reference**   · Fossett's
Internet, WWW, Software, Games... Libraries, Dictionaries, Quotations... around-the-world attempt

                                                               · July was hottest month
Education   **Regional**   on record
Universities, K-12, College Entrance... Countries, Regions, US States...
                                                                         more...

Entertainment   **Science**   **Inside Yahoo!**
Cool Links, Movies, Humor, Music... Biology, Astronomy, Engineering...
                                                               · Y! Games - chess,
                                                                 backgammon, bridge
Government   **Social Science**
Military, Politics, Law, Taxes... Archaeology, Economics, Languages... · Play free fantasy football

                                                               · Y! Autos - guide to new
Health   **Society & Culture**   and used cars
Medicine, Diseases, Drugs, Fitness... People, Environment, Religion...
                                                               · Yahoo! Store - build an
                                                                 online store in 10
                                                                 minutes
                                                                         more...

World Yahoo!s Asia - Australia & NZ - Canada - Chinese - Denmark - France - Germany
               Italy - Japan - Korea - Norway - Spanish - Sweden - UK & Ireland

Yahoo! Metros LA - NYC - SF Bay - more...   Get Local

Other Guides Autos - Computers - Games - Live Net Events - **Movies** - Personal Finance
              Real Estate - Seniors' - Sports - Travel - Y! Internet Life - Yahooligans! for Kids

Smart Shopping with VISA

How to Suggest a Site - Company Info - Privacy Policy - Contributors - Openings at Yahoo!

Figure 3.2   Yahoo!: Pre-coordinate approach
Source: Yahoo!: ⟨http://www.yahoo.com/⟩.

achieved by comparing the item numbers on two or more cards in order to identify items in common. Mechanized systems are implemented by using punched cards of various shapes and sizes, and coordination devices such as knitting needles or light sources. In practice, in a modern multimedia environment, computerization is the only efficient way of achieving post-coordination. If manual or mechanized methods are of interest, the reader will find further details in standard information retrieval textbooks, such as Kemp (1988), Rowley (1992) and others.

Computerization of the items or their surrogates does not automatically enable post-coordination. The computer software must create indexes to the surrogates based on simple search concepts, and it must enable the searcher to specify the co-occurrence of two or more concepts. This is done using Boolean operators to coordinate the concepts. (The theory underlying Boolean operators will be discussed and illustrated schematically in Chapter 6.) As a prerequisite to these search features, the data must be structured in such a way as to maximize the exploitation of the information in each record. In practice, this means that it is usually of benefit to divide the item or surrogate record into distinct entities known as fields, and to allow for searching on specific fields in addition to across the whole record. (The topic of records and fields will be expanded in Section 6.2.2.)

Coordination of concepts is not limited to subject retrieval only; it is possible to link as many characteristics of the information item as are allowed by the computer system. This may be illustrated by searching a library OPAC for books on a specific topic, by a specific author, and published since a certain date in a specific country, or by using an Internet search engine such as AltaVista.[3]

3.4   Multi-coordinate mechanisms

In traditional pre-computerized environments, and in the earlier implementations of computerized systems, the mechanism belonged neatly to one or other of the approaches of pre- or post-coordinate retrieval. The increasing use of more flexible computer software and the advances in information retrieval research now allow for the implementation of systems which can offer both pre- and post-coordinate retrieval of a collection of items. For example, hypertext (which will be discussed more fully in Section 6.4.7) allows items to be accessed and retrieved in both pre- and post-coordinate ways, and in a variety of ways which lie somewhere in between. The concept of hypertext arises from associative memory systems, or the way that human memory works.

3.5   Comparison of pre-, post- and multi-coordinate approaches

The distinction between pre- and post-coordinate approaches is best illustrated by the fundamentally different ways in which they handle complex subjects. Let us consider a situation where an item may deal with a complex subject which encompasses three different concepts: A, B and C. The complex subject might be: 'Use of *computers* in *universities* in *Europe*', where the concepts are represented by letters as follows: A = Europe, B = computers, C = universities.

In a pre-coordinate system, we would expect a ready-made slot to be provided in a linear arrangement, and this slot would reflect the fact that the item deals with these three concepts. For example, if words linked by hyphens are used to build complex subjects, the preferred slot for this item might be:

Universities-Computers-Europe

This label would be one of a sequence of pre-arranged labels, in the sequence shown in Table 3.1. The corresponding hierarchical or tree structure is illustrated in Figure 3.3. (The details of the filing sequence will be discussed in Section 5.3.4.)

Note how scattered the items which deal with concepts A AND B are in the pre-coordinate sequence, at positions 3 and 7. Searching for items about 'computers in Europe' would be unsatisfactory, as these concepts are scattered in the sequence. On the other hand, items which deal with the concept of 'universities' all come together in the sequence.

In the alternative post-coordinate approach, the position in a linear arrangement is unimportant. The items could be arranged in any sequence, but the mechanics of the system should enable the indexer to describe the

Table 3.1   *Illustration of pre-coordinate retrieval*

Item no.	Deals with concepts	Pre-coordinate filing sequence	Example
1	A	A	Europe
2	B	B	Computers
3	AB	BA	Computers-Europe
4	C	C	Universities
5	AC	CA	Universities-Europe
6	BC	CB	Universities-Computers
7	ABC	CBA	Universities-Computers-Europe

Note: The corresponding hierarchical or tree structure is illustrated in Figure 3.3.

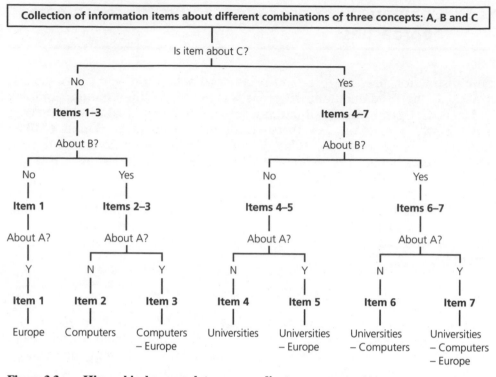

Figure 3.3   Hierarchical approach to pre-coordinate arrangements
Note: The item numbers and the structure correspond to those in Table 3.1.

item as dealing with each of the concepts, and allow the users to coordinate these concepts when they are seeking information. The post-coordinate system should have ready-made slots for each possible concept, as follows:

- Computers
- Europe
- Universities.

It should also provide a mechanism for combining these concepts. The items which would be retrieved by searching under various combinations of concepts are identified in Table 3.2.

The features of pre-, post- and multi-coordinate mechanisms are summarized in Table 3.3. All of the features in the left-hand column, with the exception of 'Roles, links' have been introduced already. This feature refers to the ability of the mechanism to show the role played by a concept, and to maintain the links between concepts. Taking the earlier example of 'computers-universities-Europe', several possible meanings arise, depending on how these words are combined. These include:

Table 3.2   *Illustration of post-coordinate retrieval*

Item no.	Deals with concepts	Retrieved by post-coordinate search for	Example
1	A	A	Europe
2	B	B	Computers
4	C	C	Universities
3	AB	A AND B	Europe AND Computers
5	AC	A AND C	Europe AND Universities
6	BC	B AND C	Computers AND Universities
7	ABC	A AND B AND C	Europe AND Computers AND Universities

Table 3.3   *Features of pre-, post- and multi-coordinate mechanisms*

Feature	Pre-coordinate	Post-coordinate	Multi-coordinate
Browsing	Easy	Difficult	Easy, can get lost
Helpful arrangement of items	Helpful	Unhelpful	Unhelpful
Linking of concepts to give specific retrieval	Inefficient	Efficient	Inefficient
Items accessible by	Primary concept	Many concepts	Many concepts
Roles, links	Maintained	Ignored	Partially maintained
Applications	Printed products Menus in computer systems	Computer databases	Hypertext Hypermedia

- the use of computers by students in universities in Europe;
- the teaching of computers in universities in Europe;
- the use of European computers in universities;
- computer practicals for European Studies programmes in universities;
- levels of computerization in European universities.

In a pre-coordinate system, the role and links are maintained through the order in which the concepts are coordinated, and the inclusion of prepositional phrases to indicate meaning, as was done in the phrases above. Roles and links can be contrived in a post-coordinate system through the development of elaborate thesauri (see Section 5.3.3), but to do so contradicts the flexibility of post-coordination.

3.6   Supermarket food analogy for conceptual approaches

The general arrangement of goods in stores (supermarkets, bookshops, record and video rental shops) is basically pre-coordinate, and encourages browsing. As with many information retrieval systems, items can be 'retrieved' using both pre- and post-coordinate methods. Shoppers looking for garlic bread can opt for a pre-packaged product (one in which the components have been combined in advance by the manufacturer) or can elect to purchase the basic ingredients separately and combine them using their own favourite recipe when cooking at home.

Shoppers may assume that garlic bread will be found somewhere in an arrangement of different varieties of bread. They are seeking a pre-coordinate product in a pre-coordinate arrangement. However, depending on store policy and varieties of the product, garlic bread may be displayed either as a fresh product in the bread section, or as a frozen product in the frozen foods section. We already see one of the disadvantages of having only one linear arrangement – because bread may be fresh or frozen, or indeed chilled, the shoppers have to look in two or possibly three places because of the different physical locations which result for the 'same' foodstuff.

On the other hand, the shoppers might decide to create their own garlic bread from a personal recipe, so they would know that they needed to buy the components of garlic bread: crusty white bread, butter or equivalent, and garlic. They would seek out each of these ingredients, where it exists as an item in its own right in the pre-coordinate arrangement, and later they would blend them together to make a tasty and aromatic side dish: they would post-coordinate the ingredients to create a new item.

The same analogy could be applied to buying ready-baked bread compared with making bread, or to buying a pre-packaged oven-ready meal as opposed to creating one from the various ingredients. Post-coordination in the creation of food products allows for the development of new products which cater for rather unusual tastes: for example, garlic and chocolate bread! Similarly, post-coordinate retrieval systems allow for combinations of search terms which were never thought of at the time the system was developed. The multi-coordinate approach is reflected by the inclusion of a product such as 'cook-in sauce' with a display of fresh meat, with a sign which says: 'You will find a full selection of tasty sauces in our gravies and sauces section.'

3.7   Application of conceptual approaches to sample collection

When presented with the task of organizing a collection of information items in some way, a choice must be made between pre-, post- and multi-coordinate mechanisms for both the items and their surrogates. Thus the following questions must be asked about the broadcast news agency described in Section 1.8:

• Is a linear arrangement of items or surrogates required?

- Which is most important: browsing or specific retrieval?
- Are the queries likely to require coordination of several concepts?
- Are the users generalists or specialists?
- Can a simple linear approach (or several of these) be combined with a post- or multi-coordinate retrieval facility?

It is likely that some combination of both pre- and post-coordinate retrieval will be required, with one approach considered more significant than the other. Browsing is often more important for generalist users, while specialist users frequently require more precise retrieval. So a sensible approach is to organize the information items – or if this is not possible, their surrogates – in some logical way. Other perspectives are accommodated through the provision of additional access points to the surrogates. So what will the simple linear arrangement be, and what type of post-coordinate mechanism will be added? If we have to store the information items, some logical arrangement will be helpful. One option is a method dictated by the requirements of the various physical media. (This aspect is discussed in depth in most textbooks on handling audio-visual or computerized media, and is only treated briefly here.) For example, it is not realistic to try to inter-file books, pamphlets, newspapers, cassette tapes, video tapes, CDs, LPs and various sizes of computer disk or computer printout. It is likely that most of the formats mentioned will be located in separate storage, thus creating a need for these items to be linked through their surrogates. This will result in savings of space, and may also be appropriate for the storage requirements of particular media (dust-free, away from electromagnetic radiation, standing upright, etc.). There may be logical reasons created by the storage or display environment which suggest separate sub-collections (by school or country in an art gallery, by themes in a museum, etc.). Again, this suggests the importance of alternative access mechanisms provided by the surrogates. Even within these 'physical sequences', there may be scope for the application of some logical method of arrangement, as indicated below.

The other possible arrangements include:

- by creator name – this is very useful for situations where the creator is clearly identifiable and plays a significant role, but it may be difficult to define a creator uniquely for some material;

- by some logical subject-based arrangement – this will facilitate browsing by the selected criteria, but can be frustrating if users have to rely on it as the only access mechanism and this is not appropriate for them or for the material (further details of these options will be discussed under 'Subject Access' in Chapter 5);

- by title – this is useful, but it may be difficult to define a unique title for some material;

- by creation date – this is helpful for weeding out older material, and also facilitates historical or current awareness approaches to the collection;

- by accession date – this facilitates the addition of new items;

- by physical characteristics, such as size or preservation requirements – this is the most efficient for minimizing storage space;

- by frequency of use – this speeds up retrieval of heavily used items at the expense of less used ones;

- by some other administratively convenient method linked to the requirements of a specific collection and its users.

As a result of these deliberations, it is likely that the original items in the broadcast news agency will be arranged by medium, with further subdivision into a chronological sequence. Some additional access mechanisms should be provided on a computer. This combination of approaches will be needed regardless of whether the original items are stored in traditional formats or electronically.

3.8   Summary

The conceptual approaches of pre- and post-coordinate retrieval may be applied to collections of non-textual information. The physical requirements of the items may make additional demands on storage; browsing may not be as automatic or as convenient an option as for most textual items (for example, one can't browse audio tapes as easily as magazines). Retrieval from the linear arrangements is possible either when there is some mechanism for scanning or browsing the content of the items, or when there is an associated post-coordinate retrieval system for the surrogates. A popular combination is a logical, linear arrangement of the items, supplemented by computerized post-coordinate retrieval of surrogates.

A chief concern is the purpose or objective of the retrieval system – it may vary from one application to another. The criterion or criteria which are used to organize the material should be dictated by the purpose of the collection and the interests of the users. In most situations, both retrieval of specific items and browsing are required.

The type of users and their information needs will also affect the organization of the collection in the following way. The general public tends to want fairly simple browsing facilities and direct access to original items; specialists are more prepared to put effort into construction of a complicated search strategy, and may be willing to have an additional retrieval step. This may result in retrieval of a reference which states where the source information can be found, with a separate procedure for obtaining the original item. It is possible, and usual, to use pre- and post-coordinate systems in conjunction: for example, a logical classified sequence, supported by keyword access to surrogates.

3.9 Practical assignments

You are encouraged to attempt to answer the following questions for one or more of the retrieval systems listed in Section 1.11:

1. Is the system concerned with the organization of original information items, or surrogates, or both?
2. What are the information items and the surrogates?
3. Is there a linear arrangement of items and surrogates?
4. What purpose(s) appear(s) to underlie this/these linear arrangement(s)?
5. Are items and surrogates arranged in the same way?
6. Are browsing and specific retrieval possible?
7. If both are possible, does one approach predominate?
8. Do you consider the system to be pre-, post- or multi-coordinate? Explain why.
9. Have the users any specialist knowledge of the collection, or are they generalists?
10. Are computers used to manage this information retrieval system?
11. Is any mechanical equipment used to manage this information retrieval system (e.g. punched cards or optical coincidence cards)?
12. If you were given responsibility for redesigning this information retrieval system from the perspective of conceptual approaches, would you make any changes?

You should try to give detailed answers, rather than simply responding with 'Yes' or 'No'. Sample answers are given in Section 3.12.

3.10 Notes

[1]   AERTEL teletext page 101: ⟨http://www.rte.ie/aertcl/index.html⟩.
[2]   Yahoo!: ⟨http://www.yahoo.com/⟩.
[3]   AltaVista: ⟨http://www.altavista.com/⟩.

3.11 References and further reading

Bush, Vannevar (1945) 'As we may think', *Atlantic Monthly*, July, 101–8.
Ellis, David (1996) *New Horizons in Information Retrieval* (2nd edn), London: Library Association.

Foskett, A.C. (1996) *The Subject Approach to Information* (5th edn), London: Library Association.

Kemp, D. Alasdair (1988) *Computer-based Knowledge Retrieval*, London: ASLIB.

Lancaster, F.W. and Warner, A. (1993) *Information Retrieval Today*, Arlington: Information Resource Press.

Nelson, Theodor Holm (1988) 'Unifying tomorrow's hypermedia', *Proceedings of the 12th International Online Meeting* (6–8 December 1988, London, England), Oxford: Learned Information, 1–7.

Rowley, Jennifer E. (1992) *Organizing Knowledge* (2nd edn), Aldershot: Ashgate.

Turner, Christopher (1987) *Organizing Information: Principles and Practice*, London: Bingley.

3.12   Sample answers to the practical assignments

3.12.1   The OPAC of a specific library, and the items in the same library

1.   Is the system concerned with the organization of original information items, or surrogates, or both?

The system is concerned with the organization of both original information items and their surrogates.

2.   What are the information items and the surrogates?

The information items are the books, journals and other media held by the library. The surrogates are the records in the OPAC.

3.   Is there a linear arrangement of items and surrogates?

There is a linear and logical arrangement of items, and a linear and random arrangement of surrogates. The items are generally arranged primarily by physical format: books together in one sequence, journals in another sequence, audio-visual media in another sequence. In some libraries, the different media may be completely integrated. Regardless of which practice is adopted, the next level of arrangement is usually by some logical classification scheme, such as the Dewey Decimal Classification. This enables users to browse the collection while also facilitating retrieval of specific items, provided the user knows the classification code. The surrogates are arranged in a random sequence on a computer storage medium, with a sophisticated indexing system which allows the OPAC software to retrieve the appropriate record(s) in response to a user search.

4. What purpose(s) appear(s) to underlie this/these linear arrangement(s)?
The purposes are quite different: for the items, it is to facilitate browsing with some possibility of specific retrieval; for the surrogates, it is efficient and quick direct access to specific records.

5. Are items and surrogates arranged in the same way?
No, items are arranged by a classified approach. Surrogates are arranged in random order.

6. Are browsing and specific retrieval possible?
Browsing is possible for the arrangement of items on shelves. It may also be possible in sections of the catalogue: for example, browsing through an author index or keyword index on the OPAC. Retrieval of a specific item is possible by identifying its shelf location. Coordination of search terms is also possible by combining them in the OPAC.

7. If both are possible, does one approach predominate?
Browsing predominates for the items, specific retrieval for the surrogates.

8. Do you consider the system to be pre-, post- or multi-coordinate? Explain why.
The arrangement of items is pre-coordinate; the OPAC is post-coordinate. There is no multi-coordinate retrieval.

9. Have the users any specialist knowledge of the collection, or are they generalists?
Most users are generalists, although there will usually be a percentage of specialists, particularly in special libraries and information centres.

10. Are computers used to manage this information retrieval system?
A central computer, or a series of networked computers, is normally used to manage the retrieval system. Microcomputers are generally used by staff and users to access the OPAC.

11. Is any mechanical equipment used to manage this information retrieval system (e.g. punched cards or optical coincidence cards)?
Mechanical equipment is rarely used to manage an OPAC nowadays.

12. If you were given responsibility for redesigning this information retrieval system from the perspective of conceptual approaches, would you make any changes?
As the shelf arrangement and OPAC encompass the benefits of both pre- and post-coordinate systems, there is not much scope for improvement. However, the following suggestions have a role to play, and have already been implemented in some systems:

- addition of hypertext links as part of a multi-coordinate system – for example, from books about someone to books created by the same person, and vice versa; these would also link different manifestations of the same items in different media;
- inclusion of other more specialized databases as part of the OPAC.

3.12.2   *The printed telephone directories (name and classified) for your country or region*

1.   Is the system concerned with the organization of original information items, or surrogates, or both?
The system is concerned with the organization of surrogates only.

2.   What are the information items and the surrogates?
The original items correspond to the people and businesses with telephone numbers listed in the directories. The surrogates are the entries in the directories.

3.   Is there a linear arrangement of items and surrogates?
The surrogates are arranged differently in the alphabetical and classified directories. The alphabetical listings arrange entries in alphabetical order, with some simplifications: for example, the prefixes 'Mac' and 'Mc' may be treated as equivalent. In the classified directory, there will be an arrangement of entries under predetermined subject headings. Under the appropriate subject headings, entries are then listed alphabetically by name of business or service.

4.   What purpose(s) appear(s) to underlie this/these linear arrangement(s)?
For the main directory, the purpose is retrieval of telephone numbers when one knows the surname, and ideally the first name(s) or initials of the phone owner. For the classified directory, it is to enable easy finding of a business by general category.

5.   Are the items and surrogates arranged in the same way?
The issue of the arrangement of original items does not arise.

6.   Are browsing and specific retrieval possible?
The alphabetical directory permits browsing by family name. This may be useful for tracing your ancestors or identifying how unusual your family name is, but doesn't fulfil any real function, other than retrieval of a phone number by a person's family name. The classified directory facilitates identification of a specific category of business (e.g. restaurants) and then enables browsing within that category.

7.   If both are possible, does one approach predominate?

Retrieval of specific items predominates in the alphabetical directory; browsing predominates in the classified directory.

8.   Do you consider the system to be pre-, post- or multi-coordinate? Explain why.

This system is pre-coordinate, as it does not allow for any coordination of search terms by the user. For example, it is difficult to find the phone number of someone for whom you know the family name and the post code, but not the first name. Similarly, while the category 'restaurants' may be subdivided by ethnic type, one can't search for restaurants in a specific area or price range.

9.   Have the users any specialist knowledge of the collection, or are they generalists?

The users are generalists.

10.   Are computers used to manage this information retrieval system?

Computers are used to compile these directories. Usually, a combination of a database management system and word-processing or publishing package is used. Computers are not used by ordinary users of the system.

11.   Is any mechanical equipment used to manage this information retrieval system (e.g. punched cards or optical coincidence cards)?

No mechanical equipment is used to manage this information retrieval system.

12.   If you were given responsibility for redesigning this information retrieval system from the perspective of conceptual approaches, would you make any changes?

It is quite wasteful that the quantity of information contained in these printed directories is only available in this form. In some countries, the public have access to computerized searching of the data if the directories are sold on CD-ROM or are accessible on the Internet (e.g. the Minitel system in France). It may also be provided through directory enquiry services. This enables post-coordination of search terms, and satisfies the following queries:

- a common user name and house name or postcode;
- a subject category and location or other criterion.

Users can then tailor searches to their own specific needs. This retrieval could be extended through the use of hypertext links: for example, having found a theatre in an area, one could then click on the area to find out more about other facilities such as restaurants, hotels and taxis in that area.

3.12.3   Internet resources and the AltaVista search engine

1.   Is the system concerned with the organization of original information items, or surrogates, or both?

The distinction between original information items and surrogates is a complex one for Internet resources. The general consensus is that the pages created by an individual or an organization for the Internet are original information items. The summaries of these pages which are retrieved by a search engine are the surrogates. However, one could argue that most Internet information resources are in fact surrogates of other information items.

2.   What are the information items and the surrogates?

The information items are the digitized information resources in various formats. These may include Web-based resources such as HTML text files and other media objects. The surrogates include entries for these pages in Internet search engines, in catalogues which include Internet resources, in Internet gateways and directories, and in bookmarks in a browser such as *Netscape* on a user's computer.

3.   Is there a linear arrangement of items and surrogates?

The information items are arranged in a completely random way, where the URL is the mechanism for locating an item. The surrogates may be arranged in a variety of ways, of which the following are the most useful:

- In a search engine such as AltaVista, they are organized in random order. The surrogates retrieved in response to a user's search are usually listed in a pre-coordinate sequence based on relevance to the search query.
- In a search directory such as Yahoo!, or as a user's collection of electronic bookmarks, they are organized in a logical, pre-coordinate sequence, a linear arrangement.

4.   What purpose(s) appear(s) to underlie this/these linear arrangement(s)?

The purpose is identification of specific Internet resources in response to a user's need.

5.   Are items and surrogates arranged in the same way?

Items and surrogates are arranged in different ways.

6.   Are browsing and specific retrieval possible?

Both browsing and specific retrieval are possible.

7.   If both are possible, does one approach predominate?

Neither approach predominates: the complexity of the Internet facilitates a variety of approaches.

8. Do you consider the system to be pre-, post- or multi-coordinate? Explain why.

Information retrieval on the Internet enables pre-, post- and multi-coordinate approaches. The AltaVista search engine uses post-coordination.

9. Have the users any specialist knowledge of the collection, or are they generalists?

Information retrieval on the Internet is complicated by the diversity in personal characteristics, cultural backgrounds, educational levels and languages of the users. They may include subject specialists, but in general, the Internet must be considered a tool for generalists.

10. Are computers used to manage this information retrieval system?

Networked computers are the heart of the Internet. These range from large, high-performance computers for sophisticated mathematical and engineering applications to hand-held personal organizers with browser software.

11. Is any mechanical equipment used to manage this information retrieval system (e.g. punched cards or optical coincidence cards)?

The network links between the computers, which range from twisted wire cabling to microwave transmission, correspond to mechanical equipment.

12. If you were given responsibility for redesigning this information retrieval system from the perspective of conceptual approaches, would you make any changes?

Given the flexibility of the conceptual approaches, one cannot fault this aspect. However, there are deficiencies which arise more from the lack of standardization of the information items and their surrogates, which have adverse effects on the efficiency with which the conceptual approaches work.

Chapter 4

Surrogates

4.1 Introduction

This chapter considers the issues involved in the creation of surrogates, examines current standards, and presents guidelines for the creation of the components of surrogates which are applicable across a range of media and applications. If one wants to produce a list, a catalogue or a database of items in a collection, or in a number of related collections, it is necessary to create surrogates of the individual items. They play an essential role in situations where it is impossible or difficult to work with original items.

4.2 Definitions and examples

A surrogate is a replacement for an original item, which enables the existence of the item to be established from a number of different perspectives, gives some description of the original item, and usually includes details of where the original is located or how it can be obtained. The term 'surrogate' also encompasses the term 'record' (in a database), 'entry' (in a catalogue) and 'metadata' (for Internet resources).

Typical surrogates are:

1. student record;
2. curriculum vitae;
3. holiday description in a brochure;
4. course module description;
5. entry in an auction catalogue;
6. entry for a photograph in the contents list of a collection, an exhibition or a book;
7. catalogue entry for a work of art;
8. advertisement for an item for sale;

Full Record Display

Document 1 of 2

Title Details: Electronic children : how children are responding to the
                        information revolution / edited by Tim Gill

Publisher: London : National Children's Bureau, c1996
Physical Desc.:   x, 122p ; 22cm, pbk
ISBN/ISSN: 1874579741

Subject(s):   Information storage and retrieval systems - Social aspects
                        Technology - Social aspects
                        Education - Data processing
                        Computers and children
Language: English

Holding Libraries: Cambridge - contact Cambridge University Library ;
                        1997.8.265;
                        Leeds - Brotherton Library, West Building ; Education
                        371.67 GIL;

Figure 4.1   Surrogate example: Book in a library catalogue
Source: COPAC – document display: ⟨http://copac.ac.uk/copac/old/author.html⟩. Found by searching for
electronic children as title words, and **1996** as publication date.

  9. record of a museum item in a database;
10. record of a newspaper article in a database;
11. record of an architectural drawing in a linear filing system;
12. entry in the inventory of a sound archive;
13. record of a film in a video archive;
14. link to, and description of, a Web page;
15. entry for a book in a library catalogue;
16. entry in a bibliography or an abstracting or indexing service.

Surrogate types 15 and 16 are highly standardized. Examples of surrogate
types 14–16 are given in Figures 4.1–4.3.

    All of these examples share the common characteristics of one or more
access points, and some identifying details of the original item. These
details may be:

- a description of the features of the item;
- a reference to a surrogate of a related item;
- a reference to a source of further information;
- a reference to the location of the original item;
- a link which enables the original item to be retrieved and used.

4.3   Components

Surrogates have three components:

- access points (creator, subject, other);
- description (physical, subject);
- location indicator.

Personal Library Software

This document, ranked number *1* in the hitlist, was retrieved from the *ericdb* database.

```
-ERIC_NO-
EJ379093
-TITLE-
Information Policy and the Discovery Process.;
-AUTHOR-
Rowe, Richard R.;
-JOURNAL_CITATION-
"Information Services and Use; v7 n6 p189-99 1987";
-LANGUAGE-
English;
-DESCRIPTORS- Access to Information Electronic Publishing Ideology Information_Systems
Intellectual_Property Library_Role Publishing_Industry Discovery_Processes Futures Global_Approach
Information_Technology Science_and_Society Social_Change
-IDENTIFIERS-
Information Society;
Information Policy;
-ABSTRACT-
Reviews past information revolutions, describes the technologies of the current revolution, and discusses
the impact of technology on broader social dynamics. Topics discussed include future roles for publishers
and libraries, the impact of social trends on the discovery process, and the need for a global information
policy. (CLB);
-CLEARINGHOUSE_NO-
IR518902;
-PUBLICATION_TYPE-
"080; 120; 150";
-PUBLICATION_DATE- 1987
```

Figure 4.2   Surrogate example: ERIC abstracts for education
Source: PLWeb document: ⟨http://ericir.syr.edu/ERic/⟩. Found by selecting 'Search ERIC Database' and
searching for **information policy** and **discovery process**.

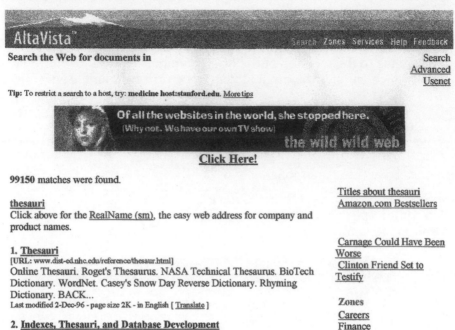

Search the Web for documents in

Search
Advanced
Usenet

Tip: To restrict a search to a host, try: **medicine host:stanford.edu**. More tips

Click Here!

99150 matches were found.

thesauri
Click above for the RealName (sm), the easy web address for company and product names.

1. Thesauri
[URL: www.dist-ed.nhc.edu/reference/thesaur.html]
Online Thesauri. Roget's Thesaurus. NASA Technical Thesaurus. BioTech Dictionary. WordNet. Casey's Snow Day Reverse Dictionary. Rhyming Dictionary. BACK...
Last modified 2-Dec-96 - page size 2K - in English [Translate]

2. Indexes, Thesauri, and Database Development
[URL: www.niso.org/pcindex1.htm]
Z39.19-1993 Guidelines for the Construction, Format, and Management of Monolingual Thesauri. This standard is the authoritative guide for constructing...
Last modified 23-Jul-97 - page size 7K - in English (Win-1252) [Translate]

3. KeyWord Thesauri
[URL: www.mp.usbr.gov/geospat/mdext/kwd_intro.html]
Pat Horn Fell and David T. Hansen. KeyWord Thesauri. Available Thesauri and KeyWord Lists. SUBJECT KEYWORDS. The subject keywords in this list are...
Last modified 31-Mar-98 - page size 7K - in English [Translate]

4. Thesauri Web Links
[URL: www.milan.k12.in.us/thesauri.htm]
Thesauri Web Links. WordNet - on-line lexical reference where English nouns, verbs, adjectives and adverbs are organized into synonym sets, each...
Last modified 1-Aug-97 - page size 2K - in English [Translate]

5. Language Dictionaries and Thesauri
[URL: mel.lib.mi.us/reference/REF-dict.html]
SEARCH. MAIN MENU. ABOUT MEL. FAQ. HELP. Dictionaries and Thesauri Related to Language. See Also the MEL Humanities section Language Resources menu. The...
Last modified 31-Mar-98 - page size 12K - in English [Translate]

6. Dictionaries and Thesauri
[URL: cal.bemidji.msus.edu/WRC/DictsandOthers.html]
On-Line Dictionaries and Thesauri. Writing Resource Center Bemidji State University. We have included multiple source when available. Sites (especially...
Last modified 1-Apr-98 - page size 6K - in English [Translate]

Titles about thesauri
Amazon.com Bestsellers

Carnage Could Have Been Worse
Clinton Friend Set to Testify

Zones
Careers
Finance
Health
News by ABC
Travel
Wild Wild Web

Services
AltaVista Discovery NEW!
Browse Categories
Create a Card NEW!
Find a Business
Find a Person
Free Email
Maps
Translation

International
Our Search Network
Search in Chinese
Search in Japanese
Search in Korean

Figure 4.3   Surrogate example: AltaVista search results for search term 'thesauri'
Source: AltaVista – simple query: ⟨http://www.altavista.com/⟩. Found by searching for **thesauri** (first page). DIGITAL, AltaVista and the AltaVista logo are trademarks or service marks of Digital Equipment Corporation. Reproduced with permission.

The *access points* are keys which enable the surrogate to be identified or retrieved. These might include the creator(s) of the item, the subject content, and unique keys which may be appropriate for certain collections, such as an employee number, an International Standard Book Number (ISBN), geographical coordinates, etc. In a manual retrieval system, such as a card catalogue or printed listing, the access points correspond to the heading under which the surrogate is filed. In a computer database, they correspond to the search terms which may be used to retrieve data.

The *description* includes a summary of the subject content of the item and/or an account of its physical characteristics. It may also include a review of the item, or some assessment of its quality or its target audience. For example, the description of a CD-ROM product in a sales catalogue indicates the subject matter according to some recommended standard, the physical dimensions and playback requirements of the disk, and the age and educational level for which it is intended.

The *location indicator* enables the original item to be traced. It may consist of the location code for the item in some physical or electronic arrangement, or contact details of where and how it can be obtained. Examples include a shelf mark in a library, and a URL (Uniform Resource Locator) on the Internet.

In traditional manual (card-based) retrieval systems, the distinctions between these three components are significant. In post-coordinate computerized retrieval systems, considerable overlap may occur, as all appropriate sections of the surrogate may become access points. The description of physical characteristics may be significant for location of the item in computer storage, and for the technical specifications needed to view or play it.

There may also be different levels of surrogate for the same item, or surrogates of surrogates may be required. The former are exemplified by the entries in different catalogues for the same book, or by the entries in different World Wide Web search engines for one resource. The latter are exemplified by the details of the recording on the cover notes of a music CD, and the entry for the same CD in the publisher's catalogue; or an entry for a library catalogue in a directory, and the entries for individual books in the catalogue.

4.4 Functions

The chief purpose of surrogates is to provide an easily accessible description of an information item. They fulfil the following more detailed functions:

- They allow for items to be organized in one way and surrogates in another – for example, items may be pre-coordinate and surrogates post-coordinate.

- Surrogates themselves may be:
  - organized in different ways – for example, multiple pre-coordinate sequences;
  - accessed by multiple users;
  - distributed as multiple copies;
  - used in different locations.
- They identify the item being described, and give sufficient information for the user to be able to identify or locate it.
- They overcome the difficulties of accessing the original to some extent. It may be unavailable, or it may be inaccessible because special equipment is required to use it, or it may be in a foreign language, or it may require a certain minimum computer configuration to operate, or it may be in a fragile condition which limits handling by users.
- They may draw together items which are scattered by their physical arrangement.
- They provide a link for the integration of multimedia components.

4.5   Surrogate standards

Standards for surrogates have developed independently for different types of information items and different applications. These developments have been driven by cataloguers, archivists and indexers in a variety of libraries, bibliographic agencies and information services. Those which have more detailed structures and which have gained international acceptance for different applications are:

- bibliographic records (books and other library holdings) – ISBD, AACR2, MARC, UNIMARC;
- reference books and directories (abstracting and indexing services, directories of people, products, services) – ANSI, ISO abstracting standards;
- museums – MDA, CIDOC;
- Internet resources – URC, URI, Dublin Core, TEI.

Standards such as the International Standard for Bibliographic Description (ISBD), the Anglo-American Cataloguing Rules (AACR2), Machine Readable Cataloguing (MARC) and those of special libraries, art galleries and museums concentrate on author access and physical description. It is not feasible to develop one generally applicable surrogate standard, but developers of multimedia retrieval systems can learn from the strengths of the surrogates described in the following sections.

The International Federation of Library Associations (IFLA) developed the ISBD as a set of requirements to delimit elements of description, their order of presentation and punctuation (IFLA, 1977). It is a framework which serves as the basis for the description of all types of media using the ISBD (G) (General). It is also used as the basis for specialized ISBDs for individual media, for example the ISBD (NBM) for non-book materials (IFLA, 1987a). (Some details of this standard are presented in Section 4.7.1.)

In the second edition of AACR2, the same basic set of principles have been applied to description and entry for all materials (Gorman and Winkler, 1993). Chapter 1 of the code deals with the description of media in general. The procedures of this chapter are then applied to the several individual chapters covering specific media, and thus serve to bring about an 'integrated and standardized framework for the systematic description of all library materials'. Access points are treated independently of description, so these rules are independent of the specific medium. The concise edition of AACR2 presents the same principles in a less intimidating volume, yet with sufficient detail for most general applications (Gorman, 1989).

MARC is a format which is used by many libraries world-wide for records in their computerized catalogues (IFLA, 1987b; UKMARC, 1990). The range of libraries is very diverse, including the majority of national and academic libraries, many public libraries and a number of special libraries. Its use for both the Prints and Photographs Library and the Recorded Sound Library in New York Public Library illustrates its versatility. More importantly, it is used by various providers of catalogue records to libraries, including the British Library and the Library of Congress. It is compatible with AACR2 and with the Dewey Decimal Classification scheme.

Over the years, variations have evolved between the versions of MARC used in different countries, so the UNIMARC format was developed for international exchange of catalogue records (Avram and McCallum, 1982; Holt et al., 1987). The IFLA UBCIM (Universal Bibliographic Control International MARC) Programme supports UNIMARC so that catalogue records may be exchanged internationally and converted locally to national formats. UNIMARC complies with ISO 2709, the international standard for bibliographic record exchange on magnetic tape.

In spite of the apparent similarity between library catalogues and abstracting/indexing services, attempts at developing standards for the latter have been less successful. Thus competing abstracting/indexing services may use different surrogate components, and may present these components in different sequences. This variation persists across the range of databases offered by an online host service operator (e.g. Dialog). Most services apply in-house standards for consistent creation of surrogates; a typical example is presented in Figure 4.2, which is influenced by the following international standards:

- The *UNISIST Reference Manual* assigns content designators to the bibliographic description of various items, in a similar, but different, fashion to UNIMARC. The Common Communications Format was developed as a specific implementation of ISO 2709 in order to enable bibliographical information from different sources to be exchanged (Dierick and Hopkinson, 1981).

- Standards organizations such as ANSI and ISO have developed standards for abstracts, particularly for scientific research publications (American National Standards Institute, 1979; International Standards Organization, 1976).

There is less incentive for co-operative development of standards for museums compared with libraries, as their holdings are more unique, and shared cataloguing is not feasible. The following initiatives are significant:

- The Museum Documentation Association (MDA) in the UK has defined SPECTRUM, a common data standard for description of museum objects, which is widely used by museums in the UK (Museum Documentation Association, 1980, 1991; Cowton, 1997).

- A detailed Data Model has been developed by David Bearman of Archives & Museums Informatics.[1]

- The Canadian Heritage Information Network (CHIN) has identified common information requirements of different kinds of museums by constructing a unified data dictionary, documenting in one format the fields of information used in databases of their many users for different applications (Canadian Heritage Information Network, 1986).

There are a number of proposed and competing standards for Internet resources, all of which attempt to cope with the inherent conflict between the need for increased management of the variety of resource formats and the desire to maintain the freedom of individuals and institutions to make information available quickly and easily without the constraints of standards. These codes are likely to evolve rapidly during the lifetime of this book, so readers are advised to examine the current picture by checking on the Internet. At the time of writing, the most relevant standards are described as 'templates' containing 'metadata' about World Wide Web resources. The simplest definition of 'metadata' is 'data about other data'; a more sophisticated definition describes it as the identifying descriptive information found at the start of an electronic file.[2] Emerging metadata standards include the Uniform Resource Identifier (URI), Dublin Core and TEI Header.

The Dublin Core is a set of 15 basic information elements designed for use in Web pages to enhance indexing and retrieval. These elements are: title, creator, subject, descriptions, publisher, contributor, date, type, format, resource identifier, source, language, relation, coverage, rights. Weibel (1997) gives a clear account of the objectives and elements of the Dublin Core,[3] and full, up-to-date details are available through the Web page.[4]

There are several initiatives to standardize resource names and to manage changes in locations of Internet-based resources, including: URIs and Persistent Uniform Resource Locators (PURLs). The URI family of standards has been developed by the Internet Engineering Task Force (IETF) to enable reliable naming, description and addressing of Internet resources (Schwartz, 1997); it includes URLs, Uniform Resource Names (URNs) and Uniform Resource Characteristics (URCs). The components of the URC, which are broadly similar to those of the Dublin Core, are: URN, title, author, subject, abstract, location, version, review, access control, signature.

The components of both the Dublin Core and the URC give a much fuller and more consistent surrogate than currently provided for most Internet resources (see the example in Figure 4.3 of a surrogate on the AltaVista search engine). The objectives of PURLs and URNs are broadly similar, in that they both aim to overcome the problem of frequent changes in Internet addresses as owners of resources move information items from one computer to another, or change the structure of their Web pages. Both involve the automatic development and updating of indexes which link names of resources to their correct addresses.

4.6   Access points

Access points provide the basis for finding surrogates, regardless of whether they are in a pre-, post- or multi-coordinate arrangement. Both creator and subject are common access points; other less usual keys are based on the specific characteristics of individual items or on unique identi-fiers of items. Control or standardization of access points is often important in order to provide consistent retrieval, and authority files of recommended terms may be developed.

4.6.1   Creator access points

The key questions regarding the provision of creator access points are:

*   Who is the creator – who is responsible for the intellectual content of the original item?
*   Did additional people or groups make different types of contribution?
*   How is the name or title of the creator best represented – what form of the creator's name should be used?

The answer to the first question may be very obvious in some cases: the creator may be one person who is the author of a report, or the artist of a painting, or the creator of a sculpture, or the speaker of a monologue, or the creator of a home-made video. In addition, the creator may be one individual, a number of individuals or a corporate body. The item may be a manifestation of an original item. A sculpture may involve input from different people at various stages of the creative process: for example, the routine work may be done by a junior under the supervision of a renowned sculptor who puts the finishing touches to the object. It is possible to be a creator who carries out the complete work oneself (e.g. an artist or a sculptor), alternatively, the physical execution of the item may be carried out by someone else, with the person who created the original idea being credited with creatorship (e.g. a designer, architect or photographer whose work is developed or constructed by a technician). It becomes difficult to resolve the question of who is the primary creator versus additional contributors consistently.

The complexity of the second question increases as more media are integrated into a product. It is difficult to identify the principal creator of a film which has an author of the dialogue, actors, a director, a producer and contributions from support staff. One can adopt a simplistic solution which advocates the creation of access points for all creators, but even in a flexible, multi-access system, this is likely to create problems in terms of indexing effort and storage space. For example, how important is it to be able to identify every film for which Brush & Comb did the hair styling? It may also be important to identify the primary creator in order to produce linear sequences which list items by principal creator (e.g. an inventory of holdings).

When dealing with manifestations of items, one needs to decide who has made the greatest intellectual contribution to an item, and do this consistently for a specific collection and user population. One choice of entry may not be superior to another: it is impossible to generalize even within one collection. The most satisfactory approach is one which allows users to distinguish between the original item and its manifestations, yet creates links between them.

Library cataloguing codes are primarily concerned with decisions on identifying the primary and secondary creators, and on examining the ways in which they should be represented. While the comprehensive instructions in these codes may be far too detailed for many applications, one can learn much from the general principles. For example, AACR2 gives guidance on identification of the primary author, items created by a number of individuals and by corporate agencies. The fuller definition of a 'personal author' in Rule 21.1A1 of the 1978 version of AACR2 is very satisfactory for multimedia items:

A personal author is the person chiefly responsible for the creation of the intellectual or artistic content of a work. For example, writers of books and composers of music are the authors of the works they create; compilers of bibliographies are the authors of those bibliographies; cartographers are the authors of their maps; and artists and photographers are the authors of the works they create. In addition, in certain cases performers are the authors of sound recordings, films, and videorecordings. (Gorman and Winkler, 1978, p. 284)

The third question, form of name, is dealt with comprehensively by AACR2 and other cataloguing codes. The general philosophy is that the form which is most likely to be sought by the users should be used.

4.6.2   Subject and other access points

For full exploitation of surrogates, it is necessary to provide a range of subject-based access points. These allow for a subject-based arrangement of the surrogates in a pre-coordinate system, for post-coordinate retrieval based on combining subject terms, and for multi-coordinate linking by subject. Examples include the use of Dewey or other classification schemes, the use of subject headings lists or thesauri, and the generation of index entries from words in titles and abstracts. (These options for subject access will be addressed more fully in Chapter 5.)

Depending on the specific application, other access points may become important. It is necessary to identify these, and to establish some guidelines for their standardization. Possible additional access points include:

- dates;
- names of people or organizations other than the creator – for example, the funding source;
- characteristics of the physical medium – for example, photographs taken with a wide-angle lens;
- coding system specific to the items or medium – for example, ZIP codes;
- unique identifiers for items – for example, ISBNs for books, or tax/social insurance identifiers for people;
- indication of level or target audience – for example, general, introductory, undergraduate, postgraduate, research.

The guidelines may involve developing sets of rules, such as using the format YYYY-MM-DD for dates so they can be sorted easily by computer to allow for easy manipulation, or using a limited list of physical media terms, such as AACR2's list of General Material Designations, as described in Section 4.7.2.

4.7   Description

The general objective of description is to enable the user to assess the potential usefulness of the original item, and to assist in its identification and location. More specifically, it should provide answers to at least some of the following questions:

- **Creator**
  - Who is responsible for creating or discovering the item?
- **Title**
  - What is the name or title of the item?
- **Source/location/identification/availability/consultation**
  - Where was the item produced or discovered?
  - When was the item produced or discovered?
  - Where is the item located?
  - What is its unique identifier or location?
  - How much does it cost to buy or consult it?
- **Physical details**
  - What is the medium or form?
  - What size is it?
  - Is any specialized equipment needed to use it?
- **Subject**
  - What is the item about?
  - Is it suitable for this user?
- **Relationships**
  - Is the item related to other items?

The details of the description are usually dictated by the nature of the items, but the experience of libraries, art galleries and museums is applicable. Particular difficulties arise when describing volatile items such as Internet resources. The key objective is consistent description, which is facilitated by the use of standards. Description may be subdivided into two distinct parts: subject and non-subject, where physical description plays a large part in the latter. Various approaches to description are described in the following sections.

4.7.1   AACR2 and ISBD

The ISBD (G) contains the following areas of bibliographic description:

1. title and statement of responsibility area;
2. edition area;
3. material (or type of publication) specific details area;
4. publication, distribution (etc.) area;

5.   physical description area;
6.   series area;
7.   note area;
8.   standard number (or alternative) and terms of availability area.

ISBD specifies that the eight areas be included in this order, and also makes recommendations for the consistent use of punctuation to distinguish between the various elements of the description. Further details of ISBDs may be found in Rowley (1992), or by consulting the original publications for ISBD (G) (IFLA, 1977) and for specific ISBDs, such as ISBD (NBM) (IFLA, 1987a). Special requirements for particular media are accommodated within ISBD (G). Some elements of description may be omitted if they are not suited to a given type of material. Thus, for example, the place of publication and name of publisher would not be appropriate for naturally occurring materials, such as a sea-shell, or for artefacts not intended primarily for communication, such as a coin.

At the same time, there are aspects essential to the description of some media which would not be considered as part of the general pattern of description, for instance the scale of a map. ISBD (G) allocates one area to be used only 'for details that are special to a particular class of material or type of publication'. The code identifies serials and cartographic materials as needing such an area, and uses it for recording numerical and chronological descriptions of serials: for example, as 'vol. 1, no. 1–'. For cartographic materials, this area is the mathematical data area, and gives the scale, projection, coordinates and equinox.

The rules for description in AACR2 are based on ISBD, and allow for three different levels of description, with each user institution free to opt for the appropriate level of description. The first and less detailed level, which is the most appropriate one for this book, is exemplified in Figure 4.1. Readers who are concerned with fuller descriptive cataloguing for academic and research libraries can obtain further details from the sources listed (e.g. Rowley, 1992). The original texts of AACR2 and ISBD are particularly useful, and Hunter's (1989) *Examples Illustrating AACR2* is a complementary guide to the rules of AACR2.

The general principles of ISBD and AACR2 provide a basis for the description of multimedia items, but most of the detailed rules are inappropriate. They enable all of the questions posed earlier in this section, except those dealing with subject, to be answered, but at the cost of long and tedious effort by the cataloguer.

4.7.2   General material designations (GMDs)

AACR2 and ISBD both provide for the description of various physical media through the optional use of General Material Designations. The intention is that these designations will prevent a proliferation of different terms, this objective is not fully realized, however, as there are two alternative lists in the AACR2. These lists, designated 'British' (List 1) and 'North American' (List 2), are organized as follows:

- **List 1**
  - braille;
  - cartographic material;
  - computer file;
  - graphic;
  - manuscript;
  - microform;
  - motion picture;
  - multimedia;
  - music;
  - object;
  - sound recording;
  - text;
  - videorecording.
- **List 2**
  - art original;
  - art reproduction;
  - braille;
  - chart;
  - computer file;
  - diorama;
  - filmstrip;
  - flash card;
  - game;
  - globe;
  - graphic;
  - kit;
  - manuscript;
  - map;
  - microform;
  - microscope slide;
  - model;
  - motion picture;
  - music;
  - picture;
  - realia;
  - slide;
  - sound recording;
  - technical drawing;
  - text;

- toy;
- transparency;
- videorecording (Gorman and Winkler, 1993, p. 21).

The main differences between the two lists are:

- List 1 uses more generic terms – for example, 'graphic' instead of specific types of graphic in List 2 (art original and reproduction, filmstrip, flash card, picture, realia, slide, technical drawing); 'cartographic material' instead of the more specific terms in List 2 (map, globe, etc.).
- Synonyms or near synonyms are used in some places – for example, List 1 uses 'multimedia' (with a rather limited definition), while List 2 uses 'kit'; List 1 uses 'object', and List 2 uses 'realia'.

There are situations in which one list will be more satisfactory than the other (e.g. List 1 is more appropriate when a general distinction between the main forms of text, audio and visual media is all that is required). If a fuller distinction is needed, perhaps because of the size of the collection, or the storage requirements of the different media, then List 2 is likely to be more suitable.

GMDs have a role to play in a multimedia environment, as it is essential to emphasize the different physical media clearly in each surrogate. They also enable a consistent surrogate structure to be used for works reproduced in different media. They may be applied successfully to various specific media, including local and Internet-based electronic files. There is much to be gained from using a standardized list, but it is discouraging that an agency such as AACR2 cannot achieve international agreement on one list.

4.7.3 Description of manifestations of an item

Difficulties frequently arise when describing a particular item which is based on another item: it may be identical to the original item, or it may be a modification or a transformation of it. For example, if we are dealing with a recorded performance of a piece of music or a play, the description should distinguish between the performance and the score or text, and should enable links to be made between these manifestations. The electronic data structures of hypertext and relational databases which will be discussed in Chapter 6 provide an efficient method of handling these related items.

ISBD and the fuller levels of description in AACR2 facilitate the distinctions and links. For example, one could name the related item, and indicate the specific nature of the relationship as an edition or translation. A facility for parallel titles may be used for translations; subsequent statements of responsibility for additional creator contributions, edition statements for revisions; the series area for items in a series, and the notes area for a range of points, including variations in title, vaguer claims on creatorship, availability of item in other formats, etc.

In many situations, it will be important to be able to distinguish between an original and its manifestation, for example between a rare work of art and postcard reproductions of this item. In other cases, the distinction may be insignificant, or it may be more practical to allow the user to browse the related items and make their own judgements (e.g. for various 'similar' recordings of a musical item). There is a need to balance the theoretical desire exhibited in the surrogate standards to catalogue every item in minute detail with the realities of an operational retrieval system.

4.7.4   Internet surrogates

The key factors of Internet surrogates are their ability to convey:

- physical characteristics of the items, and the implications of these for the user – format, size of file, whether the item consists of real data or a link to another item;
- quality and age of the data, and authority of the creator;
- the relationship to other Internet items.

The components of these standards are summarized in Table 4.1. These surrogates provide for all the questions earlier in this section, but not in a totally satisfactory manner.

4.7.5   Subject description

The objective is to give some description of subject content in order to enable decisions to be made about the potential usefulness of an item. The subject description may also be used to automatically generate subject access points. A broad interpretation of subject description includes:

- abstracts and various other types of summary;
- review or quality evaluation;
- indication of target audience.

An abstract is defined as a concise summary of the contents of an item; other types of subject representation – paraphrase, digest, abridgement – attempt to summarize the subject content in slightly different ways. The surrogates in an abstracting service provide a good example of an abstract, as shown in Figure 4.2. Reviews or quality evaluation are less widely used, but are becoming more important, particularly in computerized environments. They may be linked to entries in library catalogues or in World Wide Web search engines. There may be one 'official' review or 'Seal of

Table 4.1   *Internet surrogate components*

Components	URC Template	IAFA Template	Dublin Core	TEI Header
Access to resources				
Location or locations	URN	URI	URN	
Format of resource		Yes	Yes	
Hardware/software needs		Yes	Yes	
Size of resource		Yes		Yes
Restrictions on use	Yes			Yes
Mutability of resources				
Data elements for record		Yes		Yes
Version information	Yes	Yes		Yes
Publication date		Yes	Yes	
Revision date		Yes		
Evaluating resources				
Statement of responsibility	Yes	Yes	Yes	Yes
Source of resource			Yes	Yes
SOAPs	Yes			
Relationship to other objects				
Relation			Yes	
Subject approach				
Classification	Yes	Yes	Yes	
Index terms	Yes	Yes	Yes	
Abstracts	Yes	Yes	Yes	

Source: Devlin (1996).

Approval' (SOAP), or users of the system may be allowed to add their own individual reviews for perusal by others. Target audience codes are used by publishers to indicate that books or multimedia are intended for a particular market: reference use, for children, for general readers, for undergraduate students or for researchers. They have been tested successfully in experimental user applications.

Subject description of Internet resources is frequently based on the initial portion of an item, leading to inefficient retrieval. The template standards identified in Table 4.1 attempt to overcome these difficulties. The issue of original and manifested items also causes complications for subject description and subject access points. The principles of subject analysis and representation will be covered more fully in Chapter 5.

4.8   Location indicators

The function of location indicators is to lead the user from the surrogate to the location of the original item, or to a fuller surrogate of that item. The location may be in a manual storage system such as a filing cabinet, or in electronic form on a computer storage medium. The form of the location indicator is totally dependent on the arrangement of these items. The alternative arrangements, and the justifications for each one, were presented in Section 3.7. Suitable forms of location indicator for each of these arrangements are as follows:

- **Creator** – full form of creator's name, or modified form, for example:
  - MILLER or
  - MILLER, Frank or
  - MILLER01 (first MILLER item) or
  - MILLER92 (year is 1992).

- **Subject** – class number is more satisfactory than long alphabetical subject phrases; the class number may be further subdivided by creator, for example:
  - 300MILLER (where 300 is a Dewey class number for Social Sciences).

- **Chronological** – by date or running number, for example:
  - 10/2/92 or
  - 259 (259th item in sequence).

- **Physical form** – this will indicate physical sequence; it is likely to be subdivided by some of the other arrangements in this list, for example:
  - PHOTO – Miller; VIDEO – Miller or
  - PHOTO – 300; VIDEO – 300.

- **Random** – a running number may be assigned as items are processed, for example:
  - 259 (259th item in sequence).

Location indicators are important in computer systems, as they enable physical storage locations to be identified. They are also extremely significant in maintaining the complex network of links on the World Wide Web. Sample forms of Location Indicator are included in the surrogates in Figures 4.1, 4.2 and 4.3.

4.9 Summary

Surrogates are a means to an end; their quality is particularly significant where the original item is not immediately accessible. Thus they play an important role in an environment where the World Wide Web is touted as the ultimate information store, enabling initial filtering of its resources.

The consistent creation of all three surrogate components – access points, description and location indicator – is essential. The specific details of all three components will be dictated by the needs of the users and the particular collection. External standards such as ISBD, AACR2 or SPEC-TRUM may be considered, possibly in a simplified or highly modified form. The principles on which these standards are based should also be used as guidelines for the development of internal standards.

The fuller levels of description in AACR2 contain elements which may be applied to any object: titles and statements of responsibility, information concerning edition and state, the publishers, printers, distributors and dates, the physical description, and whether the item belongs to a series or a collection. Notes take account of any historical or critical facts. Regardless of whether one is describing paintings, sculpture, audio tapes or computer files, the same type of description applies. Although many developers of information retrieval systems may baulk at the details of AACR2, it does provide a useful reference source.

Specific attention should be given to the various levels of manifested items, perhaps through a relational database or a hypertext structure. However, for practical reasons, it may be necessary to limit the effort devoted to these finer distinctions. A conflict exists between sophisticated approaches which require a lot of human intellectual analysis and which may be feasible for small experimental systems, and the impossibility of implementing these in large-scale operational information systems.

For the broadcast news agency described in Section 1.8, it is likely that no single standard will be appropriate, but the designer of the retrieval system must make conscious decisions about the level of surrogate details, and develop guidelines to ensure consistency in each of the components. The actual outcome of decisions made about surrogates is relatively insignificant compared with the following requirements:

- The designer must be aware that these decisions must be made.
- The decisions must be implemented consistently.
- The users must be aware of the effects of the decisions for finding information.

4.10   Practical assignments

You are encouraged to answer the following questions for one or more of the retrieval systems listed in Section 1.11:

1. Is there a standard surrogate structure which is used for all items in the collection?

2. Identify clearly the components of the surrogate structure, including the following:
    –   access points;
    –   description;
    –   location indicators;
    –   other (any not covered by the first three).

3. Identify the various types of access points, including:
    –   creator;
    –   subject;
    –   other.

4. Identify the various types of description, including:
    –   physical;
    –   subject;
    –   other.

5. Explain how the location indicators work, and assess their effectiveness.

6. Are any standards used for the component parts of the surrogate?

7. Does the collection include various manifestations of an item (e.g. different versions of a computer file, or a printed book which is also on CD-ROM)? If so, how do the surrogates for original items and their manifestations differ?

8. Does the collection include multi-part items? If so, are there surrogates for the whole or the parts?

9. If you were given responsibility for redesigning this information retrieval system from the perspective of surrogates, would you make any changes?

You should try to give detailed answers, rather than simply responding with 'Yes' or 'No'. Sample answers are given in Section 4.13.

4.11   Notes

[1]   Bearman, David (1994) *Towards a Reference Model*: 〈http://
www.lis.pitt.edu/ ~nhprc/prog6-5.html〉.
[2]   UKOLN metadata: 〈http://www.ukoln.ac.uk/metadata/〉. W3C resource
description framework: 〈http://purl.org/w3c/rdf〉. Digital libraries –
metadata resources: 〈http://www.nlc-bnc.ca/ifla/II/metadata.htm〉.
[3]   Weibel, Stuart (1996) *A Topology of Metadata (Based Loosely on
David Bearman's Reference Metadata Model)*: 〈http://www.oclc.org/
~weibel/〉. See also Weibel (1997).
[4]   Dublin Core metadata element set – resource page: 〈http://purl.org/
metadata/dublin_core/〉.

4.12   References and further reading

American National Standards Institute (1979) *American National Standard
for Writing Abstracts* (Z39.14-1979), New York: ANSI.

Anderson, D. (1989) *Standard Practices in the Preparation of Bibliographic
Records*, UBCIM Occasional Paper 13, London: IFLA.

Avram, H.D. and McCallum, S.H. (1982) 'UNIMARC', *IFLA Journal*, **8**
(1), 50–4.

Baer, N.L. and Johnson, K.E. (1988) 'The state of authority', *Information
Technology and Libraries*, 7, 139–53.

Berman, Sanford (ed.) (1986) *Cataloging Special Materials*, Phoenix, AZ:
Oryx Press.

Bierbaum, E.G. (1990) 'MARC in museums: Applicability of the revised
visual materials format', *Information Technology and Libraries*,
December, 295–9.

Bruckman, Denis (1990) 'Le vidéodisque images de la Revolution
Française', *Bulletin des Bibliothèques de France*, **35** (2), 122–8, 130–5.

Canadian Heritage Information Network (1986) *Humanities Data Dictionary
of the Canadian Heritage Information Network*, Documentation
Research Publication 1, Revision 1, Ottawa, Ontario: CHIN.

Cleveland, Donald B. and Cleveland, Ana D. (1990) *Introduction to Indexing and Abstracting* (2nd edn), Littleton, CO: Libraries Unlimited.

Cook, Michael (1986) *Management of Information from Archives*, Aldershot: Gower.

Cook, Michael and Grant, K. (1986) *A Manual of Archive Description*,
London: Society of Archivists.

Cowton, Jeff (ed.) (1997) *SPECTRUM: The UK Museum Documentation*

Standard (2nd edn), Cambridge: MDA. Also available on: ⟨http://www.open.gov.uk/mdocassn/spectrum.htm⟩.

Dickson, J. and Zadner, P. (1989) 'Authority control in the online environment', *Cataloguing and Classification Quarterly*, **9** (3), 57–71.

Dierick, H. and Hopkinson, A. (1981) *Reference Model for Machine-readable Bibliographic Descriptions* (2nd edn) (PG1/81/WS/22), Paris: UNESCO/General Information Programme and UNISIST.

Devlin, Brendan (1996) 'An Assessment of Internet as a Reference Tool in Irish Academic Libraries', unpublished thesis submitted to the Department of Library and Information Studies, University College Dublin.

Frost, Carolyn O. (1983) *Cataloging Nonbook Materials*, Littleton, CO: Libraries Unlimited.

Gorman, Michael (1987) 'Bibliographic description: Past, present and future', *International Cataloguing*, **16** (4), 43.

Gorman, Michael (ed.) (1989) *The Concise AACR2: 1988 Revision*, Chicago, Ottawa and London: American Library Association, Canadian Library Association, Library Association.

Gorman, Michael and Winkler, Paul (eds) (1978) *Anglo-American Cataloguing Rules* (2nd edn), prepared by the American Library Association, the British Library, the Canadian Committee on Cataloguing, the Library Association and the Library of Congress, London: Library Association Publishing.

Gorman, Michael and Winkler, Paul (eds) (1993) *Anglo-American Cataloguing Rules* (2nd edn), prepared under the direction of the Joint Steering Committee for Revision of AACR, Chicago, Ottawa and London: American Library Association, Canadian Library Association, Library Association Publishing. (Note: *The Anglo-American Cataloguing Rules* (2nd edn, 1998 revision) is published jointly by the same publishers in paperback and CD-ROM.)

Hagler, Ronald (1991) *The Bibliographic Record and Information Technology* (2nd edn), Chicago, IL: ALA Publishing Services.

Holt, B.P. et al. (eds) (1987) *UNIMARC Manual*, London: IFLA International Office for UBCIM.

Hunter, E.J. (1989) *Examples Illustrating AACR2: 1988 Revision*, London: Library Association.

IFLA (1977) *ISBD (G): General International Standard Bibliographic Description: Annotated Text*, London: Working Group on the General International Bibliographic Description, IFLA International Office for UBCIM.

IFLA (1987a) *ISBD (NBM) International Standard Bibliographic Description for Non-book Materials* (rev. edn), London: IFLA International Office for UBCIM.

IFLA (1987b) *International Guide to MARC Databases and Services* (2nd edn), London: IFLA International MARC Project.

International Standards Organization (1976) *Documentation: Abstracts for Publication and Documentation*, Geneva: ISO.

Lancaster, F.W. (1991) *Indexing and Abstracting in Theory and Practice*, London: Library Association.

Miller, Rosalind E. and Terwillegar, Jane C. (1990) *Commonsense Cataloguing: A Cataloguer's Manual* (4th edn), New York: H.W. Wilson.

Museum Documentation Association (1980) *Data Definition Language and Data Standards*, Cambridge: MDA.

Museum Documentation Association (1991) *A Brief Guide to the MDA Data Structure Standard*, Cambridge: MDA.

Plessard, M. (1990) 'The Universal Bibliographic Control and International MARC Programme', *International Cataloguing and Bibliographic Control*, July/September, 35–7.

Rogers, Jo Ann V. and Saye, Jerry D. (1987) *Nonprint Cataloging for Multimedia Collections: A Guide Based on AACR2*, Littleton, CO: Libraries Unlimited.

Rowley, Jennifer E. (1988) *Abstracting and Indexing* (2nd edn), London: Library Association.

Rowley, Jennifer E. (1992) *Organizing Knowledge* (2nd edn), Aldershot: Ashgate.

Schwartz, Ray (1997) 'Uniform Resource Identifiers and the effort to bring "bibliographic control" to the web: An overview of current progress', *Bulletin of the American Society for Information Science*, **24** (1), 12–14.

UKMARC (1990) *UKMARC Manual* (2nd edn), London: British Library, Bibliographic Services Division.

Weibel, Stuart (1997) 'The Dublin Core: A simple content description model for electronic resources', *Bulletin of the American Society for Information Science*, **24** (1), 9–11.

4.13 Sample answers to the practical assignments

4.13.1 *The OPAC of a specific library, and the items in the same library*

1. Is there a standard surrogate structure which is used for all items in the collection?

There is a broadly similar surrogate structure for all items in the collection, in that the records in the catalogue give author, title, source, date, subject headings and location of all items. AACR2 and MARC standards facilitate this consistency. However, there are variations, in that the surrogate structure will vary slightly for different physical formats (e.g. for computer floppy disks compared with books).

2.   *Identify clearly the components of the surrogate structure, including the following:*

- *Access points:* Technically, these could be all the components of the record; in practice, the access points are normally: creator, the full title or significant words from the title, the subject headings, or significant words from the subject headings or the classification code.
- *Description:* This is the physical description of the information item.
- *Location indicators:* This is the classification code, and gives the shelf location of the item.
- *Other:* There is access by date, but only as a limiting feature on a search which has already been done, otherwise searching would be slow and too many items would be retrieved.

3.   *Identify the various types of access points, including:*

- *Creator:* For books, the creator is usually the author(s) or editor(s); in some cases, it may be the name of an organization.
- *Subject:* Users can search the OPAC using a keyword search, or by using subject headings or classification codes. Search terms can be combined using Boolean operators.
- *Other:* Another option is to use the full book title.

4.   *Identify the various types of description, including:*

- *Physical:* This would include the size of the book, the number of pages, and whether illustrations are included.
- *Subject:* Controlled or uncontrolled subject terms and the classification code give the subject description. In some cases, there may be a summary of the subject content, or contents pages may be included, but this is not the norm.
- *Other:* If the book is part of a series, details on the series are usually given.

5.   *Explain how the location indicators work, and assess their effectiveness.*
The location indicators are usually based on the classification code, followed by the first three letters of the creator's name (e.g. 025.4/BUR for this book). A prefix may be used if there are different physical sequences (e.g. L025.4/BUR for a physically large book, or C025.4/BUR for a computer disk). Users may not understand these subtleties.

6.   *Are any standards used for the component parts of the surrogate?*
Standards such as AACR2, MARC, ISBD, LCSH or other subject heading lists or thesauri are consulted in creating the surrogate; a classification scheme is used to arrange the items in the library. Usually, the location indicator of the surrogate is based on the classification code.

7. Does the collection include various manifestations of an item? If so, how do the surrogates for original items and their manifestations differ?

Examples of original items and their manifestations include different editions of popular books such as the Bible, plays by Shakespeare, translations of popular works, revised editions of items, or versions in different formats (e.g. a computer disk associated with a textbook). The descriptions within AACR2 and ISBD allow these manifestations to be distinguished through their surrogates.

8. Does the collection include multi-part items? If so, are there surrogates for the whole or the parts?

The collection includes multi-part items in the following forms:

- Journals may be published in serial form, where each issue is part of a regular sequence. The surrogate is normally for the journal as a whole, although journal record systems will track arrival of individual issues. Each journal issue may be considered as a multi-part item, with the individual articles corresponding to the parts. On the OPAC, the surrogate is typically for the overall journal, whereas in an abstracting or indexing service, it is for the individual journal article;
- For conference proceedings, or a book with contributions by several creators, the surrogate is usually for the item.
- For an item which has several volumes, such as an encyclopaedia, the surrogate is usually for the item.

9. If you were given responsibility for redesigning this information retrieval system from the perspective of surrogates, would you make any changes?

Inclusion of the original item, or some summary of its content, as part of the OPAC is desirable. A necessary improvement for many OPAC systems is fuller recognition of multi-part items, and the indication of links between them.

4.13.2   The printed telephone directories (name and classified) for your country or region

1. Is there a standard surrogate structure which is used for all items in the collection?

This system is concerned with surrogates only. No named standard is adopted, but most of the surrogate entries are presented in a uniform manner.

2. Identify clearly the components of the surrogate structure, including the following:

- *Access points:* For the alphabetical residential telephone directory, the only access point is the surname, followed by first name or initial, of the

person whose phone number you require. For the classified directory, the primary access point is through the subject heading of the service or business you require. The individual surrogate entries can then be accessed by the name of the business, which is arranged alphabetically within the subject category.
- *Description:* This refers to the details contained within the surrogate entry. In the classified telephone directory, the description may include the size, range or scope of the business or service.
- *Location indicators:* These are the telephone number and address of the individual (alphabetical name directory) or the business (classified directory).
- *Other:* None.

3.   *Identify the various types of access points, including:*
- *Creator:* None.
- *Subject:* Surrogates can be accessed by subject in the classified directory only. (The classified directory also contains an alphabetical subject index.)
- *Other:* Entries can be accessed by either the name of the individual or the name of the business, depending on the type of directory.

4.   *Identify the various types of description, including:*
- *Physical:* There is no description within the entries in the alphabetical (name) directory, other than the name, address and telephone number of each individual listed.
- *Subject:* This applies only to the classified directory, where each entry is classified under the appropriate subject heading. In the classified directory, some of the entries may resemble advertisements, and may contain further descriptions and details of the business, such as opening hours and special services offered.
- *Other:* Not applicable.

5.   *Explain how the location indicators work, and assess their effectiveness*
The location indicators are the addresses and telephone numbers in the entries in both types of directory. These are effective in providing information on how to contact the person or business you are seeking.

6.   *Are any standards used for the component parts of the surrogate?*
No named surrogate standards are used. Names are entered in the form supplied, which results in a mixture of full first names and initials. The subject headings conform to a standard set for each directory product, and are updated for new editions.

7. *Does the collection include various manifestations of an item? If so, how do the surrogates for original items and their manifestations differ?*

No, manifestations do not occur.

8. *Does the collection include multi-part items? If so, are there surrogates for the whole or the parts?*

Where a business has multiple outlets, there are usually surrogate entries corresponding to each of the outlets.

9. *If you were given responsibility for redesigning this information retrieval system from the perspective of surrogates, would you make any changes?*

In both directories, subdivision of surrogate entries by location would be useful; this is often done by producing local directories. Greater standardization is desirable for the classified directory. Entries should also include in the description information such as opening hours, fax number and e-mail address of the business. However, because this information would take up considerable space, the directory should also be made available in electronic form.

4.13.3   Internet resources and the AltaVista search engine

1. *Is there a standard surrogate structure which is used for all items in the collection?*

No, individual search engines may apply their in-house standards and encourage creators of Web resources to observe certain conventions, but overall there is no standardization. There are moves in this direction, with recommended standards, for example Dublin Core and TEI, which are likely to evolve rapidly during the lifetime of this book.

2. *Identify clearly the components of the surrogate structure, including the following:*
- *Access points:* All indexed 'words' in the surrogate can be used as access points.
- *Description:* The description in the surrogate is the title of the Web site, followed by a brief outline of content, which usually indicates the creator.
- *Location indicators:* This is the URL of the information resource.
- *Other:* None.

3. *Identify the various types of access points, including:*
- *Creator:* Generally, this would not be particularly useful or important, and it is not always included as an access point. It will be an access point if it is included near the top of the page and if it is included as an

indexed term by the search engine. Users can search for an individual's name or an organization's name, which is useful for identifying home pages.

- *Subject:* The subject is not specifically identified, but is based on words from the text. There is no control of vocabulary on Alta Vista. Internet subject directories (e.g. BUBL Link or Yahoo!) provide fuller subject access.
- *Other:* None.

4. *Identify the various types of description, including:*
- *Physical:* This indicates the size of the item in bytes (computer storage units, where 1 byte is approximately equal to one text character), and indicates the file type, which has implications for the user's ability to view/hear/play the item.
- *Subject:* This includes a section of the original text, as well as subject index terms, if assigned.
- *Other:* None.

5. *Explain how the location indicators work, and assess their effectiveness.*
The location indicator (the URL) is very fully integrated into the system. It is very effective, as it is unique. By clicking on the URL, one is connected directly to the information item it represents, so that access to the original item happens seamlessly. One disadvantage is that if the URL changes, the old link may still be in the system, so the user will get the response 'URL not found', thus leading to a feeling of being sent down a blind alley.

6. *Are any standards used for the component parts of the surrogate?*
Within AltaVista, there is a standard structure. The physical description and URL are standardized, but the subject description and access points are not.

7. *Does the collection include various manifestations of an item? If so, how do the surrogates for original items and their manifestations differ?*
The Internet is a maze of manifested items. There are mirror sites which duplicate information in order to distribute usage over a number of computers in different continents. This corresponds to a type 1 manifestation (facsimile of original item/multiple identical copies). There are very similar resources, where perhaps one version is an updated edition of another: a type 2 manifestation (distinct facsimile/multiple distinguishable copies). There are type 3 manifestations (revision, translation, adaptation or interpretation of item), where the same information may be presented in a different format or a different language. In most cases, the different manifestations are found by accident, if at all; there is no conscious effort to show the relationships within the Internet. There will be differences

between the surrogates of these manifestations where they are located on different Web sites and Web pages.

8. *Does the collection include multi-part items? If so, are there surrogates for the whole or the parts?*

The Internet abounds in multi-part items. While there are surrogates for all levels of parts, the surrogates don't reflect the existence of related parts. For example, a university may have a home page on the Web; individual departments will have pages, as will individual teachers, courses, etc. There may be a general page for a course, with subsidiary pages for a class session, with pages corresponding to each screen display or overhead transparency in a particular class.

9. *If you were given responsibility for redesigning this information retrieval system from the perspective of surrogates, would you make any changes?*

Encouraging creators to adopt a surrogate structure which reflects the contents accurately and consistently is crucial. This corresponds to a voluntary code of practice for Web page creators – if it's worth putting up information, it's worth making it retrievable. Ensuring that key components such as names of individuals, organizations and consistent subject terms are included in the early portion of the text facilitates this data being picked up by search engines such as AltaVista.

Chapter 5

Subject content

5.1 Introduction

Subject content analysis and representation have long been issues of major concern to designers and users of information collections. The experience of librarians and other information professionals in developing consistent approaches to solving these problems is valuable, but many unresolved issues remain. Traditionally, the main concerns have been with the description of printed items which consist mainly of text, with the result that 'aboutness', which may be defined as the overall subject theme of an item, is normally heavily influenced by the words contained in the item. These words may be used directly as the basis for information retrieval in a full-text system, or they may subconsciously influence the assignment of descriptive words or phrases by a human indexer.

Even for these text items, there are many problems in determining subject content, which are exacerbated by the variety of perspectives which users with different backgrounds will bring to a subject area, and by the influences of different cultural attitudes. The problems of subjectivity and individual user perspectives increase when one has to deal with audio, visual and multimedia items. The convenience of being able to use words from a text to automatically describe subject content no longer exists.

5.1.1 Stages in subject content

Working with subject content involves two distinct stages:

1. **subject analysis** – perusal of the item to decide what subject it is 'about' or 'of';
2. **subject representation** – description of the concepts identified in the first stage, using the appropriate subject vocabulary or code.

The results of each stage are presented in the example below; the details of how these results are derived are explained later in this chapter.

5.1.1.1   Example

Subject analysis indicates what an item is about, using informal language:

- use of computers in universities in Europe.

Subject representation may then produce the following:

- thesaurus terms – computers, universities, Europe;
- subject headings – universities and colleges – Europe;
- classification scheme – 378.4.

5.1.2   Applications of subject content

Organization of information by subject has three significant applications:

1. arrangement of items and/or surrogates in a pre-coordinate sequence by subject, in order to facilitate storage and browsing; the most likely types of subject vocabulary are controlled ones, for example
   - classification schemes;
   - alphabetical subject terms.
2. retrieval of items and/or surrogates by post-coordination of subject terms, in order to provide for precise retrieval of specific items; the most likely types of subject vocabulary are
   - alphabetical subject terms;
   - natural words or phrases.
3. assessment of the usefulness of the subject content before deciding whether to track down the original item, based on its subject description in the surrogate; the most likely types of subject vocabularies are
   - abstract;
   - extract.

The specific subject vocabularies mentioned above will be described in detail in Section 5.3.

5.1.3   Relationship with indexing

The term 'indexing' is used widely to describe many methods of information retrieval, particularly in relation to subject content. The term arose originally for printed works, but is now used in a much broader context, especially for computer databases. The contents of this chapter apply to all types of subject indexes in existence: back-of-the-book indexes, abstracting and indexing services, indexes to World Wide Web pages, etc. The definition of 'indexing' from Wellisch (1991, pp. xxiii–xxiv) places the term in context:

> An operation intended to represent the results of the analysis of a document by means of a controlled or natural indexing language.

Comprehensive details on indexing are contained in a number of sources, notably Foskett (1996), Rowley (1988 and 1992) and Wellisch (1991). This book doesn't treat indexing as a distinct activity, but the terms 'indexing' and 'indexer' will be used occasionally, as a convenient way of referring to the activity and the person who carries out the subject analysis and representation.

5.2 Subject analysis

Subject analysis involves the indexer in the following steps:

1. familiarization with the overall indexing policy for the information retrieval system, as identified in instructions to indexers or derived from material indexed already;

2. familiarization with the item to be indexed; the item should be examined closely, making notes of key headings, sections, objects or scenes; this may involve scanning, browsing, perusing, listening to, watching, or exploring the item, depending on the medium; the significant areas for specific media are
   - printed items: headings, first sentences, last sentences, etc., in all parts and sections; then overall analysis;
   - still images: focus of image, foreground, background, etc.; then overall analysis;
   - moving images: individual frames as for still image; then overall analysis;
   - audio recordings: individual items; then core themes.

3. possible consultation of external reference sources;

4. identification of the key subject concepts which should be indexed; these may include the overall theme of the item, and various subsidiary themes which appear in significant parts of the item; these concepts should be co-extensive with the content of the item being indexed.

5. decisions on appropriate depth of analysis; as discussed in Section 5.2.1;

6. analysis of the item as being 'of' and 'about' some concepts, as described in Section 5.2.2, may be helpful;

7. facet analysis may also help itemize concepts; this involves asking questions beginning with the following words about the item: what, who, when, where, how, etc. (This process is discussed in Section 5.2.3.)

5.2.1   Depth of analysis

The depth of subject analysis is defined as part of a general policy on subject indexing for a collection or organization. It will be heavily dependent on the objectives and resources of the organization, and the needs of the users. The type of subject representation chosen (see Section 5.3) must also be capable of reflecting the depth of analysis. Depth of analysis is based on a number of components, of which the two most significant are:

*   specificity;
*   exhaustivity.

Specificity is based on the existence of many concepts in a hierarchy of a genus–species relation, for example:

1. Computers
2. Computer hardware
3. Personal computers
4. Apple Macintosh computers
5. Apple Macintosh Powerbook computers.

In practice, a term may belong to a number of different hierarchies: for example, 'Powerbook computers' will also be part of an 'office equipment' hierarchy. The specificity with which the item is indexed will influence retrieval: if a Web page for an Apple Macintosh Powerbook is accessible only by its name, this is of little benefit to a user who doesn't know what it's called. On the other hand, a user who wants details of this specific computer doesn't want to wade through thousands of entries for various other types of computer.

In general, the best approach is to index the item as specifically as possible, and to use other mechanisms to provide links from more general headings to the specific one. These mechanisms include:

*   thesauri (Section 5.3.3);
*   alphabetical subject headings (Section 5.3.3);
*   classification schemes (Section 5.3.4).

Exhaustivity describes the extent to which every single possible concept is indexed. For example, a Web page entry for an organization could be indexed under the name of every service or department, or it might be indexed with one general heading only. The level of exhaustivity which is desirable will be influenced by the nature of the items, the collection, and the users. For instance, a CD-ROM of Impressionist Art will be analysed by subject in very different ways for the two scenarios:

- a general information resource in a multi-purpose information service;
- a specialist service for art historians.

Similar differences arise between the creation of an internal index to provide subject access within a book, and the subject entry for that book in a library catalogue or bibliography.

5.2.2 'Of' and 'about'

It is possible to analyse items as being 'of' certain subjects, creatures, places and events, and as being 'about' certain intangibles. The terms 'hard' and 'soft' indexing are equivalent to analysing what an item is 'of' and 'about'. It is also possible to identify 'specific' and 'generic' subject matter:

- 'specific of' information can be expressed easily in words or codes as a precise search statement, is unambiguous, and deals with the concrete – for example, 'Powerbook computers';
- 'generic of' information can be expressed easily in words or codes, may result in unmanageably high recall, and often has to be made more specific – for example, 'personal computers' or 'computers';
- 'about'/'aboutness' is difficult to express verbally, as it deals with emotional responses to a stimulus, it cannot be expressed in a search statement, and is dependent on characteristics of an item as interpreted by the individual – for example, 'information society', or 'office systems'.

This approach has been developed very fully by Shatford (1986) for subject analysis of pictures, but it is applicable to all multimedia items, particularly those which have some 'soft' meaning.

5.2.3 Facet analysis

The concept of facets and facet analysis comes from consideration of the many-sided structure of gems. In the same way as a precious jewel presents many different sides to the light, and may appear to be of different colours when examined at different angles, the subject of an item may be considered as having different facets or aspects. A combination of one or more facets is normally needed to give the full picture. Facets correspond to different aspects of, or approaches to, a subject.

Ranganathan (1959) identified five primary facets – Personality, Matter, Energy, Space and Time – which are applicable to a range of subjects and types of media. These are defined as follows, including the questions which should be asked in order to identify each facet:

- **Personality** – core of a subject; primary facet
  - What is the core theme?

– What single concept best describes the item?
- **Matter** – materials
  – What objects or people are described?
- **Energy** – processes, activities or operations
  – What are these people doing?
  – How are they doing it?
  – What activities are taking place?
- **Space** – geographical regions
  – Where is this happening?
- **Time** – past, present or future time periods
  – When is this happening?

5.2.3.1 Example

An expanded version of the earlier topic, 'computers in teaching in universities in Europe in the 21st century', possesses the following facets:

- Personality – universities;
- Matter – computers;
- Energy – teaching;
- Space – Europe;
- Time – 21st century.

Shatford (1986) applies the concept of facets to the subject analysis of paintings. Her ideas are applicable to a wide range of items, not merely visual ones. She is not concerned with developing a classification scheme, but only with identifying and classifying the kind of subjects an item may have. Her basic facets are based on Ranganathan's. By asking the questions 'Who?, What?, Where? and When?', one identifies basic facets. It is not necessary to use every facet to describe every item: for example, in the case of the briefer example 'computers in universities in Europe', the Energy and Time facets would be empty. A simplified version of Shatford's (1986) approach is presented in the first three columns of Table 5.1, where each row corresponds to one of Ranganathan's five facets.

Facet analysis, with its emphasis on the representation of different aspects (facets) of the item being described and its ability to coordinate different combinations of concepts at the time of retrieval, provides a very good theoretical basis for the analysis and description of multimedia items in diverse retrieval systems. It allows the indexer to describe the item fully and precisely. In addition to its use in identifying subject concepts, a faceted approach provides a systematic framework for describing the physical characteristics of the original item, by providing a checklist of questions to be asked about each item. It is difficult to apply facet analysis to the totality of subject knowledge; it works more effectively when applied to specialized areas.

Table 5.1   *Facet analysis of subject content*

1 Ranganathan's facets	2 Questions for each facet	3 Example	4 'Specific of'	5 Example	6 'Generic of'	7 Example	8 'About'	9 Example
Personality	Who/what is the core theme?	Universities	Individually named persons, animals, things	University of Sheffield; Sorbonne University	Kinds of persons, animals, things	Universities, third-level institutions	Abstractions symbolized by people or objects	Advancement of knowledge
Matter	What objects or people are described?	Computers	Individually named persons, animals, things	Apple Macintosh computers; the Internet; Novell networks		Personal computers, networking	Abstractions symbolized by people or objects	Technology
Energy	What are the people and objects doing? How are they doing it?	Teaching	Individually named events	Practical tutorials	Actions, conditions	Learning methods; teaching methods	Emotions; abstractions manifested by actions, events	Education
Space	Where is this happening?	Europe	Individually named geographic location	Dublin, Sheffield, Paris	Kind of place, geographic or architectural	European cities	Places symbolized; abstractions manifested by locale	
Time	When is this happening?	20th century	Linear time; periods	20th century	Cyclical time; time of day		Emotions or abstractions symbolized by or manifested by time	Technological era

Note: 'Aboutness' – collaboration on teaching and learning in the EU; implications of new technology for resource allocation in education; the information society and distance learning in universities.

Source. Adapted from Shatford (1986).

5.2.4   Combination of 'of'/'about' and facet analysis

Shatford (1986) subdivides each of the facets into three components based
on 'specific of', 'generic of' and 'about'. These components are illustrated
in columns 4 and 5 ('specific of'), 6 and 7 ('generic of') and 8 and 9
('about') in Table 5.1, where the first column in each pair gives a definition,
and the second gives an example.

The Personality and Matter facets, which are shown in the first two rows
of Table 5.1, contain terms which answer the questions: 'Who, or what, is
this item "of"?' and 'Do these people or objects represent other people,
objects or ideas – what are they "about"?' The question 'Who, or what, is
this item "of"?' is further subdivided into the two questions: 'Who specifically is this of?' and 'Who generically is this of?'

The Energy facet, which is shown in the third row of Table 5.1, is composed of terms that answer the following questions:

- What are the creatures or objects in this item doing?
- What emotions are conveyed by these actions?
- What themes do these actions symbolize?

The first two questions are 'of' questions, the second two 'about' questions.

The Space facet, which is shown in the fourth row of Table 5.1, asks
'Where is the item in space?' It may also be subdivided into the three components. The Time facet, which is shown in the fifth row of Table 5.1, deals
with dates, periods and recurring time (e.g. spring, night), by asking: 'When
is this event occurring?' 'Aboutness' results from the 'ofness' of two or
more facets, and is determined by a synthesis of these facets. There is no
simple rule for determining the principal or central subject of an item, but
the indexer must make the attempt by asking the question: 'What is this
item "of", when viewed as an entity?' or 'What is this item "about", when
viewed as an entity?' This is illustrated in the note to Table 5.1. The nature
and intended use of the collection to which an item belongs, not the
subjective nature of 'aboutness', should determine whether or not 'aboutness' is to be analysed and indexed. Shatford's theory is important for multimedia items, in particular a film sequence, audio sequence or text
sequence, or a combination of these. Individual frames, clips or pages may
be about certain subjects, while the overall subject of the item may be quite
different.

5.2.5   Complex items

The subject of an original item and its manifestation may differ – for
example, a painting of a person reproduced in other formats, or a play or
film based on a book, or a live performance of a musical score. The dif-

ference may be fairly subtle: the subject of the original may be 'Elvis Presley' and that of the manifestation may be 'media pressure on Elvis Presley'.

Multi-part items may have parts which are about quite different subjects, for example:

- a newspaper, periodical, television or video or film series, newspaper cartoon series, published music series, a weekly radio programme;
- an item which consists of parts dealing with a variety of subjects – a television/radio chat show, book or report with many sections, conference proceedings;
- an item which consists of several physical parts, with different subject emphasis.

The ideal solution is to carry out subject analysis of the whole item, and of all its component parts, but this would result in:

- heavy demands for time and cost;
- underutilization of much of the analysis;
- complex record structure and database requirements;
- a difficult system to use.

A more practical solution is to take the following steps:

1. Develop definite guidelines for the extent to which subject analysis should be carried out for parts of an item.
2. Apply these guidelines consistently, and familiarize users with them.
3. Use 'aboutness' to deal with the whole item, while applying 'of' and 'about' to the components.

5.3   Subject representation

Subject representation, or translation, involves converting the subject concept(s) identified through the subject analysis to terms in the indexing language. For controlled vocabularies, the concepts will be expressed in terms from the thesaurus, subject headings list or classification scheme. Alternative terms should be considered for possible use, instead of, or in addition to, the terms first considered.

Care must be taken to avoid subjectivity or bias, as the assignment of keywords may unintentionally involve the indexer in passing judgement on the image. For example, the four terms 'freedom fighter', 'guerrilla', 'partisan' and 'terrorist' all have very similar definitions, yet each has a different meaning in public perception. This problem is exacerbated for media other than text.

5.3.1   Alternative approaches

The approaches to subject representation can be categorized using the following four characteristics:

1. **Natural or controlled** – 'Natural' refers to the type of language used in normal oral and written communication, which is not restricted in any way. 'Controlled' language limits the choice of subject terms to a predefined list.

2. **Derived or assigned** – 'Derived' vocabularies take words or other components automatically from an information item. 'Assigned' terms are not necessarily taken from the original item, they are allocated by an indexer, frequently from a controlled vocabulary.

3. **Alphabetical or classified** – 'Alphabetical' vocabularies use words, phrases or sentences to describe subjects. 'Classified' vocabularies use some type of code or notational symbols which represent a logical arrangement.

4. **Pre- or post-coordinate** – This distinction between the two approaches to organization of information, which has been discussed in Chapter 3, also applies to the coordination of subject terms. For example, the phrase 'university teaching' is pre-coordinate, while the terms 'universities' and 'teaching' may be post-coordinated.

Different combinations of these characteristics result in a number of distinct subject vocabularies. Table 5.2 shows the relationship between the vocabularies and the characteristics. For some categories, there may be a gradual progression from one extreme to the other – for example, increasing levels of vocabulary control along a spectrum from full-text words to

Table 5.2   *Categorization of subject vocabularies*

Vocabulary example	Natural or controlled	Derived or assigned	Alphabetical or classified	Pre- or post-coordinate
Full-text words	Natural	Derived	Alphabetical	Post-coordinate
Full-text phrases	Natural	Derived	Alphabetical	Pre-coordinate
Indexer's words	Natural	Assigned	Alphabetical	Post-coordinate
Indexer's phrases	Natural	Assigned	Alphabetical	Pre-coordinate
None	Natural		Classified	
Thesauri	Controlled	Assigned	Alphabetical	Post-coordinate
Alphabetical subject terms	Controlled	Assigned	Alphabetical	Pre-coordinate
Thesauro-facet	Controlled	Assigned	Classified	Post-coordinate
Classification schemes	Controlled	Assigned	Classified	Pre-coordinate
None	Controlled	Derived		

Table 5.3   *Comparison of various categories of subject representation*

Advantages and disadvantages of natural and controlled vocabularies:

Natural	Controlled
More vague/ambiguous	More precise
Changes with new developments	Difficult to keep up to date
No links/suggestions of terms	Links between related terms

Advantages and disadvantages of alphabetical and classified vocabularies:

Alphabetical	Classified
Discourages browsing	Facilitates browsing
No index needed	Requires index
One-step retrieval	Two-step retrieval
Language-dependent	International

Advantages and disadvantages of pre- and post-coordinate vocabularies:

Pre-coordinate	Post-coordinate
Becomes out-of-date	More readily kept up to date
Subject/discipline-based	Word/term/simple concept-based
Suitable for printed products	Suitable for computerized access
Longer list of terms	Shorter lists of terms
General terms	More specific terms

classification schemes. The advantages and disadvantages associated with various categories of subject representation are presented in Table 5.3.

5.3.2   Natural words and phrases

The simplest and most obvious vocabulary to use would be natural-language terms, where the words or phrases which seem appropriate are derived from the item. A stop-word list may be used to exclude frequently occurring words which have no retrieval value. These include definite and indefinite articles, some verbs, pronouns, prepositions and conjunctives, such as: the, a, an, is, are, was, were, this, that, they, when, who, what, of, in, on, etc.

This approach has many advantages, including speed of generation of subject entries, hospitality for handling new topics, and apparent ease of use, but there are also problems:

- Synonyms (different words which have the same, or almost the same, meaning) are not linked – for example, 'universities' and 'colleges'.
- Homonyms (words which have the same spelling, but different meanings) are not defined – for example, 'lead' as a heavy metal, or 'lead' as the opposite of 'follow'.
- Ambiguous words are not clarified – for example, 'computer design'.

- Scattering of related material occurs – for example, 'animals' and 'zoology'.
- Hierarchical relationships, or levels of specificity, are ignored – for example, 'computers' or 'Apple Macintosh Powerbook computers' in the hierarchy illustrated in Section 5.2.1.
- The vocabulary is language-dependent, and difficult for foreign users.
- Inconsistencies develop.
- Searching is more complicated, as the user needs to list all synonyms and possible word endings.
- Single words may be ambiguous when taken out of context.
- Retrieval is dependent on the quantity and quality of source data which is used to derive the subject entries.
- Multimedia items may not contain any helpful text and words.

Some of the disadvantages can be overcome in a computerized environment, with automatic truncation of words to word stems – for example, 'management', 'managers', 'managing', 'manage', all truncated to 'manag*'. In a rapidly growing information system, where the ideal of human analysis may be completely unrealistic, this is a practical solution. It is adopted by the majority of search engines on the Internet, with a varying amount of encouragement to designers of Web pages to include meaningful words in the early portions of their texts, which are indexed.

If this process is extended to the mechanical derivation of meaningful phrases or sentences, a pre-coordinate form of derived vocabulary results. Computer software can identify significant combinations of words in two ways:

1. semantically – based on the level of co-occurrence of two or more words;
2. syntactically – based on the grammatical structure of the sentence in which they occur.

This is the basis for printed applications such as KWIC (Key Word In Context), KWAC (Key Word And Context), and KWOC (Key Word Out of Context) indexes, which display keywords in the context of surrounding text for many traditional journal current awareness services. More recently, it has become a standard feature in World Wide Web search engines such as AltaVista to allow users to specify that search words be adjacent or located in close proximity in the source page.

Human indexers may be used to assign words and phrases, either with total freedom in the choice of these subject terms, or by following a standard set of rules for the formulation of subject terms, such as Cutter's *Rules for a Dictionary Catalog* (Cutter, 1904). Facet analysis, as described in Section 5.2.3, may influence the selection of terms and the way in which they are combined. There is a logical progression from words and phrases to the sentences and paragraphs of an abstract. These are written in natural language, with some degree of guidance as to the vocabulary used.

5.3.3 Controlled vocabularies: Thesauri and alphabetical subject terms

The problems of natural language identified in Section 5.3.2 indicate the need to introduce some sort of control on vocabulary terms. This may be done by introducing a general set of rules, without actually introducing a list of vocabulary terms, or by developing a list of subject terms for the specific application. Examples of the former include Cutter's *Rules for a Dictionary Catalog* (Cutter, 1904); the latter category is exemplified by alphabetical subject heading lists and thesauri.

Lists of subject terms may be divided into two broad categories:

1. thesauri which cover more specific subject areas; these generally involve less pre-coordination of terms, and do not employ subdivisions; examples include ERIC for Education, INSPEC for Engineering,

ball
Use appropriate term.

    USE ball (game) ✦
    SE ball (ritual) ✦
    SE chalk ball ✦
    SE musket ball ✦

---

ball (game)
A round object used in games.

    CL sports and games ✦

    UF ball
    bowling ball

---

ball (ritual)
Polished stone balls interpreted as ritual objects in the Scottish Iron Age.

    CL religion or ritual ✦

    UF ball

---

ballista ball
A stone missile fired from a ballista, larger in diameter than ballista shot.

    CL armour and weapons ✦
    BT projectile ✦

Figure 5.1   **Extract from the *MDA Archaeological Objects Thesaurus***
Source: MDA Archaeological Objects Thesaurus: ⟨http://www.open.gov.uk/mdocassn/archobj/ archobjb.htm⟩.

MeSH for Medicine, AAT for Art and Architecture, MDA for Museum Objects, *BSI Root Thesaurus* for general coverage, etc.[1] (an extract from the *MDA Archaeological Objects Thesaurus* is reproduced in Figure 5.1).

2. alphabetical subject headings lists which cover broad subject areas and have a high level of pre-coordination of terms and subdivisions of headings; examples include *Sears List*, *Library of Congress Subject Headings* (LCSH) and RAMEAU (France)[2] (extracts from the LCSH are reproduced in Figure 5.2).

Balls, Decorative
   USE Decorative balls

Balls (Parties) (May Subd Geog)
   [GV1746–GV1750]
   Here are entered works dealing with formal dances. Works concerned with less formal
       dances are entered under Dance parties.
   UF Dances
   BT Amusements
     Entertaining
   RT Dance
     Dance parties
   NT Debutante balls
     Drag balls
     Proms

Balls (Sporting goods)
   [GV749.B34]
   BT Sporting goods
   NT Baseballs
     Bowling balls
     Footballs
     Golf balls
     Medicine balls
     Tennis balls
     . . .

Decorative balls (May Subd Geog)
   [TT896.8]
   UF Balls, Decorative
   BT Decoration and ornament
     Handicraft
   NT Witch balls
     . . .

Tennis balls (May Subd Geog)
   [GV1002.5]
   BT Balls (Sporting goods)

Figure 5.2   Extract from the *Library of Congress Subject Headings*
Source: Library of Congress Classification Plus Folio Database (1998).

In practice, there may be very little difference between subject headings lists and thesauri, and the distinction is not important for this text, as it relies mainly on their different historical origins rather than their use. Subject headings lists were developed originally for use in pre-coordinate systems, while thesauri were intended for use in post-coordinate systems. Traditionally, vocabularies were coexistent with the retrieval mechanism, so the vocabularies (labels) which were used to describe items in a pre-coordinate system attempt to list in advance all the specific items which might be required. Thus a pre-coordinate vocabulary provides a label for the complex subject ABC in advance, whereas a post-coordinate vocabulary provides the components A, B and C separately, and expects the user to coordinate these when searching (see Table 3.2).

Vocabularies for retrieval systems often have a judicious amount of pre-coordination, where components that are frequently associated together are pre-coordinated. One has to assess the extent to which this is helpful, compared with the danger of creating overlapping groups while still having gaps between them. Examples of vocabularies which are intended for use in a post-coordinate way but have a certain amount of pre-coordination include most thesauri, such as *Medical Subject Headings* (MeSH), *Thesaurus of ERIC Descriptors* (for education) and *Art & Architecture Thesaurus*. (The basic distinction between pre- and post-coordination was introduced in Section 3.5; the advantages and disadvantages of pre- and post-coordinate vocabularies are presented in Table 5.3.)

A thesaurus is defined as a list of preferred and non-preferred vocabulary terms, with a strong network of references of three different types, as shown in Table 5.4.

Table 5.4   *Network of references in a thesaurus*

Preferential	Use/See	REVERSE	Used For/See Under
Hierarchical	Narrower Term/NT	REVERSE	Broader Term/BT
Semantic	Related Term/RT	REVERSE	Related Term/RT

Figure 5.1 shows the alphabetical arrangement of terms in the *MDA Archaeological Objects Thesaurus* from 'ball' to 'ballista ball'. If the indexer or the user consults the thesaurus under the general term 'ball', the instruction is to 'use appropriate term', for example 'ball (game)'. On doing this, he or she sees the context in which the term is used, and may also check the general class to which this term belongs, such as the general category of 'Sports and Games'. This gives an alphabetical listing of these terms from 'ball (game)' to 'toy', with more specific terms in some cases: for example, types of 'toy', such as 'doll', 'puppet' and 'spinning top'.

There is usually no need to develop a thesaurus from scratch; it is recommended that existing thesauri which deal with the subject area or the physical format be investigated. Thesauri may be identified by consulting the Web site listings which are maintained by organizations such as ASLIB

(OSIS – thesaurus selection) and the Museum Documentation Association's wordHOARD.[3] It is likely that the adopted thesaurus will require modification or extension, in which case guidelines for construction of thesauri should be followed. Thesauri designed for describing textual items in a specific subject area may be extended to handle visual, audio and multimedia items.

A thesauro-facet is essentially a combination of a faceted classification, which shows the relationships between subjects, and a thesaurus which provides a structured index to the classification. The principles are embodied in many modern thesauri which are used for subject content description of multimedia items, such as the AAT, and the *MDA Archaeological Objects Thesaurus*.

Subject headings were traditionally presented as a list of preferred and non-preferred vocabulary terms. Selected entries from the *Library of Congress Subject Headings* are shown in Figure 5.2. 'Balls, Decorative' is a non-preferred term, so the user is referred to 'Decorative balls'. 'Balls (Parties)' and 'Balls (Sporting goods)' are preferred terms which show how the different possible meanings of an ambiguous term are clarified. Each of these preferred terms is printed in bold typeface and forms part of an intricate network of other preferred terms, some of which are broader (BT), others narrower (NT), and some have less clearly defined relationships (RT) to the main term. Some headings may be subdivided: for example, it is possible to subdivide 'Balls (Parties)' geographically. The letters and numbers in square brackets give the classification code for headings which also occur in the Library of Congress classification scheme: for example, the code for 'Decorative balls' is TT896.8.

5.3.4   Controlled vocabularies: Classification

Classification is a very natural process, which we all apply in order to make sense of the world in which we live. It is the basis for much scientific research, particularly in areas of taxonomy. It can be applied to the supermarket analogy presented earlier, where criteria such as the storage requirements, ingredients or origins of the food, use or meal for which it is intended result in different store layouts.

The crucial aspect which distinguishes classification from any other retrieval process is the grouping of items in classes, where members of a class have at least some characteristic in common, and this characteristic is not possessed by items which are not members of this class. The objective of classification is to group items in a logical, linear fashion, which allows for browsing through the materials, moving from general aspects of a subject to more specific aspects, then to another somewhat related topic, then to a more specific aspect of that subject. Thus there is a hierarchical, branching structure which forms the core of the classification scheme.

The simple, linear arrangement might be influenced by one or more of the following overlapping traditions:

- philosophers' approach to the classification of knowledge;
- scientific taxonomies;
- general library classification schemes, such as the Dewey Decimal Classification, Universal Decimal Classification (UDC), Library of Congress (LC), Bliss Bibliographic Classification (BC);
- synthetic (faceted) library classification schemes for general and specific areas, for example Ranganathan's Colon Classification and a whole range of special schemes listed in sources such as Vickery (1968);
- hierarchical approaches used in everyday life – in offices, schools, industry, travel, etc.;
- hierarchical approaches used in some computerized information services, for example videotext and viewdata services such as CEEFAX, ORACLE, PRESTEL, MINITEL, etc.;
- Internet menus and search directories, such as BUBL Link, Lycos, Excite, NetFirst (Vizine-Goetz, 1997), etc.;[4] the Web site for the Dewey Classification Scheme lists Internet resources classified by the scheme.[5]

A classification scheme normally consists of three parts:

1. the schedules, which are the logical arrangement of classes;
2. the notation, which facilitates the implementation of this logical arrangement;
3. the index, which is an access route that allows a subject to be found in the schedules, and its notation to be identified.

The characteristics of division which are used in a classification scheme, and the order in which they are used, have a dramatic effect on the logical arrangement which results. This is illustrated in Figure 3.3, where characteristic C is applied as the first characteristic of division, and A is applied last. The linear sequence which results is shown in the bottom line of this table; it minimizes scattering by characteristic C, the most important characteristic of division. The best order for filing the items is one which always takes the user from general aspects of a subject to the more specific aspects, and which minimizes scattering by the most important characteristic. By expanding the original example in Table 3.1 and Figure 3.3, to show what happens when each of the concepts A, B and C has two different values, we can see the linear filing sequence which results in Table 5.5.

Many of the disadvantages of pre-coordinate systems can be removed by the use of synthesis in the construction of the pre-coordinate vocabulary. Synthesis allows for the building of more complex labels from component parts, by combining the parts according to a certain specified sequence. This may create the impression that a synthetic pre-coordinate vocabulary is equivalent to a post-coordinate vocabulary, but the following distinction exists: while the list of building-block components in a synthetic

Table 5.5   *Effect of the order of application of characteristics of division on a linear sequence*

Filing sequence in a linear arrangement	Example
A1	Europe
A2	USA
B1	Computers
B1 A1	Computers – Europe
B1 A2	Computers – USA
B2	Television
B2 A1	Television – Europe
B2 A2	Television – USA
C1	Kindergartens
C1 A1	Kindergartens – Europe
C1 A2	Kindergartens – USA
C1 B1	Kindergartens – Computers
C1 B1 A1	Kindergartens – Computers – Europe
C1 B1 A2	Kindergartens – Computers – USA
C1 B2	Kindergartens – Television
C1 B2 A1	Kindergartens – Television – Europe
C1 B2 A2	Kindergartens – Television – USA
C2	Universities
C2 A1	Universities – Europe
C2 A2	Universities – USA
C2 B1	Universities – Computers
C2 B1 A1	Universities – Computers – Europe
C2 B1 A2	Universities – Computers – USA
C2 B2	Universities – Television
C2 B2 A1	Universities – Television – Europe
C2 B2 A2	Universities – Television – USA

pre-coordinate vocabulary may be identical with the list of terms in a post-coordinate vocabulary, the way in which they are combined is different. In the synthetic pre-coordinate vocabulary, the components may only be combined in a fixed order, while those in a post-coordinate vocabulary may be combined in any order. The order of combination in a pre-coordinate synthetic vocabulary is predetermined because of the emphasis on placing items in one place in a linear sequence.

The distinction between pre-coordination, post-coordination and synthesis may be illustrated by the treatment of the subject 'computers in universities in Europe':

- A pre-coordinate scheme with no synthesis will have predefined terms, some of which are simple words, others will be combinations of words. For example, it might list 'computers', 'computers in universities', 'universities', 'universities in Europe', but not 'computers in Europe' or 'computers in universities in Europe', because these had not been identified as likely subject classes.

- A pre-coordinate scheme with synthesis will have predefined simple concepts only. For example, it might list 'computers', 'universities', 'Europe', and will allow these to be combined in a fixed order to describe all possible combinations of classes. Only one combination of terms will be assigned.

* A post-coordinate scheme will have predefined simple concepts, for example 'computers', 'universities', 'Europe'. Any number of these will be assigned in any combination.

The same vocabulary concepts could be used to create a synthetic pre-coordinate vocabulary and a post-coordinate one, but the way in which the vocabularies are used is totally different.

5.3.5 Subject vocabularies for non-text items

Despite the apparent dependence on the word-based derivation process, natural vocabularies are not restricted to text items. There are now equivalent signatures for many other media types, including visual pattern matching and audio byte extraction. Many of these applications derive from QBIC (Query By Image Content), which will be discussed in Section 6.4.6. In addition, virtually all visual, audio or multimedia items have some accompanying text which may be used to generate entries. Pictograms of specific shapes, icons or symbols form controlled vocabularies for visual items. Lists of sound effects or musical genres fulfil the same function for audio items.

5.4 Automation of subject analysis and representation

A high level of interest in the automation of subject content and analysis has existed since computers became widely acceptable in the 1970s. The ideas and experimental systems have been enriched by research developments in cognate areas, including machine translation, textual analysis, linguistics, natural language processing, artificial intelligence, expert systems and pattern recognition.

The ideas and pilot projects have had little impact on the routine process of subject content analysis and representation in large-scale operational systems because of the impossibility of automating the human intellectual processes involved. The most successful work has been in the area of automation of subject representation, where the same process is applied both to the user's information request and the items in the collection. The procedures neglect the complexities of subject content analysis by merging analysis and representation into one activity. In many cases, the automated system provides a crude initial filtering mechanism, which is followed by human analysis. The second stage of subject representation is more manageable in terms of formal procedures and instructions for computer systems. Some of the more successful areas include:

- expert systems for classification which assign a classification code to an item by asking the classifier to answer a series of YES/NO questions;
- automatic word analysis of text, which matches textual items to a user's request based on frequency of word occurrence;
- pattern-matching systems for digitized visual and audio items, as exemplified by QBIC;
- syntactic and semantic analysis of text arising from research into machine translation and textual analysis;
- systems which can check for key components of an article which are significant for subject content analysis, for example the introduction, methodology, results and conclusions.

These issues are discussed in current literature and in standard textbooks such as Van Rijsbergen (1979), Salton and McGill (1983) and Sparck-Jones (1981).

5.5   Summary

Facet analysis can be applied to the description of both the subject content and the physical medium of multimedia items. A combination of Ranganathan's (1959) PMEST facets, the 'of' and 'about' concepts of Shatford (1986) and facets which are specific to a particular physical medium gives a flexible and comprehensive approach. These may be used as a consistent method of assigning keywords for subject retrieval, in addition to the more usual applications of a classified arrangement. A conscious policy for subject analysis is required in order to deal with issues such as depth of indexing and complex items.

The advantages and disadvantages of the various types of subject representation discussed in this chapter are summarized in Table 5.3. If browsing is very important, then a classification scheme is needed. This may be achieved by:

- using an existing general scheme;
- using an existing specific scheme;
- modification of an existing scheme;
- development of a local scheme, using synthesis where possible.

Otherwise, subject words/phrases/headings should be developed based on thesaurus-type guidelines. By starting with simple concepts, pre-coordination may be gradually introduced. Standard reference works and other thesauri or subject heading lists may be used as guidelines. There is a need for vocabulary control; the AAT and subject-based thesauri are useful models.

The relative importance of a logical arrangement will determine whether an alphabetical or classified approach will be used in a particular situation. If browsing of items or surrogates is important, then classification by primary characteristic of division is appropriate; but if this isn't needed, subject headings are more natural and less complicated. Clearly, a linear arrangement will not meet all requirements, and must be supported by additional access points. Boolean logic-based retrieval is valuable in providing for multiple access points and their coordination.

Systems in libraries tend to depend on traditional tools such as classification schemes and alphabetical subject heading lists for all types of material, including both audio and visual. For example, the RLIN (Research Library Information Network in the USA) recommends the use of LCSH and LC Classification, but is sufficiently flexible to allow for the use of AAT by art libraries instead. Subject searching can generally be by exact matching of descriptors/subject headings, by words, and by truncated strings.

For the example of the broadcast news agency described in Section 1.8, it is usual to classify items initially by physical medium, then by the main functional divisions of the agency, for example news, sport, light entertainment, documentaries, etc., with the standard subdivisions of 'regional', 'national' or 'international' being applied to most divisions. A computerized retrieval system would also structure these options in a menu-based hierarchy, supplemented by post-coordinate search facilities using words and other subject indicators. Searching by both controlled and uncontrolled subject terms would be essential: the former would enable consistent and confident retrieval of resources which had been indexed by a human intermediary; the latter would enable quick and full access to the full content of original source material. The thesaurus of controlled terms would evolve gradually from the vocabulary used in the resources themselves, while being strongly influenced by the general examples and guidelines introduced in this chapter.

5.6   Practical assignments

You are encouraged to attempt to answer the following questions for one or more of the retrieval systems listed in Section 1.11.

5.6.1   Subject analysis

1. Does the subject analysis cover 'ofness' (concrete, objective) and 'aboutness' (abstract, subjective)?

2. Is the subject analysis specific or generic, or both?
3. Is there any evidence of facet analysis (PMEST or 'Who, What, How, Where, When, etc.')?
4. How is the subject analysis of multi-part items handled?
5. How is the subject analysis of manifested items handled?

5.6.2   Subject representation

6. Is more than one type of subject representation used? Describe this/these.
7. Are the items or surrogates arranged by subject?
8. Is there some form of direct access by subject (e.g. printed index, keyword searching of computer databases)?

Answer the following questions for each type of subject representation:

9. Are classification codes or alphabetical subject terms used?
10. Is the vocabulary controlled or uncontrolled?
11. Is the vocabulary pre- or post-coordinate?
12. If the vocabulary is pre-coordinate, does it allow for synthesis?
13. Is there any subject content description as part of the item surrogate (e.g. keywords, abstract)?

5.6.3   General

14. If you were given responsibility for redesigning this information retrieval system from the perspective of content analysis and representation, would you make any changes?

You should attempt to give detailed answers, rather than simply responding 'Yes' or 'No'. Sample answers are given in Section 5.9.

5.7   Notes

[1]   Houston, James E. (1995) *Thesaurus of ERIC Descriptors* (13th edn), Phoenix, AZ: Oryx Press. Institute of Electrical Engineers (1993) *INSPEC Thesaurus*, London: IEE. National Library of Medicine (1995) *MeSH Annotated Alphabetical List*, Bethesda, MD: NLM. Getty Art History Information Program (1994) *Art & Architecture Thesaurus* (2nd edn), New York: Oxford University Press. Museum Documentation Association, *MDA Archaeological Objects Thesaurus*: ⟨http://www.open.gov.uk/mdocassn/archobj/archcon.htm⟩. British Standards Institution (1990) *Universal Decimal Classification*, London: BSI.

2 Sears, Minnie Earl (ed.) (1997) *Sears List of Subject Headings* (16th edn), Detroit: Gale. Library of Congress (1997) *Library of Congress Subject Headings* (20th edn), Washington, DC: Library of Congress. RAMEAU: 〈http://www.abes.fr/rameau2.htm#menu〉.

3 ASLIB OSIS – thesaurus selection: 〈http://www.aslib.co.uk/osis/thesauri.html〉. MDA wordHoard: 〈http://www.open.gov.uk/mdocassn/wrdhrd1.htm〉.

4 BUBL Link: 〈http://www.bubl.ac.uk/link/〉. Lycos: 〈http://lycos.cs.cmu.edu〉. Excite: 〈http://www.excite.com〉.

5 OCL/Forest Press/DDC users/Internet resources: 〈http://www.oclc.org/oclc/fp/users/resource.htm〉.

5.8   References and further reading

Aitchison, Jean et al. (1997) *Thesaurus Construction and Use: A Practical Manual* (3rd edn), London: ASLIB.

Aluri, R., Kemp, D. Alasdair and Boll, J.J. (1991) *Subject Analysis in Online Catalogs*, Englewood, CO: Libraries Unlimited.

Cutter, C.A. (1904) *Rules for a Dictionary Catalog* (4th edn), Washington, DC: Government Printing Office. (Republished London: Library Association, 1953.)

Foskett, A.C. (1996) *The Subject Approach to Information* (5th edn), London: Library Association.

Kemp, D. Alasdair (1988) *Computer-based Knowledge Retrieval*, London: ASLIB.

Lancaster, F.W. (1979) *Information Retrieval Systems: Characteristics, Testing and Evaluation* (2nd edn), New York: Wiley.

Lancaster, F.W. (1986) *Vocabulary Control for Information Retrieval* (2nd edn), London: Information Resource Press.

Lancaster, F.W. (1998) *Indexing and Abstracting in Theory and Practice* (2nd edn), Urbana-Champaign, IL:GLIS, University of Illinois at Urbana-Champaign.

Library of Congress (1998a) *Library of Congress Subject Headings* (21st edn), Washington, DC: Library of Congress. Regular updates available on: 〈http://lcweb.loc.gov/catdir/cpso/〉.

Library of Congress (1998b) *Library of Congress Classification Plus Folio Infobase* (CD-ROM), Washington, DC: Library of Congress.

Library of Congress Cataloging Policy and Support Office, Collections Service (1997) *Library of Congress Classification H: Social Sciences*, Washington, DC: Library of Congress. Regular updates for all classifications available on: 〈http://lcweb.loc.gov/catdir/cpso/lcco/lcco.html〉.

Library of Congress, Prints and Photographs Division (1995) *Thesaurus for Graphic Materials*, Washington, DC: Library of Congress. Available on: 〈http://lcweb.loc.gov/rr/print/tgm1/〉.

Maltby, Arthur (1975) *Sayer's Manual of Classification for Librarians* (5th edn), London: André Deutsch.

Mitchell, Joan S. et al. (eds) (1996) *Dewey Decimal Classification and Relative Index* (21st edn), Albany, NY: Forest Press.

Ranganathan, S.R. (1959) *Elements of Library Classification* (2nd edn), London: Association of Assistant Librarians.

Roberts, A. (ed.) (1990) *Terminology for Museums: Proceedings of an International Conference Held in Cambridge, England, 21–24 September 1988*, Cambridge: Museum Documentation Association.

Rowley, Jennifer E. (1988) *Abstracting and Indexing* (2nd edn), London: Library Association.

Rowley, Jennifer E. (1992) *Organizing Knowledge* (2nd edn), Aldershot: Ashgate.

Salton, G. and McGill, M.J. (1983) *Introduction to Modern Information Retrieval*, London: McGraw-Hill.

Sears, Minnie Earl (ed.) (1997) *Sears List of Subject Headings* (16th edn), New York: H.W. Wilson.

Shatford, Sara (1986) 'Analysing the subject of a picture: A theoretical approach', *Cataloguing and Classification Quarterly*, **6**(3), 39–62.

Sparck-Jones, Karen (1981) *Information Retrieval Experiment*, London: Butterworths.

Van Rijsbergen, C.J. (1979) *Information Retrieval* (2nd edn), London: Butterworths.

Vickery, Brian Campbell (1968) *Faceted Classification: A Guide to Construction and Use of Special Schemes*, London: ASLIB.

Vizine-Goetz, Diane (1997) 'From book classification to knowledge organization: Improving Internet resource description and discovery', *Bulletin of the American Society for Information Science*, **24**(1), 24–7.

Weihs, Jean et al. (1979) *Nonbook Materials* (2nd edn), Ottawa, Ontario: Canadian Library Association.

Wellisch, Hans H. (1991) *Indexing from A–Z*, Bronx, NY: H.W. Wilson.

5.9   Sample answers to the practical assignments

5.9.1   *The OPAC of a specific library, and the items in the same library*

5.9.1.1   Subject analysis

1.   Does the subject analysis cover 'ofness' (concrete, objective) and 'aboutness' (abstract, subjective)?

For non-fiction items held by the library, the corresponding surrogate entries on the OPAC will in general cover 'ofness', as these items are typically objective and factual, whereas subject analysis of fiction titles is much more likely to correspond to 'aboutness', because the content is soft and subjective. However, this division can be more difficult to define in reality, where many texts, particularly in the humanities, can cover both 'ofness' and 'aboutness', or can even be wholly subjective. In reality, a general library system concentrates on 'ofness' for text items, although the American Memory project facilitates the use of 'ofness' for visual items.

2.   Is the subject analysis specific or generic, or both?
Entries on the OPAC usually include both 'specific of' and 'generic of' subject analysis. The title usually indicates what the item is specifically concerned with, whereas a breakdown of the Dewey Classification number or the Library of Congress Subject Headings will indicate what the item is 'generic of'.

3.   Is there any evidence of facet analysis (PMEST or 'Who, What, How, Where, When, etc.')?
The indexer in the library may have applied some facet analysis when deciding the appropriate Dewey Classification number or Library of Congress Subject Headings for an item. Ultimately, each item can be given only one location, so the indexer will have to identify the primary facet. The OPAC allows the user to then retrieve the surrogate using either the primary facet (the primary subject under which the item has been classified) or other facets with the keyword search facility.

4.   How is the subject analysis of multi-part items handled?
Subject analysis of multi-part items in library catalogues varies widely between institutions. For example, if a book on 'organization of multimedia resources' is in a series of books with an overall theme 'information science', it will be analysed based on its specific theme, with a note in the catalogue entry to indicate that it is part of this series. This may result in multi-part items being located in different sections of the library, with different Dewey Classification numbers.

5.   How is the subject analysis of manifested items handled?
Subject analysis of manifested items will differ: for example, subject analysis of a book and a film production of the same book also held by the library, or subject analysis of an encyclopaedia and a CD-ROM version of the same encyclopaedia. In the first example, the difference in subject analysis will depend on how true the film production is to the original. The indexer must consider the extent to which the manifestation differs from the original. For the user on the OPAC system, this would be apparent in differing search terms and different classification codes for the original and the manifestation. In the second example, subject analysis of the

manifested item will have to take into consideration the multimedia nature of the item, which includes not only text but also sound and moving images.

5.9.1.2   Subject representation

6.   Is more than one type of subject representation used? Describe this/these.
In most libraries, including the Library of Congress, there are two types of subject representation: a classified arrangement using Library of Congress or Dewey Classification, and an alphabetical representation using Library of Congress Subject Headings or a specialized thesaurus. The OPAC allows for retrieval of surrogates through a combination of these subject terms (e.g. words from subject headings).

7.   Are the items or surrogates arranged by subject?
The items are arranged by subject according to the classification scheme (e.g. the Library of Congress Classification Scheme). The surrogates on the OPAC are arranged randomly, but can be retrieved by keying in the appropriate classification code or by using the keyword search facility. It is also possible to browse alphabetical subject indexes on the OPAC.

8.   Is there some form of direct access by subject (e.g. printed index, keyword searching of computer databases)?
Yes, both items and surrogates can be directly accessed by subject.

9.   Are classification codes or alphabetical subject terms used?
Classification codes are used for both the items and their surrogates. Surrogates can also be retrieved by combining subject terms in a keyword search, by keying in truncated strings, or by browsing the alphabetical subject index on the OPAC.

10.   Is the vocabulary controlled or uncontrolled?
Both the classified and alphabetical subject vocabularies are controlled. The only type of uncontrolled vocabulary is based on searching individual words from titles or subject headings.

11.   Is the vocabulary pre- or post-coordinate?
The classification scheme and the alphabetic subject headings are pre-coordinate. The vocabulary is used in a post-coordinate way when individual words from alphabetical subject headings and other parts of the surrogate are combined using Boolean logic.

12.   If the vocabulary is pre-coordinate, does it allow for synthesis?
Both the classification scheme and the alphabetical subject headings use very little synthesis. The Dewey Classification scheme embodies more syn-

thesis than the Library of Congress scheme (e.g. Tables for Geographic Subdivisions, etc.), but this is not very evident to the user of the OPAC. The separate listing of the 'Most Commonly Used Subdivisions' in the Library of Congress Subject Headings is an example of synthesis, which could be developed much more extensively.

13. *Is there any subject description as part of the item surrogate (e.g. keywords, abstract)?*
Keywords can be used to retrieve the surrogate. However, the surrogate itself does not contain any subject description such as an abstract.

5.9.1.3 General

14. *If you were given responsibility for redesigning this information retrieval system from the perspective of subject content analysis and representation, would you make any changes?*
Further subject description, such as the inclusion of an abstract or a table of contents within the surrogate would be useful.

5.9.2 The printed telephone directories (name and classified) for your country or region

Subject content analysis and subject representation do not apply to the printed alphabetical (name) directory; these questions can only be answered in relation to the classified telephone directory.

5.9.2.1 Subject analysis

1. *Does the subject analysis cover 'ofness' (concrete, objective) and 'aboutness' (abstract, subjective)?*
The subject analysis covers 'ofness'. The classified directory is subdivided by specific subject areas which are concrete and tangible.

2. *Is the subject analysis specific or generic, or both?*
Subject analysis is generic. For example, subject headings typically include 'Car Accessories', 'Car Auctions', 'Car Dealers' and 'Car Repairing', rather than names of individual products or services. It is possible to argue that these terms are also specific, when compared with the broader theme of 'Automobiles'.

3. *Is there any evidence of facet analysis (PMEST or 'Who, What, How, Where, When, etc.')?*
There is no real evidence of facet analysis.

4.   How is the subject analysis of multi-part items handled?
The only example of multi-part items in the classified directory is where a particular company may have multiple branches or outlets. However, subject analysis is the same for all parts, and they will be listed together.

5.   How is the subject analysis of manifested items handled?
There are no manifested items in this system.

5.9.2.2   Subject representation

6.   Is more than one type of subject representation used? Describe this/these.
The subject representation used throughout the classified directory is an alphabetical subject heading list. Surrogates are subdivided by subject. The directory also contains an alphabetical subject index, which is similar to a thesaurus as it also shows preferred subject terms ('See …') and related subject terms ('See also …').

7.   Are the items or surrogates arranged by subject?
This system is concerned only with surrogates. The surrogates are arranged alphabetically by subject first, and then alphabetically by name under each subject heading.

8.   Is there some form of direct access by subject (e.g. printed index, keyword
    searching of computer databases)?
Yes, the classified directory contains an alphabetical subject index, which is usually located at the back of the directory.

9.   Are classification codes or alphabetical subject terms used?
Alphabetical subject terms are used.

10.   Is the vocabulary controlled or uncontrolled?
The vocabulary is controlled, as predefined subject terms are used. The index at the back of the directory also acts as a thesaurus, and contains alternative subject terms which point the user to the subject terms which have been used in the directory (e.g. 'Leisure Wear, See Sports Wear, page …'). The index also contains 'See also …' references to related topics.

11.   Is the vocabulary pre- or post-coordinate?
The vocabulary is pre-coordinate.

12.   If the vocabulary is pre-coordinate, does it allow for synthesis?
There is no evidence of synthesis in the subject terms used.

13. *Is there any subject description as part of the item surrogate (e.g. keywords, abstract)?*

No, although in a few cases the surrogate entry may resemble an advertisement, and describe particular features and services offered by the business.

5.9.2.3 General

14. *If you were given responsibility for redesigning this information retrieval system from the perspective of subject content analysis and representation, would you make any changes?*

Subject analysis by geographical location would be useful, as it would enable the user to determine the catchment area of a particular business.

5.9.3 Internet resources and the AltaVista search engine

5.9.3.1 Subject analysis

1. *Does the subject analysis cover 'ofness' (concrete, objective) and 'aboutness' (abstract, subjective)?*

Subject analysis can cover both 'ofness' and 'aboutness' depending on the nature of the Internet Web site and the extent to which it is intended as a personal, institutional or public resource. 'Ofness' is considerably more significant, as retrieval is usually based on mechanical extraction of keys from the information item (e.g. words or bit patterns). As searching on the Internet draws on uncontrolled natural vocabulary, both soft and hard terms can be used. Searching AltaVista by hard terms is considerably more effective than by using soft terms, which lead to the retrieval of much irrelevant material.

2. *Is the subject analysis specific or generic, or both?*

Subject analysis can be both specific and generic, depending again on the nature of the search query. This makes searching difficult, as one needs to search under both specific and generic search terms in order to be sure of retrieving all relevant items. Specificity can be enhanced by linking search terms using Boolean AND or NOT operators, and by using adjacency or proximity operators to ensure that search terms are adjacent or located in close proximity in the retrieved item(s). Generic searches can be carried out by linking synonyms and related terms using the OR operator.

3. *Is there any evidence of facet analysis (PMEST or 'Who, What, How, Where, When, etc.')?*

There is minimal evidence of facet analysis on AltaVista, although this could play a significant role in implementing a consistent approach to subject analysis on the Internet. A knowledge of facet analysis, including Ranganathan's and Shatford's approaches, will allow the user to link search terms effectively. Search engines which attempt to subdivide search results into sub-categories use rudimentary facet analysis (e.g. Northern Light or IBM's *QBIC*).

4.   How is the subject analysis of multi-part items handled?
The Internet contains a vast collection of multi-part items, but there is no intelligent linking of subject analysis for these items. When the surrogates of Web sites are retrieved on an AltaVista search, the existence of multi-part items is identified only when the same search terms are contained in the various parts. The ability to categorize results into folders on the Northern Light search engine may group related parts together. The complexity of links in the World Wide Web also helps link the related parts, but in a haphazard fashion.

5.   How is the subject analysis of manifested items handled?
This is similar to the handling of multi-part items. The Internet contains a wide spectrum of manifested items, and different levels of manifestation. However, links showing the existence of manifestations are rarely explicit. Therefore, retrieving the surrogates of manifested items will only occur if the search terms used are also found in the manifested item.

5.9.3.2   Subject representation

6.   Is more than one type of subject representation used? Describe this/these.
Many different types of subject representation are used on the Internet, including Dewey and other classification schemes, alphabetical subject heading lists and thesauri, and uncontrolled subject terms. The most frequent type of subject representation is uncontrolled and derived, with words or other keys extracted directly from the opening text of the information items (e.g. AltaVista).

7.   Are the items or surrogates arranged by subject?
Items and surrogates are arranged randomly on the Internet. Display of retrieved surrogates is normally in a logical sequence, corresponding to decreasing likelihood of relevance to the user. Surrogates are also arranged by subject within Internet directories such as Excite, Lycos and Yahoo!

8.   Is there some form of direct access by subject (e.g. printed index, keyword searching of computer databases)?
Direct access of surrogates by subject is the basis on which most Internet search engines operate. The user specifies the subject area required, and determines the degree of specificity through Boolean logic.

9. Are classification codes or alphabetical subject terms used?
Both are used widely on the Internet, and the level of use is likely to grow rapidly in the future. However, the general philosophy of information retrieval on the Internet, and on AltaVista, is based on uncontrolled vocabularies.

10. Is the vocabulary controlled or uncontrolled?
The vocabulary is largely uncontrolled, as it is based on natural, everyday language. In addition, controlled index terms may be added by the creator of the Internet resource.

11. Is the vocabulary pre- or post-coordinate?
In general, the vocabulary is post-coordinate, as surrogates are retrieved through a search engine by the user combining the search terms they decide on in a useful search strategy. However, the vocabulary of any menu-based system (e.g. search directories and gateways) is pre-coordinate.

12. If the vocabulary is pre-coordinate, does it allow for synthesis?
The pre-coordinate vocabularies in directories and gateways do not use synthesis, unless it is embodied in the underlying classification scheme (e.g. Universal Decimal Classification).

13. Is there any subject description as part of the item surrogate (e.g. keywords, abstract)?
On AltaVista, the surrogate will contain the opening text of the source item. Whether this constitutes a subject description of the source will depend on whether the designer of the Web page included meaningful, relevant words in the early part of this text. The subject description in the surrogates should indicate the creator of the Web site, and a brief outline of its content.

5.9.3.3 General

14. If you were given responsibility for redesigning this information retrieval system from the perspective of subject content analysis and representation, would you make any changes?
At present, the details of the item contained within the surrogate are entirely dependent on the designer's ability to include a useful subject description in the early part of their Web page. It would obviously be most effective if surrogates contained hard facts about the page, in the form of an abstract or list of keywords, which would allow the user to determine the relevance of a page from its surrogate. Consistent subject description is essential; this could be achieved by requiring creators of all Internet resources to include the following four types of subject descriptors: a brief abstract, a classification code, terms from controlled subject headings, and uncontrolled keywords.

Chapter 6

Electronic data structures

6.1   Introduction

The simplest view of information management assumes that items are discrete, uniquely identifiable, and that the items or their surrogates can be represented by records in flat files: the equivalent of index cards in a box. Retrieval occurs either by scanning every record until the desired one is found, or by using some method of indexing which provides random access to specific records. This is how retrieval works in manual record-keeping systems which are based on printed linear products such as textbooks, directories, indexes and personal notebooks, and in earlier generations of computerized database management systems, which assume that each item can be represented by a flat record with various access points, and that the retrieval chains which are followed are based on simple links between the same access point in different records. For example, these links might be that the paintings are by the same artists, or artists from the same school, or that a specific musical instrument is played in these sound recordings, or a number of films were produced in a particular year.

Both pre- and post-coordinate systems over-simplify the relationships between the items into a limited number of predefined dimensions. The problems of these systems include the following:

- The distinction between pre- and post-coordinate retrieval is too rigid.
- The information items may not be discrete, and it may be necessary to subdivide them artificially.
- Item surrogates are not necessarily divisible into discrete components.
- The multi-dimensional nature of the information items and of users' needs is not satisfied by pre-coordinate systems.
- Information searchers don't necessarily think in the structured terms of records, access points and indexes which are required by post-coordinate systems.

- Range searches are executed laboriously by entering the values of upper and lower limits.
- Queries are answered by segregating items into two distinct categories – those which appear to deal with the query and those which appear not to deal with it. In reality, items may have varying degrees of usefulness for a query, ranging from extremely useful to useless.
- Many systems give references, or a standard chunk of data, whereas users often want answers to questions.
- The variety of item formats in a multimedia system may be difficult to manage in a conventional pre- or post-coordinate system.

These issues may be illustrated in a practical way as a user's information needs evolve gradually, along the following sequence of statements and questions:

1. I'm interested in organ music.
2. What organ music is available for listening on this system/in this institution?
3. What is the name of the organist?
4. Who composed that piece?
5. Where did the composer come from?
6. What else did he or she write?
7. Was there a strong school of music there?
8. What musical style was associated with this school?
9. Who else worked with this group of composers?
10. Are there any concerts taking place in this area? ... Where? ... Can I see on a map? ... What bus/subway goes by there? ... Is there a restaurant/hotel near there?
11. How much are the tickets for the concert?
12. How old is the organ being used?
13. Can I hear other works by that composer?
14. What did he or she look like?
15. Were any biographies written about him or her?
16. Can I see his or her original score?
17. What is meant by 'Baroque' music?

In a traditional manual system, this involves numerous directories and reference works, card indexes, flyers, brochures, diaries, calendars, etc. In a basic computerized environment, it involves numerous different files, or a single file with a record structure where there are lots of blank fields in any one record. In order to respond satisfactorily to the 'organ music' query above, there would be files for:

- events and ticket/seat availability;
- items created;
- maps;
- people and organizations (creators);

- photographs and other visual images;
- places;
- restaurants/hotels;
- sound/music items;
- textual descriptions and definitions.

These numerous files could be created in a way which allows different concepts to be linked: for example, Mozart as a composer, Mozart as the topic for a book, Mozart as the subject for a photograph, etc. Retrieval will still take place in a very structured fashion, by searching for records which deal with 'Mozart', finding some, opening another file, doing another search on it, etc.

The systems described in this chapter allow for greater flexibility than pre- and post-coordinate mechanisms, in that they attempt to cater for the less structured ways in which information queries evolve. They allow for a multi-dimensional approach, with multiple logical orders being applied simultaneously, and with scope for creating, breaking and rebuilding an infinite number of linear trails. The most significant sequence could be used for physical arrangement of the items in electronic storage, but it is unlikely that this will be done. It is more likely that the items will be stored using the methods which are most appropriate for the various storage media involved, with a logical structure superimposed by the search software.

6.2   Terminology

It is necessary to introduce some computer terms in order to discuss electronic data structures for multimedia.

6.2.1   Analogue and digital information

Human sensory organs are analogue devices in that they can respond to a continuous range of values for colour, intensity, sound, etc. Similarly, many multimedia listening and viewing devices that can be connected to computers, such as audio systems, television receivers, video cameras, video disk players and motion picture film, are analogue devices. Because of their analogue nature, they can never be fully integrated into the computer system itself, and will always be separate hardware units. In contrast, a digital computer is designed to work with discrete values of things, based on clock pulses in electric circuitry and binary storage devices (i.e. as bits with the value 0 or 1). However, analogue devices have greater storage capacity, which makes it less likely that compression of the data they store will be necessary.

Luther (1992) and Cawkell (1996) present fuller descriptions of the distinction between analogue and digital data, and Luther identifies the following advantages of a fully digital system:

- All components can be stored and distributed on standard computer media, such as floppy disks, hard disks, digital tape, CD-ROM and computer networks.
- The components can be manipulated and analysed by computer software.
- The components can be integrated into the computer, removing the technical difficulties associated with external components or cable connections.
- Multimedia computers which contain these components are now standard (e.g. the MPC machine described in Section 1.3).

6.2.2   Database management systems (DBMSs)

A database management system is the software used for creating, editing and updating files in a database, and for answering queries and generating reports based on the data in these files.

6.2.2.1   Databases

A database is a group of related files, for example in a library, an employment agency, or the student records system in a university. The files in a database may be linked, merged or cross-referenced.

6.2.2.2   Files

A file is a collection of records in a specific application area, for example books and other holdings in a library, job-seekers in an employment agency, or students in a university.

6.2.2.3   Records

Each record is a collection of data for one item in a file. Although all records are likely to contain different data, they will have a consistent structure. For example, for books in a library, each record will allow for details of the creator(s) of the book, the title, the subject, the source and the location to be stored, even though some of this data may be absent and may vary considerably in length.

6.2.2.4 Fields

Each record contains specific elements or units of data called fields. Each of the components listed for the records of books in a library are in fact fields: creator field, title field, date field, location field, etc. A field corresponds to the smallest unit of information which one might want to treat separately in a DBMS. A key field is one that uniquely identifies a record, for example Social Security number for employees, student number in a university or accessions number for items in a library. The ISBN is a key field which identifies the existence of an information item; however, it should not be considered as a key field for multiple copies of a book. The URL is a key field for Internet sites, but the PURL is a more reliable one. The terms 'attribute' and 'data element' are used synonymously with 'field'.

The relationships between these components may be illustrated by analogy with a filing cabinet containing database files, with each card corresponding to a record:

- **Database** = collection of files for all students and staff in a university, or for books and other items in the library;
- **File** = collection of records for all students taking Information Studies;
- **Record** = details of one individual student;
- **Field** = components of a student's record, for example student ID number, family name, first name, first line of address, second line of address, third line of address, date of birth, programme of study, year of study, date study commenced;
- **Field value** = value of a field, for example 29 October 1980 = date of birth.

6.2.3 Physical and logical structures

The physical data structure describes how data is organized for maximum efficiency in a storage medium. It applies to the arrangement of the original information items, regardless of the medium in which they exist. Physical data structure refers to books on shelves, office files in cabinets, videos in a storage cabinet, and records in computer storage. The two main alternatives for electronic physical structures are sequential and random-access files, and these are described in Section 6.3.

The logical structure refers to the relationships which are imposed on the information items so that they may be manipulated and retrieved. They provide the logical access routes which enable users to exploit the data. The options under this heading, which are discussed in Section 6.4, are: inverted files and Boolean logic, retrieval software, database management systems, relational databases and Binary Large Objects (BLOBs), probabilistic methods, Query by Image Content, hypertext, expert systems, and multimedia authoring software. Logical structures are of more interest than physical ones for the purposes of this book, but since a logical structure must be implemented physically in order to create an actual system, it is necessary to examine some features of physical structures.

6.3   Physical structures

There are two main types of physical structure for computer files: sequential and random-access.

6.3.1   Sequential files

The traditional method of organizing records in data files is as a linear sequential arrangement in a file. Sequential files can only be accessed sequentially. This was particularly appropriate when magnetic tape was the primary storage medium and when access was normally on a batch basis, with queries by different users to the database being combined into batches which were matched as a set against the database. When a match occurred, the matching records were stored separately and sorted by user. The records could be filed in various sequences on the storage medium, including random order, by accession date, or by any significant field value. The latter arrangement facilitates access by that field, but otherwise gives poor access to individual records. Usually, all of the records have to be scanned by a computer in order to find the relevant ones. It is not an appropriate method for instant access to multimedia items.

6.3.2   Random-access files

When access to individual records is required, a more satisfactory approach is to structure them so that they can be retrieved on the basis of their key, and other, fields; in other words, to provide random access to individual records. Random-access files allow records to be accessed directly without having to scan each one sequentially. The searcher, who may be the requester of the information, will search directly at a computer workstation, displaying or printing search results as they are found. This has the advantage that a search can be modified if the initial results are unsatisfactory. Technically, random access can be implemented in two ways: as indexed sequential files, or as direct-access files.

Indexed sequential files have records in a sequential sequence on magnetic disk storage, with an index at the beginning of the file which gives the physical location of each record. The index assigns a unique disk address that identifies the record location by its surface number, track number, and sector or cylinder number. There is a direct analogy with finding a topic in a book by consulting the book's index, as opposed to scanning the book page by page, from the beginning.

In direct-access files, the computer accesses records directly by converting a key field, through some arithmetic calculation, into an actual address that identifies the surface, track, and sector or cylinder number. There is no need to search an index. Direct file access is faster than indexed sequential access because there is no need to look up an address in an index, but it may require more programming. A simplistic form of direct access would store the records in the sequence of the key field values. No conversion would be required from key field value to address, as the record with a key field value of 1 would be placed at the first disk location, the record with a key field value of 2 at the second location, and so on. In practice, more complex arithmetic calculations, such as hashing, are used to lead directly to the storage location of the record. The most basic hashing algorithm divides the key field value by the number of storage locations, and uses the remainder to locate the storage location.

6.4   Logical structures and software

It is usual to combine the benefits of direct-access file structures with various methods of indexing the values of the fields in the records. This procedure is best illustrated by considering inverted file mechanisms for access to records in bibliographic and other databases.

6.4.1   Inverted files and Boolean logic

An inverted file is an index which identifies, for every searchable field value, the unique identifier of every record which possesses this field value. The searchable fields might include words, creators' names, subject terms, etc. The entries in the inverted file are normally arranged in alphabetical or numerical order. Sometimes there is one integrated inverted file for all the fields in a record; in other applications, there may be separate inverted files for each field. The inverted file may also contain the number of occurrences of each field value, or this may be held in a separate but interconnected postings file. The first stage of a search – finding out how many records contain each search term – is executed by the computer using only the

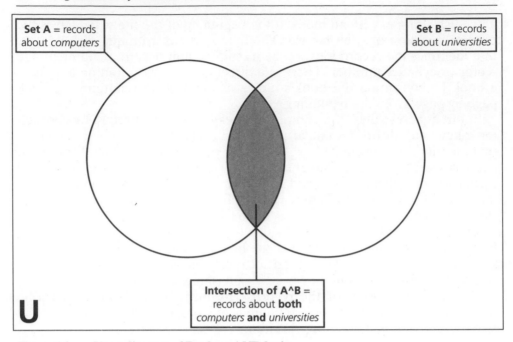

Figure 6.1   Venn diagram of Boolean AND logic

inverted file. It is only when the user asks to view an item than the main file of computerized records is accessed.

Retrieval from inverted files is based on using Boolean operators to combine search terms together in a logical fashion. The efficient implementation of post-coordinate retrieval, Boolean logic, is named after the mathematician George Boole. It is a combinatorial system for representing logical relationships between sets. A set of search concepts represents a search query. During searching, a set of search terms is matched against terms in the inverted file. Lists of items retrieved are combined, based on the Boolean operators used.

In order to illustrate the sets of records that would be retrieved, or not retrieved, by a search statement, a visual representation known as a Venn diagram is used, as illustrated in Figure 6.1. The universal set – the set of all records in a file – is represented by a rectangle labelled 'U' for universe. Labels, such as A and B, are used to represent subsets of U: subsets of the universal set of records in a file. The area that contains records in common (i.e. where A and B intersect) is labelled $A^{\wedge}B$, and is illustrated in Figure 6.1. This intersection of two sets is known as AND logic. For example, if a user wants information on 'computers in universities in Europe', the Boolean search statement might be:

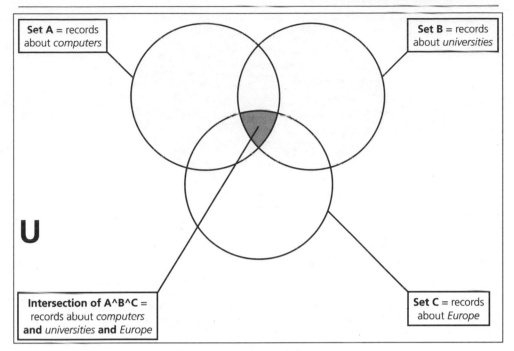

Figure 6.2   **Venn diagram of Boolean AND logic for three sets**

Computers AND Universities AND Europe.

This search statement is shown schematically in Figure 6.2. This example assumes that the words 'computers', 'universities' and 'Europe' are the appropriate search terms.

Two other types of Boolean logic enable more complex search statements to be developed. OR logic identifies records which are members of at least one set, and is described as the union of two sets. It is illustrated in Figure 6.3. It facilitates the grouping of synonyms to retrieve records which contain any one of a range of synonymous or near synonymous terms. For example, replacing the rather vague term 'Europe' by the names of specific countries in the example above would generally improve retrieval:

Europe OR United Kingdom OR Ireland OR France OR Germany OR Finland OR . . .

NOT logic identifies records which are members of one set but not of another, and is known as the exclusion operator. It is shown schematically in Figure 6.4. The search above might retrieve too much material dealing

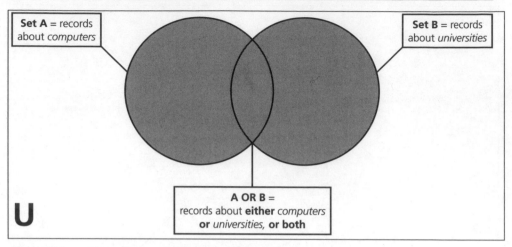

Figure 6.3   Venn diagram of Boolean OR logic

with teaching the subject Computer Science in universities. Using the NOT operator to exclude Computer Science will overcome this problem:

Computers NOT Computer Science.

Thus the full search statement becomes:

(Computers NOT Computer Science) AND Universities AND (Europe OR United Kingdom OR Ireland OR France OR Germany OR Finland).

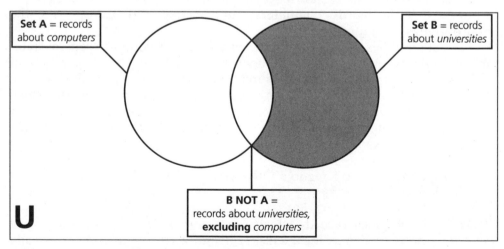

Figure 6.4   Venn diagram of Boolean NOT logic

While different software packages apply the operators in different sequences, the sequence NOT, AND, OR is the most common order of application. It is often advisable, if not essential, to enclose some terms within parentheses in order to ensure that the overall logic is maintained. The parentheses are necessary in the sequence above – if they were not used to combine countries in the example above, the search would retrieve a lot of items dealing with specific countries, such as 'United Kingdom' or 'Finland', but not necessarily having anything to do with 'computers' or 'universities'.

6.4.2   Retrieval software

The database creation and search software may be a general, multi-purpose records management package such as *DBASE, DATAEASE* or *ORACLE*, or it may have been developed for a particular sector of the market: *INMAGIC* or *Pro-Cite* for bibliographic data, *MODES* for museums, etc. The majority of software packages which were designed for handling bibliographic or full-text records are based on this logical structure of an inverted file and a retrieval mechanism with Boolean operators.

There is no major conceptual difference in objectives, structure or facilities which distinguishes these packages from the database management systems described below, but they represent opposite ends of the software spectrum. In general, the bibliographic packages cope better with MARC record structure and with multiple subject headings. Table 6.1, which is based on Kemp (1988), identifies some of the main differences.

Table 6.1   *Comparison of text retrieval and database management systems*

Criterion	Text retrieval software	Database management systems
Handles full text?	Well	Poorly
Variable field lengths?	Well	Poorly
Repeating/multi-valued fields?	Well	Cumbersome
Multimedia items?	Variable	Improving
Frequent updating?	Bad	Good
Ranked output/relevance feedback?	Good	Bad

Source: Based on Kemp, p. 134 (1988).

6.4.3   Database management systems

Database management systems are ubiquitous in business and commercial applications. They operate by separating the physical and logical data structures, so that once the data structure is defined, it can be viewed and accessed from a variety of perspectives by different users. In addition to simple file management systems, there are four predominant types of logical database model:

* hierarchical;
* networked;
* relational;
* object-oriented.

Simple file management systems are the computerized equivalent of card indexes. They enable records to be sorted, filtered, printed and displayed in various sequences and formats. They are not true DBMSs because data in one file cannot be linked easily to data in another. Examples include the *Windows* accessory *Cardfile*, *Sidekick*'s *Cardfile*, Symantec's *Q&A* and Claris's *Filemaker Pro*. Spreadsheet packages may be used as simple file managers, where columns are used to define fields, and each row corresponds to a record.

The hierarchical data model may be easily understood by considering hierarchical approaches to classification. It is like an inverted tree, with one root at the top, and multiple branches growing down from this root. The structure may also be compared to a family tree, and the terms 'parent' and 'child' are used to describe branches. In a hierarchical database, each child has only one parent, but each parent can have many children. This has quite a lot to offer for applications where hierarchical access is important, but problems arise because the structures are so rigidly defined. As an item can only be a member of one hierarchy, a 'child' may not be associated with multiple 'parents'. When searching, the search software may have to negotiate up and down hierarchies to bring related material together.

The network data model is rather more flexible, and bears some similarity to hypertext links (see Section 6.4.7). It allows for multiple links from one item to other related items. It can be used to link items in multiple files based on field values. The 'parent–child' relationship is applied again, but both one-to-many and many-to-one relationships between parent and child are allowed. It can represent more complex relationships, but these must be defined when the database is first constructed.

The relational database model consists of the entities, or information items, the field values or attributes of those entities, and the relationships between entities. Key fields within records link, or join, any number of files, through tables. It is a very flexible approach, which allows virtually any type of relationship between fields. Data models identify the structure of the information in a system and the operations performed on it. The structure of information systems data is documented in data dictionaries. Entities, fields and relations are the three structural features of a data model.[1]

An object-oriented model has an aggregation hierarchy in which each object is an abstraction of all the objects below it. In general, the database has three components: logical structure, layout structure, and content. The logical structure provides a method for representing the conceptual organization of the database and its semantic properties. The layout structure provides a means for organizing the syntax of the data, for example laying it out in pages and sections, managing the synchronization of temporal data for audio or motion video, and spatial information for graphics. Content is the actual information, the bits comprising the text, images or sound. A content generator, in the form of an algorithm from which content can be derived, may be supplied instead of the actual content.

6.4.4   Relational databases and Binary Large Objects

Feldman (1991) describes a realistic model for multimedia database design which combines text and images in a range of database types, including CD-ROM. Pointers in searchable text fields provide links to the images for retrieval. However, in a true multimedia database it becomes necessary to store very large, unstructured data objects, such as photographs, diagrams, motion video, spreadsheets, program code and digitized sound, as fields in a database record. The database can then offer any combination of fields, whether they are data, images, motion video, text or sound objects. A key difference between conventional and multimedia relational databases is the large size of data objects (hundreds of megabytes) which the latter must handle. These data types are known as Binary Large Objects (BLOBs).

Since BLOBs can be so large, each BLOB is normally located on its own separate portion of a disk, or on its own magnetic or optical disk. This logical area, which is known as 'blobspace', may be located on one or more physical devices, perhaps spread over a number of disks. The field in a database record corresponding to a particular BLOB will always point to its location. The actual physical location of the BLOB does not affect an application. Being able to store BLOBs separately has two advantages: firstly, it ensures that the database can be used without retrieving BLOBs, and with no loss of speed in an application because of the presence of BLOBs within records; secondly, it provides a choice of storage media for BLOBs, which may have advantages of cost and convenience.

6.4.5   Probabilistic methods, ranked output and relevance feedback

The disadvantage of all the methods described above is that they treat everything as black or white, whereas the matching of an item to a specific request is not usually so clear-cut. In fact, there is normally a gradation in suitability from a complete match (an item which appears to be very useful) to a complete mismatch (an item which appears to be useless), with the majority of items falling somewhere in the range in between.

Probabilistic retrieval methods allow for this by indicating the probability that retrieved items will be relevant to a particular request. This requires more sophisticated search mechanisms than the simple inverted file systems described above, which may use one or more of the following techniques:

- ranking retrieved items based on the level of similarity of each one to the user's search request;
- weighting of search terms to indicate the relative importance of each one to the user;
- weighting of terms in the database to attach greater importance to unusual terms.

In theory, these methods are very applicable to multimedia items, where assessment of relevance is even more imprecise than for textual items. In practice, because they are so dependent on patterns of word occurrence, they have little application outside the full-text area. However, if the equivalent of 'words' can be identified in non-textual items, there is considerable scope for sophisticated retrieval. (A practical implementation of these methods is discussed in Section 6.4.6.)

The presentation of items retrieved by a search in some approximate order of decreasing usefulness is of tremendous benefit for large search results. This can become particularly important in any situation where precise specification of a search request is difficult, such as when describing a need for visual or audio items. If these items have some characteristics which may be measured quantitatively, for example colour density or loudness of sound, then ranking is possible. Ranking of items is exploited more fully through relevance feedback, where the user gives an assessment of the usefulness of each retrieved item. This information is interpreted by the search software, and incorporated automatically into a modified search strategy. Again, this is particularly useful for situations where users have difficulty in expressing a search request.

6.4.6   Query by Image Content

Query by Image Content, an IBM search and access development, allows users to search a collection's media objects by colour, texture, shape and size. A query is expressed graphically, for example by specifying colours from a colour wheel or selecting textures from a list of sample images.[2] Then, if a user decides a retrieved item matches their needs, they can then request other items which are similar to it, based on any of the search criteria. Users may try QBIC demonstrations for several sample databases on the Web.[3]

QBIC is incorporated into two IBM commercial products: *Digital Library* (IBM digital library) and *DB2 Universal Database Extenders.*[4] *Digital Library* enables multimedia libraries to be created, distributed across networks, and accessed from a variety of perspectives. *DB2 Extenders* takes database applications beyond traditional numeric and character data to images, video, voice and complex documents, even to fingerprints. The user can bring these types of data together in one SQL (Standard Query Language) query. For example, a user can retrieve all items dealing with 'computers', regardless of the format in which these occur. (The specific features of extenders for individual media, including the image, video and audio extenders, will be discussed in Chapters 7 and 8.)

6.4.7 Hypertext

The concept of hypertext as computer software which allows items to be accessed and retrieved in both pre- and post-coordinate ways, and in a variety of intermediate ways, was introduced in Section 3.4. The idea of multiple links between information items pre-dated the computer technology which enabled it to become a reality. Vannevar Bush was influenced by the way human memory works when he anticipated the basics of hypertext in 1945:

> The human mind ... operates by association. With one item in its grasp, it snaps instantly to the next that is suggested by the association of thoughts, in accordance with some intricate web of trails carried by the cells of the brain ... the speed of action, the intricacy of trails, the detail of mental pictures, is awe-inspiring beyond all else in nature. Man cannot hope fully to duplicate this mental process artificially, but he certainly ought to be able to learn from it. (Bush, 1945)

The term 'hypertext' derives from the Greek words for 'text-over-text'. It is essentially non-linear, although it can allow the creator or the user to create a multiplicity of linear trails. The information may be accessed by alternative paths, as opposed to a fixed path or structure in conventional retrieval systems. Schematic illustrations of hypertext mechanisms are presented in Figures 6.5 and 6.6. Figure 6.5 shows the two key elements of a hypertext system:

• the items of information which are to be linked;
• the links between these items.

Figure 6.6 illustrates how hypertext works in practice, for example of a popular photograph and associated items from the US National Archives. The central item is the overview of the meeting between US President

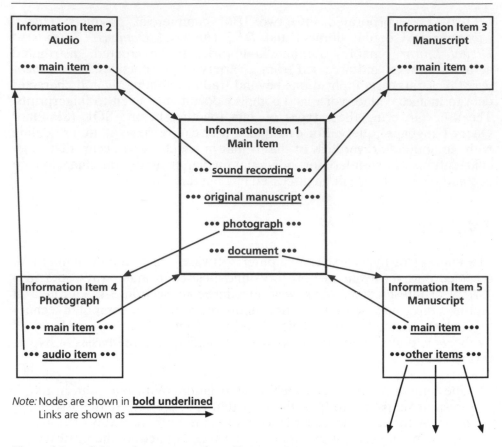

Figure 6.5   Schematic representation of hypertext structure

Nixon and singer Elvis Presley. There are links from each of the terms which are bold and underlined to related items: the photographs, the account of the meeting, other correspondence, and the National Security Archive. There will be further levels of links which enable users to read or view individual items. There could also be links to other resources, in addition to those shown in the figure, for example to biographies of either participant, to more information about the White House, or the political context in which the meeting occurred, etc.

Hypertext allows for the establishment of a database of records which superficially appears to be a normal records management system, and which does allow for standard coordination of search terms in fields. In addition, it allows for the creation of links between items by the database designer which are not at the rigid field-to-field level of a normal post-coordinate system. For example, it can show the connection between Elvis

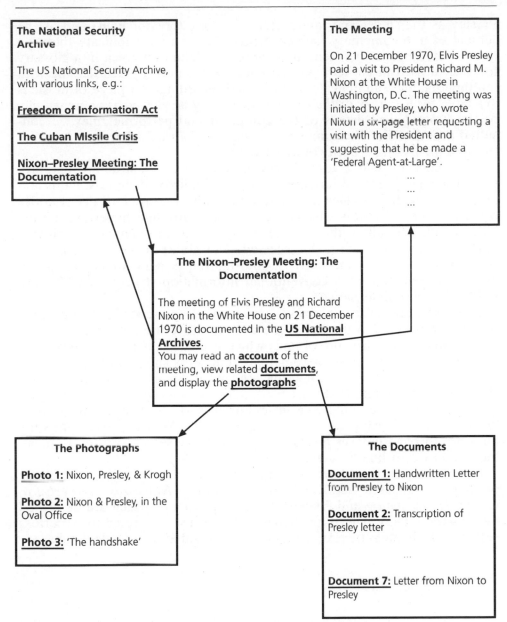

The National Security Archive

The US National Security Archive, with various links, e.g.:

Freedom of Information Act

The Cuban Missile Crisis

Nixon–Presley Meeting: The Documentation

The Meeting

On 21 December 1970, Elvis Presley paid a visit to President Richard M. Nixon at the White House in Washington, D.C. The meeting was initiated by Presley, who wrote Nixon a six-page letter requesting a visit with the President and suggesting that he be made a 'Federal Agent-at-Large'.
...
...
...

The Nixon–Presley Meeting: The Documentation

The meeting of Elvis Presley and Richard Nixon in the White House on 21 December 1970 is documented in the **US National Archives**.
You may read an **account** of the meeting, view related **documents**, and display the **photographs**

The Photographs

Photo 1: Nixon, Presley, & Krogh

Photo 2: Nixon & Presley, in the Oval Office

Photo 3: 'The handshake'

The Documents

Document 1: Handwritten Letter from Presley to Nixon

Document 2: Transcription of Presley letter

...

Document 7: Letter from Nixon to Presley

Figure 6.6　Example of hypertext structure based on a Web page
Source: The Nixon–Presley meeting: ⟨http://www.seas.gwu.edu/nsarchive/nsa/elvis/elnix.html⟩.
Reproduced with permission of the National Security Archive.

Presley as the singer and interpreter of a song (creator field) and as the subject of a documentary (subject field). Thus one can indicate that one item is cited by another item; that there is a definition given in a glossary for a term used in an item, etc. Of even more interest when dealing with multimedia, one can indicate that a sound recording of a piece of music is available for listening, or the original score may be viewed as an image file, or the biographical details of the composer and performer may be consulted as a text file. The complex structure of Figure 2.1 becomes a reality through the linking capacity of hypertext.

A graphical browser gives an overview of the network structure, and prevents users getting too disoriented by the multiplicity of choices. Paths and filters can also help reduce disorientation. Paths are ordered sets of nodes or recommended routes which guide the user through hypertext. Filters hide detail, and allow the user to skip quickly through nodes without having to examine each node accessed. The ability to associate multiple structures with the same body of information is a major advantage of hypertext compared with conventional information structures, which are rigid and mono-dimensional.

The difficulty of categorizing hypertext as pre-coordinate or post-coordinate resulted in the use of the term multi-coordinate in Section 3.4. Depending on the structure of links which is created, hypertext may result in either a pre- or a post-coordinate system, as is shown in Figure 6.7. If these links are created along one or more linear sequences, a pre-coordinate system results (Figure 6.7A). A superimposed structure may linearize access to the underlying information, and result in a conventional linear or hierarchical presentation (Figure 6.7B). Alternatively, if the only links are through indexes for each field which are searched using Boolean logic, a post-coordinate system results (Figure 6.7C).

Hypertext principles have been implemented in a number of software packages, databases and catalogues, including *Notecards*, *HyperCard*, *Guide*, *Hypercatalog* and *Hyperties*, the first three of which are described by Rowley (1992). The term 'hypermedia' is used to refer to hypertext systems which integrate text, data, images and sound on a single database.

6.4.8   Expert systems

Expert systems are computer programs which attempt to interact with a user in the same way as a human, in order to provide advice or a solution to a problem. As part of this process, expert systems structure data in a number of ways which may also be used in their own right to develop logical data structures. An expert system can be used to formalize a structure or several structures which are deemed appropriate for a collection of information. There are four main types of data structure used in commercial expert systems software:

A: Pre-coordinate and linear

Item 1 ——— Item 2 ——— Item 3 ——— Item 4 ——— Item 5 ——— Item 6

B: Pre-coordinate and hierarchical

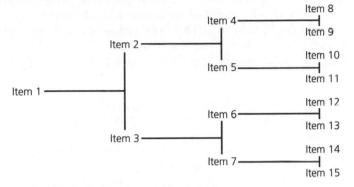

C: Post-coordinate (Positions are not significant.)

Item 6

Item 3

Item 1

Item 5   Item 4

Item 2

Figure 6.7   Hypertext as pre- and post-coordinate

- frames;
- networks;
- predicate calculus;
- rules.

Frames may be seen as analogous to record-based structures, networks to hypertext systems, and predicate calculus and rules to logical hierarchies and classification schemes. It is unrealistic to predict complete expert systems for the organization and retrieval of multimedia, but the data structures provide a logical framework. Kemp (1988) describes these data structures in the context of computer-based retrieval.

6.4.9   Multimedia authoring software

Multimedia applications are created by assembling the components in a way which suits a particular task, in a process known as 'authoring'. The applications may be written in a general-purpose programming language such as C, or they can be created with less knowledge of programming by using an authoring program. The authoring system is not necessarily needed for playback or use of the application.

In general, an authoring system for multimedia has four main requirements:

1. maintaining a logical description of the product;
2. allowing editing of that structure via a physical view of the product;
3. maintaining the structural validity of the product;
4. converting between the product's own internal format and a format appropriate for storage and interchange.

Detailed descriptions and comparative evaluations of individual authoring systems are provided by Cawkell (1996), Luther (1992) and Raskin (1990). Authoring systems have tools for incorporating the various components needed – audio, video, image, and data files. The term 'assets' is used to refer to the components. The authoring system may perform audio, video or image capture from live-input signals, editing of those assets, management of asset files and directory structures, maintaining storyboards, and many other tasks.

Most authoring systems take a flowchart approach that allow developers to specify the elements they wish to incorporate, and to string them together in the desired sequence. Transitions from one image to another can be specified, or animations can be created using clip or frame animation techniques. Motion video is integrated by specifying the beginning and end points of each video clip, and video tools allow titles and text to be overlaid on the clip. Audio control ranges from simple playback from a video disk audio track to complex musical notation systems. They enable the developer to specify branch points and conditional events where users can make choices about how to proceed with the presentation.

The most flexible authoring systems use hypertext structures for maximum flexibility in accessing information. An object-oriented design also facilitates audio and video presentations. Clicking on a hypertext button can play a sound or video clip just as easily as it can display a picture or jump to a text window. The entire knowledge domain of a chosen topic must be clearly structured, and the necessary links between related ideas, concepts and topics must be identified, so that the information-seekers are permitted to browse non-sequentially, without following any predetermined path.

6.4.9.1 Topology and structures

Luther (1992, p. 59) identifies the following six types of generic application structures:

1. linear presentation;
2. data-driven engine;
3. hierarchical menu;
4. information retrieval;
5. hypermedia;
6. simulation.

Figure 6.7 illustrates schematically how these structures reflect the different conceptual approaches to information retrieval identified in Chapter 3. The characteristics of each approach, including advantages, disadvantages and ideal applications, also apply to these structures.

The linear presentation corresponds to one pre-selected pre-coordinate sequence which has been identified as most appropriate for the application. The user has to follow this sequence to get to the desired information. It is very suitable for a user who is completely new to a subject and needs a general overview. The data-driven menu introduces elements of choice into a linear presentation, including moving backwards to an earlier part of the presentation, or quitting it completely. Both of these structures correspond to the sequence in Figure 6.7A. The hierarchical menu in Figure 6.7B is based on a pre-coordinate structure, using a classified approach. It is particularly appropriate when the multimedia content can be segregated into discrete parts, with clear choices between the parts.

Full retrieval requires a multimedia database, which might include text, audio, video or images. The user is given various access routes to the database, such as searching by creator, title, subject or other access point. The search results may be displayed as a list or a group of icons which can be quickly browsed by the user. The user can then either select one or more items for controlled display/listening, or modify the search strategy. This post-coordinate approach is shown in Figure 6.7C. The hypermedia class enables multi-coordinate retrieval of the items in the database. If a linear trail of hypertext links is created, the users can search in a pre-coordinate way. If they opt to search the database using access points which may be combined, the approach is post-coordinate. If a varied network of links is created, then users may click on highlighted items, and follow links to related items. In many cases, these links will be from an item in one format to other items which deal with the same concept in different formats. It requires the existence of all three structures in Figure 6.7. The simulation class is not relevant for information retrieval.

6.4.9.2 Multimedia assets

The files in which data, image, audio, animation and video items are stored on hard disk or on optical storage media are known as multimedia assets. All asset files contain file headers, which are data structures placed at the start of the file to give some information about the file. The software that is going to use a file must know the format of its header in order to read the actual asset data from the file. To help keep track of asset files without having to open them to read header data, many file standards use a file-name extension code to identify the file type: '.txt' for text, '.gif' for images, '.wav' for audio, etc. The management of asset files is discussed in detail in Luther (1992).

Audio and video (and, to a lesser extent, animation) present special problems because they have a temporal dimension lacking in other media. Such media are referred to as isochronous: they are essentially continuous, with built-in timing constraints on the arrival of individual information units. Video is, in fact, a series of raster images, called frames, shown fast enough to simulate motion. Both audio and video are normally digitized, and usually compressed, for delivery to the user appliance.

The bandwidth capacity required to transmit, or space required to store, current media increases along the sequence: text, vector graphic images, raster images, audio, animation, and video. Several orders of magnitude separate the lowest from the highest. For a rough comparison: the text of this book, 10 seconds of high-fidelity music, and a single frame of video are all approximately the same size, at around 5 Mb (megabytes). The high storage requirements of multimedia assets have also resulted in the need for methods of data compression. This technique also lowers the data transfer rates between storage devices, main memory and visual display or audio playback devices. (The question of digital image input, storage and output is discussed in Section 7.6.1; the representation of audio images in computer storage in Section 8.6.)

6.5   Summary

As the range of technological implementations of electronic data structures is evolving rapidly, the reader is encouraged to consult up-to-date resources such as current issues of published journals and the ever-changing resources on the Internet in addition to this book. Irrespective of the apparent sophistication of a technological solution, it is likely to be based on a combination of one or more of the components identified in this chapter.

Many commercial multimedia systems allow for a very low level of user interaction in selecting paths; there are very few real databases which provide for retrieval in a flexible, Boolean way. A logical data model can co-exist with an object-oriented approach. The best combination for a multi-media structure is either a relational database model with BLOBs or an object-oriented database. Hypermedia systems are dependent on the same logical structure as multimedia, with hypertext browsing merely providing an additional access route to the database.

The following issues are crucial to the design of multimedia:

- How are the various media linked, and how does this effect their retrieval?
- How well does the technology allow for simultaneous display of different component media?
- How well does the technology provide for logical and physical organization of items so as to maximize retrieval efficiency (both specific and browsing)?
- How can software developments take into consideration
  - the different physical media in use and their physical characteristics?
  - the requirements of the information from the point of view of subject description of its contents?
  - the ability to link the different media and use their content descriptors in combination – words from text, physical shapes from visual images, and audio patterns from sound?

It is useful to summarize the range of possible solutions, and to identify their implications for the broadcast news agency described in Section 1.8. Both the medium and large-scale solutions are appropriate for this setting, with the large-scale solution corresponding to a more futuristic scenario.

The small-scale solution entails the following:

- A simple file management package is used to identify photographic slides or CDs.
- Allocation of access points is done manually (intellectually).
- Retrieval is very definite – either items are retrieved in response to a query, or they aren't.
- The AND operator is the only Boolean operator which may be used.
- Records in the file are accessed sequentially.

The medium-scale solution involves the following:

- A full-text database package, which enables hypertext links, is used to store and manage text and images.
- Allocation of access points is done manually (added keywords and hypertext links) and mechanically (automatic analysis of words in text).
- Retrieval is fuzzy/probabilistic, with retrieved items presented in rank order, based on likely match with the query.
- The three Boolean operators AND, OR, NOT may be used.

- There is random access to records in the file, based on indexes which have been constructed by the database package.

The large-scale solution has the following features:

- An enhanced relational database is used to manage text, audio, image, video and other files of a prominent information organization.
- Identification of access points requires some manual input, but there is also considerable automatic input, in a similar system to QBIC.
- Retrieval is probabilistic, with retrieved items presented in rank order. There is a lot of scope to modify queries, and to search by example. Searching is available on attributes specific to the medium, for example colour, texture and contrast in a picture, or number of channels, length and sampling rate in an audio clip.
- All Boolean operators may be used; proximity searching and other advanced search features are available.
- There is random access to the full information content of the records in the file.
- The system facilitates viewing of, and listening to, the retrieved information, as appropriate.
- The organization maintains a significant Web presence.

6.6   Notes

[1]   Bearman, David (1994) *Towards a Reference Model*: ⟨http://www.lis.pitt.edu/~nhprc/prog6-5.html⟩.
[2]   *IBM QBIC*: ⟨http://wwwqbic.almaden.ibm.com/stage/index.html⟩.
[3]   *IBM QBIC* demo: ⟨http://wwwqbic.almaden.ibm.com/stage/demo.html⟩.
[4]   *IBM Digital Library*: ⟨http://www.software.ibm.com/is/dig-lib/⟩.
      DB2 Extenders: ⟨http://www.software.ibm.com/data/db2/extenders/⟩.

6.7   References and further reading

Bush, Vannevar (1945) 'As we may think', *Atlantic Monthly*, July, 101–8.
Cawkell, A.E. (1993) *Encyclopaedic Dictionary of Information Technology and Systems*, London: Bowker-Saur.
Cawkell, A.E. (1996) *The Multimedia Handbook*, London: Routledge.
Ellis, David (1996) *Progress and Problems in Information Retrieval*, London: Library Association.
Feldman, Tony (1991) *Multimedia in the 1990s*, BNB Research Fund

Report 54, Boston Spa: British Library.

Humphrey, Suzanne M. and Melloni, Biagio John (1986) *Databases: A Primer for Retrieving Information by Computer*, Englewood Cliffs, NJ: Prentice-Hall.

Kemp, D. Alasdair (1988) *Computer-based Knowledge Retrieval*, London: ASLIB.

Luther, Arch C. (1992) *Designing Interactive Multimedia*, New York: Bantam Books.

Maurer, Hermann and Tomek, Iavan (1990) 'Broadening the scope of hypermedia principles', *Hypermedia*, **2**(3), 201–20.

Raskin, Robin (1990) 'Multimedia: The next frontier for business?' *PC Magazine*, July, 151–92.

Rowley, Jennifer E. (1992) *Organizing Knowledge* (2nd edn), Aldershot: Ashgate.

Stern, Nancy B. and Stern, Robert A. (1996) *Computing and the Information Age* (2nd edn), New York: Wiley.

Tenopir, Carol (1990) *Full Text Databases*, New York: Greenwood Press.

Chapter 7

Visual information

7.1   Introduction

This chapter investigates and evaluates the alternative approaches to the storage and retrieval of visual images and their surrogates, with particular reference to computerized systems. Visual images are defined as items which convey information in the form of symbols which are interpreted by the naked eye, and which are not dependent on words or text for their meaning.

Examples of visual images include the following: paintings, art prints and drawings; photographs; posters; slides; trademarks; logos; architectural, engineering and electronics plans; maps; slides; items of correspondence; films, videos (still frames and continuous); cartoon strips (sequences); graphics, design symbols, icons, drawings, models and specimens dealing with medicine, biology, science, archaeology, engineering and architecture; museum artefacts; globes, and multimedia items. These may exist in hard copy only, in electronic form only, or as both. For example, a map may exist as internal computer code which a mapping software package displays on a computer screen.

The questions which were introduced in Section 1.8 apply to visual items, and must constantly be borne in mind when designing a retrieval system for visual information. This chapter will extend the theory and the practical solutions of earlier chapters to a broad range of visual items.

7.2   Features and categorization of visual items

The following characteristics of visual items are relevant to their organization and retrieval:

- They differ from textual items in that they convey information using symbols other than words.

- They may exist in many varied formats – two- or three-dimensional, discrete or continuous, or in different physical media. One or more formats may be combined in an integrated product, possibly in a multimedia system.

- They may be original items, or manifestations thereof. For example, we could be dealing with a real item such as a stone, a building, a painting or a person, or a photograph of the stone, an architectural drawing of the building, a reproduction of the painting on a postcard, or a portrait of the person. This creates problems for describing and exploiting the item, as there may be many levels of related items, which must be linked and differentiated. Thus a photograph of a portrait of a famous person may be of interest from the point of view of the photographer, or the artist, or the person portrayed.

- There is a distinction between subjective images, where the interpretation of meaning is subjective and where the object has some aesthetic value, and the more objective content of architectural models and engineering drawings.

- It is much more difficult to describe the subject content of visual images than textual ones, particularly when the possible uses of a collection span a range of disciplines. A picture may truly be worth a thousand words. For example, an autumnal tree may be an example of a particular species, in a particular state of growth, for the botanist; for the film-maker, it may be a shot which is evocative of death, harvests, short days and cold nights, etc.

- Visual items are subject to changes in state and variants (reprinting and modifications) as well as repeated uses in different products (print reused in a number of items, a page from a periodical distributed as a single sheet, an original photograph used as an illustration in a book, etc.).

- Visual images are usually stored as bit-mapped data, with implications for storage requirements, input and display equipment, and retrieval.

- Different disciplines generate needs for diverse types of access to visual information. In some areas such as art history or archival research, the medium may be the main interest; in others, such as botany or social history, the content is the primary concern. Some quantitative mechanisms concentrate on the physical aspects of the items, for example the size, scale or position of objects, or the degree of resolution. Other mechanisms emphasize qualitative aspects of both form and content – a particular artistic, photographic or architectural style, the objective or purpose underlying the work – in addition to more objective features, such as the objects represented in an image.

Despite the variety of visual information resources, they fall into distinct categories, where each category poses specific problems for the design of an information retrieval system. The following characteristics define the categories of visual items, and correspond to the columns in Table 7.1:

- Category number (No.)
- Examples in this category (Examples)
- Is the item two-dimensional or three-dimensional? (2D/3D)
- Is the item discrete or self-contained, or one which is continuous and contains a succession of images? (Discrete/Continuous)
- Is it an original item, or a manifestation of an original? (Original/Manifestation)
- Is the subject matter of the item mainly objective (an image of something) or mainly subjective (vaguely about something)? (Objective/Subjective)
- Is the content of the image of interest, or is the medium through which it is conveyed of importance? (Medium/Content)
- Do the users of the items have any specialist knowledge of the medium or the content? (Generalist/Specialist)

The 21 categories which result span the interests of libraries, museums, galleries and many specialist information agencies.

The description in the surrogate of a visual item will vary depending on whether the item is two- or three-dimensional. Procedures and standards for creating a description are discussed in Section 7.3.3. Surrogates, creatorship, subject analysis and representation will be handled differently for a discrete, self-contained image, compared to a continuous one which contains a succession of images. These aspects are dealt with in Sections 7.3, 7.4 and 7.5. An item may be an original in its own right, or a manifestation of something else: for instance, a sculpture or a painting may be an abstract creation which only has this identity, or it may be a manifestation of something else, such as a person, a building or an event. The additional questions of description and creatorship which arise when dealing with a manifestation of an original item are discussed in Sections 7.3.3.2 and 7.4.2. Depending on how objective or subjective the subject matter is, various challenging aspects of subject access arise, particularly the questions of what the image is 'of' and what it is 'about'. These are investigated in Section 7.5.

The relative importance of medium and content have implications for subject analysis and for description in a surrogate. It is worth noting from Table 7.1 that no items are identified where only the medium, and not the content is of interest. Description of medium is examined in Section 7.3.3 and subject content in Section 7.5. Whether the users of the items have any

Table 7.1   *Characteristics and categorization of visual items*

No.	Examples	2D/3D	Discrete/ Continuous	Original/ Manifestation	Objective/ Subjective	Medium/ Content	Generalist/ Specialist
1	Trademark	2D	Discrete	Original	Objective	Content	Both
2	Letter	2D	Discrete	Original	Objective	Both	Both
3	Cartoon	2D	Discrete	Original	Both	Both	Both
4	**All original items without any specific subject matter:**						
	Letter	2D	Discrete	Original	Subjective	Both	Both
	Painting (subjective)	2D	Discrete	Original	Subjective	Both	Both
	Poster (subjective)	2D	Discrete	Original	Subjective	Both?	Both
5	Icon	2D	Discrete	Manifestation	Objective	Content	Generalist
	Sign	2D	Discrete	Manifestation	Objective	Content	Generalist
6	**Manifestations of things with very specific subject matter and with specialist users:**						
	Architecture plan	2D	Discrete	Manifestation	Objective	Content	Specialist
	Design symbol	2D	Discrete	Manifestation	Objective	Content	Specialist
	Engineering drawing	2D	Discrete	Manifestation	Objective	Content	Specialist
	Logo	2D	Discrete	Manifestation	Objective	Content	Specialist
7	Map	2D	Discrete	Manifestation	Objective	Both	Both
8	**Manifestations of specific things, with objective and subjective content, interest in both the medium and the content, for generalist and specialist users:**						
	Painting (specific)	2D	Discrete	Manifestation	Both	Both	Both
	Photograph	2D	Discrete	Manifestation	Both	Both	Both
	Poster (specific)	2D	Discrete	Manifestation	Both	Both?	Both
	Slide	2D	Discrete	Manifestation	Both	Both	Both
9	Letters	2D	Continuous	Original	Objective	Both	Both
10	**All continuous originals with no definable subject:**						
	Letters	2D	Continuous	Original	Subjective	Both	Both
	Film (subjective)	2D	Continuous	Original	Subjective	Both	Both
	Video (subjective)	2D	Continuous	Original	Subjective	Both	Both
11	Cartoon sequence	2D	Continuous	Original?	Both	Both	Both
12	Film (specific)	2D	Continuous	Manifestation	Both	Both	Both
13	Medical specimen	3D	Discrete	Original	Objective	Content	Specialist
14	Stuffed animal	3D	Discrete	Original	Objective	Both	Both
15	Sculpture (subjective)	3D	Discrete	Original	Subjective	Both	Both
16	Globe	3D	Discrete	Manifestation	Objective	Content	Both
17	Museum artefact	3D	Discrete	Manifestation	Objective	Both	Both
18	Sculpture (specific)	3D	Discrete	Manifestation	Both	Both	Both

No.	Examples	2D/3D	Discrete/ Continuous	Original/ Manifestation	Objective/ Subjective	Medium/ Content	Generalist/ Specialist
19	Multimedia	3D	Continuous	Original	Objective	Both	Both
20	Multimedia	3D	Continuous	Original	Subjective	Both	Both
21	Multimedia	3D	Continuous	Manifestation	Both	Both	Both

Table 7.1   continued

specialist knowledge of the medium or the content will affect whether they search by primary or secondary subject matter. For example, with medical or architectural drawings, non-experts may know the name of the disease or the architectural style, but may not recognize its specific features even if they see them. For art, non-experts are likely to itemize things which may be seen in a painting, but may not interpret them in any way. The expert will be capable of both levels of access, the novice of only one. Table 7.1 shows the high number of cases where both generalists and specialists use a shared information resource. Ways of facilitating these two levels of users are discussed in Section 7.5.4. When establishing a retrieval system for any collection of visual items (including those not listed in Table 7.1) which may not yet be invented, it is essential to identify the general categories to which they belong before applying the principles which are developed in this chapter.

7.3   Surrogates

7.3.1   Surrogate components and examples

The three components of surrogates – access points, description and location indicator – which were established in Chapter 4 also apply to visual items. There are no specific points which arise for location indicator other than those discussed in Chapter 4, but new issues occur for both access points and description.

Some familiar examples of surrogates of visual items include:

- an entry for a photograph in the contents list of an exhibition, a book or a collection;
- a catalogue entry for a work of art;
- an entry for a film in a movie database on the Internet;
- a record for a painting or drawing in a visual arts database;
- a record of a museum item in a database;
- a record of an architectural drawing in a linear filing system.

Figures 7.1–7.3 present examples of surrogates for three different types of visual image accessible on the Internet.

Collections

European Paintings

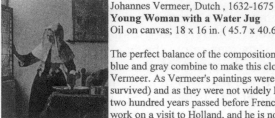

Johannes Vermeer, Dutch , 1632-1675
Young Woman with a Water Jug
Oil on canvas; 18 x 16 in. (45.7 x 40.6 cm)

The perfect balance of the composition, the cool clarity of the light, and the silvery tones of blue and gray combine to make this closely studied view of an interior a classic work by Vermeer. As Vermeer's paintings were few in number (fewer than 35 accepted works have survived) and as they were not widely known, he was forgotten soon after his death. Almost two hundred years passed before French critic Theophile Thore rediscovered Vermeer's work on a visit to Holland, and he is now one of the most esteemed Dutch painters. The **Young Woman with a Water Jug** is characteristic of his early maturity and dates from the beginning of the 1660s.

Marquand Collection, Gift of Henry G. Marquand, 1889

Back to Floor Map   Back to Listing of Art

Home Membership Calendar Collections Info News Shop Education FAQ

Home Membership Calendar Collections Info News Shop Education FAQ

(c) 1998 The Metropolitan Museum of Art.

Figure 7.1   Surrogate example: Painting from the Metropolitan Museum of Art
Source: Metropolitan Museum of Art: ⟨http://www.metmuseum.org/htmlfile/gallery/ second/euro5.html⟩. Reproduced with permission. © 1997 The Metropolitan Museum of Art.

7.3.2   Access points

It is essential that consistent internal or external standards be followed for the generation of subject and creator access points. The guidelines for facet analysis and generation of keywords should be followed for subject entries. Similarly for creator access, guidelines for deciding on the type and form of entries must be followed. Depending on the type of material, additional

AMERICAN MEMORY | PREVIOUS | NEXT | ITEM LIST | NEW SEARCH

By Popular Demand: Portraits of the Presidents and First Ladies, 1789-Present

Photograph 1 of 8

For a larger reference image, click on the picture. Click here for unsharpened high resolution image (1,286 kilobytes)

[Abraham Lincoln, head-and-shoulders portrait, facing front]
CREATED/PUBLISHED
[photograph taken 1863 Nov. 8, c1900]
NOTES
Copyright by M.P. Rice, Washn., D.C.
Original photograph by Alexander **Gardner**.
SUBJECTS
Lincoln, Abraham,--1809-1865.
Portrait photographs--1860-1870.
Photographic prints--1900.
RELATED NAMES
Gardner, Alexander, 1821-1882, photographer.
MEDIUM
1 photographic print.
CALL NUMBER
Item in PRES FILE - Lincoln, Abraham -Portraits--Meserve Collection--No. 59
REPRODUCTION NUMBER
LC-USZ62-13016 DLC (b&w film copy neg.)
REPOSITORY
Library of Congress Prints and Photographs Division Washington, D.C. 20540 USA
DIGITAL ID
(b&w film copy neg.) cph 3a53289

AMERICAN MEMORY | PREVIOUS | NEXT | ITEM LIST | NEW SEARCH

Figure 7.2   Surrogate example: Photograph from the American Memory Collection
Source: Portraits of the Presidents and First Ladies home page: ⟨http://lcweb2.loc.gov/ammem/
odmdhtml/preshome.html⟩. Found by searching on **Lincoln** and **Gardner**.

access points may be important. For visual items, these might include medium, date, size or technical details. All, or selected, fields from the surrogates in Figure 7.1 could be used as access points.

AMERICAN MEMORY | PREVIOUS | NEXT | ITEM LIST | NEW SEARCH

Before and After the Great Earthquake and Fire: Early Films of San Francisco, 1897-1916

Movie 1 of 5

Arrest in Chinatown, San Francisco, Cal. / Thomas A. Edison, Inc.

Information about Video Playback

View this film.
(*AVI Format....5,586,454 bytes*)...*To download the film for future viewing, be sure to set your browser to the "load to disk" or "retrieve to disk" option.*

CREATED/PUBLISHED
United States : Thomas A. Edison, Inc., 1897.

NOTES
Copyright: Thomas A. Edison; 25Oct1897; 60596.

Duration: 0:48 at 15 fps.

This film shows the **arrest** and conveyance of a Chinese man in Chinatown, watched by a crowd of onlookers. The precise date of this film and the **arrest** charge are uncertain. It is possible that the **arrest** was connected with the smuggling of illegal immigrants from China. By mutual agreement between China and the United States, a small quota of merchants and students were allowed to immigrate yearly, but few legal immigrants actually were of these professions, and illegal immigration continued. One of the San Francisco residences for new arrivals was located at 830/832 Washington Street, the general location from which the **arrest** party ascends at the start of the film. A second possible cause for the **arrest** is tong activity. Chinatown at this time was plagued with warfare between various tongs (gang associations of rootless and under-enfranchised immigrants and non-family members). The murder of tong kingpin Fong Ching - called "Little Pete" - in January 1897 set off a flurry of tong violence that continued for months. The practice of tying the queue up on the head, a fashion supposedly confined to tong "hit men" called "highbinders" was in fact common among laborers. The **arrested** man has followed this practice and his rough canvas jacket suggests he is a peddler or shophand by (legitimate) profession. A third possible

Figure 7.3   Surrogate example: Motion picture from the American Memory Collection
Source: San Francisco home page: ⟨http://lcweb2.loc.gov/ammem/papr/sfhome.html⟩. Found by browsing Subject Index, then searching on Arrest - - California - - San Francisco.

arrest charge may involve illegal gambling. Stout's Alley was lined with gambling houses, many owned by the late Fong Ching. Pawnbroker shops were nearby. The circular sign seen at left in the first part of the film is a pawnbroker's sign. All of the local streets had Chinese names. Washington Street was Wa Sheng Shong Hong ("Waystation to Prosperity Street"), Stout's Alley was Lou Shong Hong ("Old Spanish (Mexican Gambler) Alley") and Waverly Place was Ten How Mui Gai ("Ten How Temple Street"). These names are still in use.

The following is a scene-by-scene description of the film: [Frame: 0002] The camera was placed at the northwest corner of Washington Street and Stout's Alley (Now Ross Alley), midway between Stockton Street and Grant Avenue. The first scene shows the **arrested** man being led by a police officer west up the north side of Washington Street to Stout's Alley. A group of pedestrians, mostly white, watch the man's unwilling **arrest** [0037]. A detective is seen pointing the cameraman toward the police cart waiting in Washington Street [0391]. The next scene shows the departure of the police cart with the **arrested** man, policemen, and triumphant detective, who waves to the camera [0572]. The cart turns east and begins down Washington Street as a mostly Chinese crowd watches from the south side of Washington Street and the intersecting Waverly Place [0680].

Received: 10/25/1897; paper pos; copyright deposit Paper Print Collection.

SUBJECTS
Police--California--San Francisco.
Horse-drawn vehicles--California--San Francisco.
Police vehicles--California--San Francisco.
Streets--California--San Francisco.
Commercial buildings--California--San Francisco.
Chinatown (San Francisco, Calif.)
Shorts.
Actualities.

RELATED NAMES
Thomas A. Edison, Inc.
Paper Print Collection (Library of Congress) DLC

MEDIUM
1 roll (68 ft) : si., b&w ; 35 mm. paper pos.

CALL NUMBER
LC 992 (paper pos)

REPOSITORY
DLC M/B/RS

DIGITAL ID
(m) lcmp003 m3a15145

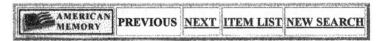

Figure 7.3   continued

7.3.3   Description

The elements of description outlined in Chapter 4 are applicable to visual items. Bruckman (1988) argues strongly that the elements of bibliographic description which apply to books can be applied to any item. AACR2 and ISBD provide for titles and statements of responsibility, information concerning edition and state, the publishers, printers, distributors and dates, physical description, and whether the visual item belongs to a group of items or a collection. Notes take account of any historical or critical facts. The founder takes the place of the printer, the surface or weight correspond to height or width, etc. Although many developers of information retrieval systems may baulk at the details required by AACR2, it does provide a useful reference source for description of visual items.

7.3.3.1   Examples and standards

The principle of consistent description identified in Section 4.7 is important. Typical descriptions are shown in the surrogates of visual items in Figures 7.1–7.3. The main activities in libraries have been from the perspective of cataloguers, archivists and indexers. Standards such as AACR2, Library Association Rules for Audio-Visual Materials, ISBD, MARC, and those of art libraries provide the basic guidelines. A general format such as ISBD may be modified, or versions of it developed for different media. The edition statement in ISBD and AACR2 may be used to distinguish related items from one another. An equivalent of the MARC format (described in Section 4.5) is available for the exchange of computerized records for visual items between institutions. The *Thesaurus for Graphic Materials I: Subject Terms* (Library of Congress, 1995a), and the *Thesaurus for Graphic Materials II: Genre and Physical Characteristic Terms* (Library of Congress, 1995b) cover many aspects of surrogate creation, including the description of physical and subject content.

Consistency of treatment and the form of entries is important for film libraries. Harrison (1973) identifies the following features of a film which should be noted on a catalogue record:

- title;
- subject and/or classification number;
- production details (production company, place and date);
- production and performance credits;
- physical format, including length;
- production or location number;
- summary or synopsis;
- notes, including such details as restrictions on future use.

7.3.3.2   Description of original or manifested item

Distinguishing between an original item and its manifestations through the description is essential in order to differentiate between an original work of art and postcard reproductions, for example. It must be recognized that each item will have a different description, and a description of a mixture of the two items should be avoided. By distinguishing between the original and the manifestation, both can be described accurately. For example, when dealing with a photograph or a painting of some person, object or event, it is necessary to handle the description at different levels, with separate sections for each of the levels, as illustrated in Table 7.2. This basic distinction can be achieved using AACR2 and ISBD. Shatford considers the problem of description and subject analysis of pictures from the perspective of existing cataloguing, classification and indexing tools (Shatford 1984 and 1986).

Table 7.2   *Layers in a manifested item*

Manifested item:
Level 1: The Custom House Dublin, by Lord Snowdon
B&W photograph; 5″ × 7″; matt finish; 1970.
Is a manifestation of the original architectural design:
Level 2: The Custom House Dublin, by James Gandon
Details of architectural style, date etc.

However, we need to allow for description of the different manifestations of an item within one record: a description of the postcard in hand and also of the original painting, for instance. The only efficient way of doing this is with an appropriate data structure for items and their surrogates, such as a relational database or hypertext. In a relational database, there would be a relational file based on titles of original items; hypertext would allow links to be created between specific items.

The concepts of related manifestations, related translations, and related editions of an item discussed in Chapter 2 may be applied to visual items. It may be very important that the retrieval system draw these together in order to allow for the answering of general and specific queries. Manifestations of an item are equivalent to 'pictures' of an item; translations correspond to various etchings, engravings and drawings relating to an original painting. Editions could be used for items that are copied or adapted from each other, but that remain in the same medium. These related pictorial items are presented in Table 7.3. The various manifestations of a movie film may be seen in a movie database on the Internet: for example, searching on the title of a movie on the Reel Web site leads to details of availability in different formats and editions, for sale or rent.[1]

Table 7.3   *Pictorial manifestations*

Term	Definition	Examples
Manifestations	Pictures/reproductions of the original work	Portrait/building
Translations	Copies or adaptations of the original work, done in a different medium	Woodcuts based on a painting
Pictorial editions	Copies or adaptations of the original work, done in the original medium	Portraits of a famous person; copies of a famous painting

7.4   Creatorship

7.4.1   Introduction

The key issues which arise when considering creatorship were identified in Section 4.6.1. An additional issue for visual items is that creatorship may be by origination or by assumption. The former occurs when a person actually creates an item; the latter when the creative input is provided by one person, with the physical execution of the item carried out by someone else. An artist or photographer who originates a item would come under the first category; a designer, an architect or a photographer whose item is developed and printed by someone else all fall into the second category. Problems of different creators are also likely to arise because of the importance of manifestations of original items. It is necessary to reflect these varied contributions for certain applications, for instance for credits in the film industry.

Library standards and experience should be used as a general guide, rejecting any portions which are not appropriate. At a minimum, they raise the issues which need to be examined, even if the libraries' solutions are not necessarily adopted, and they also provide the basis for the development of consistent in-house standards.

7.4.2   Manifested item

If a visual item is a manifestation, one needs to decide who has made the greatest intellectual contribution, and to do this consistently for a specific collection and user population. In particular, the type 4 manifestation identified in Section 2.4, which corresponds to 'adaptation/interpretation of an item in a new medium', occurs frequently for visual items.

A manifested item need not necessarily be two-dimensional: it may be a piece of sculpture, a building, a theatrical performance, or an object or an event that can be described as a creative or intellectual item. A significant issue is whether primary access should be by the person responsible for the original item, or its manifestation. For example, should it be by an original sculptor and/or the artist or photographer of a sculpture? It is not possible to answer this question categorically, even for one collection, but the choice of which entry or entries to make must be linked to the needs of the users of the collection.

AACR2 deals with adaptations of art works as follows (from Gorman and Winkler, 1993):

> Enter an adaptation from one medium of the graphic arts to another under the heading for the person responsible for the adaptation. If the name of the adaptor is not known, enter under title. Make a name-title added entry for the original work. [Rule 21.16A]

> Enter a reproduction of an art work (e.g. a photograph, a photo-mechanical reproduction, or a reproduction of sculpture) under the heading for the original work. Make an added entry under the heading for the person or body responsible for the reproduction ... [Rule 21.16B]

Reproductions of two or more art works are handled as follows:

> Enter a work consisting of reproductions of the works of an artist without accompanying text under the heading for the artist. [Rule 21.17A]

> If a work consists of reproductions of the works of an artist and text about the artist and/or the works reproduced, enter under the heading appropriate to the text if the person who wrote it is represented as the author in the chief source of information ... Make an added entry under the heading for the artist. Otherwise, enter under the heading for the artist. In case of doubt, enter under the heading for the artist. If the work is entered under the heading for the artist, make an added entry under the heading for the person who wrote the text if his or her name appears in the chief source of information. [Rule 21.17B]

These rules identify some of the problem situations, with the underlying philosophy of identifying the person who is chiefly responsible for the intellectual creation of the work as the creator. For type 1 manifestations, the original artist is the chief responsible person, whereas for types 2 and 3, where another creator substantially enriches or modifies the work, he is responsible. The decision as to which is the main entry and which are added entries is of minor importance compared with the need to ensure that all necessary entries are made, particularly in a computerized environment.

7.4.3   Form of creator's name

The creator may be an individual, a number of individuals, or a corporate body. The issues which arise have been identified in Section 4.6.1, for example varying forms of name, changes of name, parent and subordinate bodies, related bodies. Which decision is made on a particular point is less important than the fact that the designer of the retrieval system should be aware that a decision is needed, and that decisions should be consistent. Internal or external name authority lists encourage consistency. These might include the cataloguing codes described in Chapter 4, or codes developed internally in order to cover local interests.

7.5   Subject content analysis and representation

7.5.1   Introduction

Subject analysis and representation are necessary both for a helpful linear arrangement and for specific retrieval. It is decidedly more difficult to describe definitively what visual items are 'of' or 'about' than in the case of text. The subject content of textual documents is normally determined by the words in the text, which are used either directly as the basis for information retrieval in a full-text system, or indirectly through keywords assigned from a controlled or uncontrolled vocabulary. Even so, there are many problems in determining 'aboutness', which have been discussed in Chapter 5. These problems are exacerbated by the varying perspectives which users with different backgrounds will bring to a subject area, by the influences of different cultural attitudes, and by changes in users' needs with time.

Visual items possess no intrinsic cue words for the generation of subject description or retrieval keys. Subject access to visual items should be related to the purpose or use of these items. Any item may contain a variety of information: a painter, an art historian, a sociologist, a botanist, a potter and a chemist would all obtain different but complementary information from a subject such as an Impressionist painting of a bunch of wild flowers in a pottery jug on a kitchen table. As visual perception is a subjective process, individual user characteristics will have a strong bearing on interpretation. This creates problems for subject analysis, but it also provides scope for the incorporation of user profiles into the retrieval process.

7.5.2   Subject analysis issues

The assignment of keywords may unintentionally involve the indexer in passing judgement on an image. For example, any of the terms 'march', 'parade', 'procession', and 'walk' might be used to describe a photograph, yet each has a different meaning in public perception. The indexer has made moral, political and intellectual decisions, and has informed users to some extent what he or she believes the subject of the picture to be. For text, the indexer tends to be influenced by the author's actual words, and there is less danger of subjectivity in subject analysis.

In general, an item should be indexed as specifically as possible. For example, a video of Nôtre Dame Cathedral in Paris should be indexed by its specific name. The structure of the subject vocabulary should alert the information-seeker who thinks of more general terms such as 'France', 'cathedrals', 'churches', 'Gothic churches' or 'thirteenth-century cathedrals' to this specific term. The example of a generic-to-specific hierarchy presented in Section 5.2.1 also applies to visual items.

The difficult subjective aspects of indexing visual items are illustrated by a particular theme which could be represented by more than one keyword: in the case of 'universities', such themes could be 'elitist educational systems', 'ivory towers', 'vibrancy of youth' or 'concrete ghettos'. The indexer can resolve this dilemma by attempting to identify the objectives of the creator of a visual item, and of the potential users of the item.

Continuous items such as film present additional challenges for subject analysis. Even feature films may contain a series of separate sequences only loosely linked together by one or more themes. In addition, the film may have been shot in several locations, on different dates, and may contain shots of several personalities involved in the main story. The film can be indexed as a whole, or may be broken down into specific sequences which have an interest of their own. The cataloguer may index the whole film, separate sequences and/or individual shots. Harrison (1973) provides further details on film library techniques.

7.5.3   Levels of meaning and iconography

Subject analysis is enriched by the principles of iconography, 'the study of subject matter or meaning in art' (Panofsky, 1962, p.3). Panofsky's theories may be applied to all visual items, spanning a broad spectrum of subject interests, and are not limited to art. This art historian developed a theory which describes three levels of meaning in a work of art which may be applied to any representational visual item. In the analysis of an artwork, the iconographer distinguishes three levels of subject matter:

1. primary subject matter;
2. secondary subject matter;
3. iconographical interpretation.

These three levels of meaning are summarized in Table 7.4.

The first level of meaning is 'pre-iconography', which is defined as: 'primary or natural subject matter, subdivided into factual and expressional'. Factual and expressional meaning is derived from practical experience of the world. Factual meaning describes what the picture is 'of'; expressional meaning describes what it is 'about'. Factual meaning is easy enough to identify and index, whereas the expressional component of mood or emotion is much more difficult. Panofsky employs Leonardo Da Vinci's *Last Supper* to explain how to identify primary subject matter. The *Last Supper* shows 13 men sitting around a table, eating dinner and engaged in conversation. This enumeration of objects, events and expressional qualities is a pre-iconographical description of this artwork. The only knowledge needed to formulate a pre-iconographical description is practical experience of everyday life.

Secondary subject matter is: 'the identification of themes or concepts manifested in images, stories, and allegories' (Panofsky, 1962, p.6). It requires familiarity with specific themes and concepts; it incorporates identification of specific (not generic) objects, for example the people or place shown in a photograph; it also incorporates the identification of images rep-

Table 7.4   *Levels of interpretation in the visual arts*

Levels of interpretation	Pre-iconographical description	Iconographical analysis	Iconological interpretation
Object of interpretation	Primary or natural subject matter: factual and expressional, constituting the world of motifs	Secondary or conventional subject matter, based on images, stories, and allegories	Tertiary or intrinsic meaning or content, based on symbolic values
Equipment for interpretation	Practical experience (familiarity with objects and events)	Knowledge of literary sources (familiarity with specific themes and concepts)	Synthetic intuition (familiarity with the human mind and personal psychology)
Example of sample photograph	'Of' men queuing at a doorway; 'about' anticipation, hope, queuing, patience	Opening of new employment centre in a Georgian building in Waterford City (Ireland) on 3 March 1910	Social implications of unemployment

Source: Panofsky (1962).

resenting certain ideas, themes or concepts, as in stories or allegories. Secondary subject matter recognizes that the gathering of these 13 men depicts Christ's last supper with his disciples. The identification of secondary subject matter is known as iconographical analysis. The iconographer relies upon his or her own knowledge of literary sources, customs and cultural traditions peculiar to a certain civilization.

Panofsky's final level of meaning he calls 'iconology', and he defines it as the intrinsic meaning of content. As this third level of meaning requires a high degree of interpretation, it cannot be indexed consistently. Iconographical interpretation is: 'the identification of underlying principles which reveal the basic attitude of a nation, period, religion, class, or philosophical persuasion' (Panofsky, 1962, p.7). It involves aspects such as the interpretation of the painting as a reflection of the artist's personality, or of the cultural, social, religious or political standards of the period.

Panofsky's three levels of meaning correspond to a fuller implementation of the principles of subject analysis based on 'ofness' and 'aboutness', as described in Chapter 5. 'Ofness' corresponds to primary subject matter and pre-iconographical description. 'Aboutness' corresponds to secondary subject matter and the iconological analysis. Overall 'aboutness' of the item as a whole corresponds to iconological interpretation. A combination of 'ofness/aboutness' with facet analysis is applied to the example of the photograph of the meeting between President Richard Nixon and Elvis Presley in the White House in 1970 in Table 7.5. The subject content of this photograph may be described simply as follows:

- specific 'of' – Elvis Presley meeting President Nixon;
- generic 'of' – famous people; US presidents; rock and roll singers;
- 'about' – interaction between politics and music, etc.

The fuller level of analysis for each facet ('Who?; What?; When?; Where?') is also shown in Table 7.5.

Table 7.5   *Application of 'ofness'/'aboutness' and facet analysis to the Nixon–Presley photograph*

Ranganathan's facets	Question	Shatford's specific 'of'	Shatford's generic 'of'	Shatford's 'about'
Personality	Who?	Richard Nixon	US presidents	Politicians
		Elvis Presley	Rock & roll singers	Entertainers
Matter	What?	Concert	Entertainment	
Energy	What are they doing?	Talking, smiling, shaking hands	Meeting Negotiating	Friendship Co-operation
Space	Where?	Washington, DC	Capital cities	
Time	When?		The 1970s	

'Aboutness' (non-facet-specific): politics and entertainment; drugs control

The distinction between 'of' and 'about' indexing is incorporated into the *Library of Congress Thesaurus for Graphic Materials I: Subject Terms* (Library of Congress, 1995a). An example is a cartoon from the collections of this institution, depicting a woman sweeping with a long broom, which was drawn in the period 1910–20. The image is *of* 'sweeping and dusting'; it is *about* 'women's suffrage'.[2]

7.5.4   Linking of primary and secondary subject matter

Many of the difficulties of subject analysis of visual items arise from the inconsistent use of different levels of analysis by indexers, and the natural tendency of different user groups to apply different levels.

Markey (1983) has developed a *Thematic Catalog of Primary and Secondary Subject Matter* as a search aid for iconographical research collections. Its purpose is to help users of these collections who do not have knowledge of the symbolic implications of artworks' representational elements. Consulting the search aid, users can translate representational elements (primary subject matter) into the appropriate symbolic theme or concept (secondary subject matter) before starting a search. Iconographers often use different terms to express the same theme, for example 'The Dormition' or 'The Assumption' to describe the Roman Catholic doctrine concerning the end of the life on earth of Mary, the Mother of Jesus. The thematic catalogue also lists synonymous terms for secondary subject matter.

This linking of primary and secondary subject matter has applications far beyond the works of art for which it was originally developed. It may be applied to any collection of visual items where there are different levels of users, for instance specialist and generalist, or expert and novice. If the primary and secondary subject matter are linked, the user has the option of searching at either level. Depending on their level of knowledge, the user selects the appropriate approach. Thus, for a collection of archaeological drawings, a novice might use terms corresponding to particular components of the drawing, whereas an expert might be familiar with the overall nomenclature associated with that phenomenon. For architecture, a novice might merely specify an interest in images which possess such features as ornate designs, sweeping curves, elongated and graceful plant-forms, etc., while an expert would be capable of describing his or her interest as 'Art Nouveau'. In some situations, the process may operate in reverse: a novice might want drawings of Art Nouveau structures to see what they look like, yet not be capable of spelling out the specific features.

It is important to resolve the following issues before setting up a retrieval system for visual items:

1.   Identify whether primary or secondary meaning, or both, are required for a specific collection of items and users.

2. Decide whether the input of expertise necessary to link primary and secondary meaning is justified.
3. Develop guidelines for the description of primary and secondary meaning.

For the sample application of a broadcast agency in Section 1.8, both types of meaning are required, but it is debatable whether the efforts required to link primary and secondary meaning are justified: it may be worthwhile for an internationally accessible information service on the Internet, but not for a purely in-house system. For Internet resources, directory services targeted at specific user groups could play an active part in developing links between the two levels for specific subject disciplines. Potential areas of application include Architecture, Art, Biology, Engineering and Medicine.

7.5.5   Facet analysis of subject content

Facet analysis, with its emphasis on the representation of different aspects of the item being described, and its ability to coordinate different combinations of concepts at the time of retrieval, provides a very sound theoretical basis for the analysis and description of visual images in both manual and computerized retrieval systems. It allows the indexer to describe the photograph fully and precisely, using a controlled vocabulary which can also be used for searching in a post-coordinate system. In addition to its use in identifying subject concepts, a faceted approach is essential when describing the physical characteristics of an item.

Facets such as entities, their properties, activities, agents of those activities, location in space or time, and media for storage may be used in order to represent single characteristics of a complex topic. Other facets would be used to represent the concepts represented by the visual item as a whole. In addition, facets are used to describe the physical details of the photograph, as shown in Table 7.6.

Enser et al. have analysed user queries in a range of collections of still and moving images by image content, identification and accessibility (Enser, 1993 and 1995; Armitage and Enser, 1997). Their research projects

Table 7.6   *Facet analysis of a photograph*

Facet	Term
Colour	B&W
Angle of shot	Horizontal
Lens	50 mm
Negative size	35 mm
Print size	3 inches by 5 inches

show that there are similarities in query formulation for a range of different libraries, and that a general categorization of queries can be formulated in spite of the variations in functions, contents and users across these collections. The categorization successfully combines Panofsky's three levels of meaning, the specific/generic distinction and facet analysis. They suggest that the application of this categorization to images and queries as part of the user interface of a retrieval system would allow automatic mediation of queries and filtering of results (Armitage and Enser, 1997).

The following guidelines should be followed when carrying out subject analysis of visual items:

- Use some combination of objective (factual = 'of') and subjective (interpretative = 'about') description. A greater level of interpretation is acceptable than for textual items.

- A distinction between primary and secondary subject matter is usually helpful.

- It may be useful to list (itemize) objects which are seen in an item as part of the objective description.

- Parts of items should be listed only if they are useful in their own right.

- It may be helpful to subdivide the item into areas as part of the objective description, for example foreground, background, left, right, centre.

- A checklist of points, based on a faceted approach, is helpful, for example
  - Who/what is shown?
  - What is happening?
  - Why is it happening?
  - How is it happening?
  - When is it happening?
  - Where is it happening?

- Some interpretation may be possible, such as the mood engendered by the colour of a painting. It may be necessary to do some guesswork and make some assumptions. This is acceptable in certain situations, provided the user can distinguish between fact and hypothesis.

- Add specific analysis dependent on the type of material (e.g. botanical drawings, architectural renderings, impressionist paintings or cartoon strips) to give secondary and tertiary analysis.

7.5.6 Subject representation

Once subject analysis has been carried out, the most suitable form of vocabulary must be established. A decision must be made regarding the most appropriate form of vocabulary control. Consistent and unambiguous selection of keywords is very difficult because of the subjective nature of interpretation of visual items. A range of alternative approaches to subject representation for all items has been presented in Section 5.3. These general solutions – for example, keywords and classification schemes – are applicable to visual items. In addition, very detailed specialized subject systems may be developed for these collections.

Both pre- and post-coordinate retrieval are important for visual items: pre-coordination because it enables the retrieval of sets of visual items which users may then browse and filter, post-coordination because it gives scope for access to items from a number of different perspectives. The use of Boolean operators for multiple co-ordination of subject headings or key-words is widespread in interactive computer systems.

7.5.7 Natural words and phrases

One approach is to generate index entries automatically, based on words in titles or captions of visual items. This will work more satisfactorily for items which fall into the objective category than for subjective ones. The results are very dependent on the accuracy and detail of the captions.

For abstracts, the background of the abstracter has a strong influence, and abstracts may be slanted in order to reflect the interests of the users of the information system. Lack of background subject knowledge, and/or ignorance of the creator's intention is very limiting. Great care is needed to avoid inaccurate or over-general description. Consultation with subject experts, or of reference works, may be required. Examples of the abstracts which result are included in the surrogates in Figures 7.1–7.3.

If the approaches of 'of' and 'about', and facets, are used to analyse subject content, they should also be used for the construction of the abstract. Thus, for the photograph of the meeting between a political leader and a rock and roll singer, which is analysed in Table 7.5, an informative abstract might read:

> This B&W photograph shows the meeting between Elvis Presley, the world famous Rock & Roll star, and President Richard M. Nixon, in the White House in Washington DC on 21 December 1970. They are shown in a relaxed mood in the Oval Office with presidential aide Egil 'Bud' Krogh. Presley initiated the meeting in a letter in which he suggested that he be made a 'Federal Agent-at-Large' in the Bureau of Narcotics and Dangerous Drugs.

7.5.8   Controlled vocabularies: Thesauri and alphabetical subject terms

Thesauri designed for describing textual items in a specific subject area may be extended to handle visual items, or specialized thesauri may be developed. A large number of lists of controlled terms have been developed for the visual arts. In general, these reveal the special characteristics of the collection for which they were constructed. For primary subject matter, the emphasis is on objects, expressional qualities and events, with date and place also significant. Important agencies in these developments include:

- the Library of Congress, with the *Thesaurus for Graphic Materials I: Subject Terms* (Library of Congress, 1995a) and the *Thesaurus for Graphic Materials II: Genre and Physical Characteristic Terms* (Library of Congress, 1995b), in addition to its *Library of Congress Subject Headings* list;
- the Getty Information Institute, with the *Art & Architecture Thesaurus* (Getty Art History Information Program, 1994), the *Union Lists of Artists' Names* (ULAN) and the *Getty Thesaurus of Geographic Names* (TGN).

Both thesauri for graphic materials were compiled and edited by the Prints and Photographs Division of the Library of Congress in 1995. TGM I consists of over 6,000 terms, with numerous cross-references for indexing visual materials. The companion volume, TGM II, consists of 600 terms based on input from the Library of Congress and other archival image repositories. Both thesauri may be consulted on the Internet, and there are also some very informative examples of their use as part of the same Web site.[3]

Library of Congress Subject Headings are widely used for cataloguing films and videos. While there are structural weaknesses in this list, the use of broad headings facilitates generic searching. The particular perspective – feminist, Christian, pacifist, Baha'i, etc. – may be indicated. Dwyer (1986) discusses the use of subject headings for moving images in detail. Local sets of subject headings have also been developed: for example, those at the Picture Collection of the Newark Public Library have evolved gradually since the 19th century. A sample section of these subject headings is presented in Table 7.7. Despite the theoretical criticisms which one could make of the LCSH and *Picture Collection Subject Headings*, they work well in situations where loose subject groupings are required. Specific criticisms of the *Picture Collection Subject Headings*, some of which may be seen in Table 7.7, include:

- There is very little use of facets, as illustrated by the listing of 'Preservation' as a subdivision of 'Meat'.
- Access points are very limited, for example there is no entry directly under 'River(s)'.

Table 7.7   *Extract from the Picture Collection Subject Headings at Newark Public Library*

FLOWER ARRANGEMENT
FLOWER STUDIES
FLOWERS
        Subdivided by names of flowers and the following:
        State
        Wild
FOOD
        Bakery
        Breakfast
        Candy
        Dairy
        Dessert
        Dinner and Supper
        Fish
        Fruit
            See also Fruit; Fruit growing
        Meat
            See also Meat
        National
        Preservation
        Salad
        Soup
        Vegetables
            See also Vegetables; Vegetable growing
FORESTRY
FORMS OF LAND AND WATER
        Bay
        Brook
        Canyon
        Cape
        Cave
        Cliff
        Desert
        Geyser
        Glacier
        Harbor
        Island
        Isthmus
        Lake
        Marsh
        Mountain
        Natural Bridges
        Ocean
            See also Oceanography
        Peninsula
        Plain
        Plateau
        Pond
        Promontory
        Rapids
        River
        Strait
        Valley
        Volcano
        Volcano – old prints
        Waterfall

Source: The Picture Collection Subject Headings (6th edn) © 1968 by William J. Dane. Reprinted by permission of The Shoe String Press, Inc.

- There is overlap between headings, for example 'Vegetables'.
- Different types of subdivision are used; these are mainly alphabetical, as for 'Food' and 'Forms of land and water', but some are chronological.

One of the most significant developments in vocabulary control of visual items is the *Art & Architecture Thesaurus* project, which was initiated in order to overcome the lack of any comprehensive and standardized vocabulary for art and architecture. The result of the project is a list of subject headings which are linked through a hierarchical structure similar to MeSH. Figure 7.4A shows the AAT terms which result for a search on the term 'computers'. Figure 7.4B shows the Hierarchical Display for the same term, as displayed on the Web. Figure 7.4C shows the Term Record Display, which clarifies the scope and meaning of the term 'computers'. The AAT may be searched on the Web.[4] Other Getty-supported vocabulary control initiatives deal with the standardization of names and places.[5]

7.5.9   Controlled vocabularies: Classification

7.5.9.1   Objectives of classification

The threefold objectives of classification were discussed in detail in Chapter 5, and are merely summarized here:

- storage of items and surrogates;
- browsing of items and surrogates;
- specific retrieval of items and surrogates.

The application of classification for the arrangement of visual items is totally dependent on the nature of the physical storage medium and the facilities which it provides. If the arrangement is such that items can be scanned by the naked eye or are otherwise accessible in a sequential order (e.g. with a video disk player linked to a database of records on a microcomputer), a logical sequence becomes important. Even if the physical storage locations are not important, logical locations may be. For example, with a hierarchical, menu-based system, it isn't important for the user to know where the images are stored on disk, but the computer software must do so.

Because of the difficulties of accurate and consistent description of visual items, browsing becomes even more significant than for textual items. Ideally, larger sets of items should be retrieved for the user, who then makes the final selections by browsing through the set, filtering the items, based on their usefulness. Multiple thumbnail images may be displayed on-screen for visual browsing by the user. The user may request full-size

New
Search   THE GETTY INFORMATION INSTITUTE
HOME   INDEX   SEARCH   E-MAIL

A: Terms which are found by searching on 'computers'

Exact match search:

```
computers-------------------> computers
```

Keyword match search:

```
computers-------------------> computers
computers, home-------------> microcomputers
computers, laptop-----------> laptop computers
computers, mainframe--------> mainframes
computers, micro------------> microcomputers
computers, personal
hardware (computers)--------> computers
home computers--------------> microcomputers
lap-size computers----------> laptop computers
laptop computers
mainframe computers---------> mainframes
microcomputers--------------> microcomputers
micro computers
miniature computers---------> minicomputers
minicomputers
mini computers
personal computers----------> microcomputers
programming (computers)-----> computer programming
terminals (computers)-------> computer terminals
```

B: Tools and Equipment Hierarchy

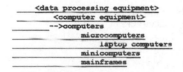

```
        <data processing equipment>
            <computer equipment>
        -->computers
                microcomputers
                    laptop computers
                minicomputers
                mainframes
```

Note: The printed thesaurus gives a fuller hierarchical structure

C: Term Record Display

Descriptor: **computers**

Hierarchy: **Tools and Equipment [TH]**

Scope note - **Devices or systems capable of carrying out a sequence of operations in a distinctly and explicitly defined manner. DOC**

Alternate Forms of Speech {ALT}:

computer

Synonyms and spelling variants {UF}:

hardware (computers)

You may also be interested in the following related concepts {RT}

computerized composition

Figure 7.4   Extract from the *Art & Architecture Thesaurus*
Source: Art & Architecture Thesaurus: ⟨http://www.gii.getty.edu/aat_browser⟩. Used with permission of the Getty Information Institute.

images of individual thumbnails, and may also ask to see extra images which are similar to the ones retrieved.

Classification is not the most effective way of achieving specific retrieval, yet a classified approach, particularly the logical application of facets, provides a very sound basis for the subject analysis of visual items (e.g. for the development of a thesauro-facet or guidelines for subject description, as outlined in Section 7.5.8). The order of application of the characteristics of division is essential, as appropriate broad categories must be established for specific groups of users. This may require the application of multiple, distinct, logical hierarchies to a collection of visual information items.

7.5.9.2 Classification schemes

General classification schemes like Dewey and the Library of Congress Classification are not aimed at visual items. It is interesting to see how they treat an area such as fine arts (see Table 7.8).

Table 7.8   *Comparison of the Dewey and Library of Congress classification schemes*

Dewey		Library of Congress	
700	The arts, Fine and decorative arts	N	Visual arts (general)
710	Civic and landscape art		
720	Architecture	NA	Architecture
730	Plastic arts, Sculpture	NB	Sculpture
740	Drawing and decorative arts	NC	Drawing, Design, Illustration
750	Painting and paintings	ND	Painting
760	Graphic arts, Printmaking and prints	NE	Print media
		NK	Decorative arts, applied arts
		NX	Arts in general
770	Photography and photographs	TR	Photography

Knight (1986) concludes that the two systems are very similar, with the Library of Congress scheme being based on Dewey's arrangement for the arts. It means that individual artists will be classified in several different places, unless they manage to channel all their creative energies through one artistic format.

Two of the best-known classification schemes for visual items, TEL-CLASS and ICONCLASS, are based on general classification principles. TELCLASS has its roots in the Universal Decimal Classification (UDC), and is used in the BBC film archive. ICONCLASS is used in many libraries which deal with the history of art. An example of its use by the ICON-CLASS Research and Development Group in the Netherlands is presented in Figure 7.5.

© Copyright ICONCLASS Research & Development Group

Introducing ICONCLASS

Example

The following picture shows a printer's device used by the 17th-century Dutch printer Boutesteyn ("sturdy stone"). The subject of the image is indexed with four ICONCLASS notations, from divisions 2, 4, and 7. The short description says: 'House built upon a rock, house built upon sand': landscape with castle on rock; windmill in background.

```
Printer 712
Boutesteyn, Cornelis

Alias:

Residence:
Leiden from 1679 until 1710

Device 186
ICONCLASS:
25H1123
41A12
47D31
73C7455
       'House built upon a rock, h
       built upon sand': landscap
       castle on a rock; windmill i
       background
```

Notation (Code)	Textual Correlate (Meaning)
25H1123	rock-formations
41A12	castle
47D31	windmill
73C7455	'house built upon a rock; house built upon sand' « doctrine of Christ on love, etc. (Matthew 7:24-27; Luke 6:47-49)

Figure 7.5   Example of the ICONCLASS Scheme
Source: Introducing ICONCLASS: (http://iconclass.let.ruu.nl/texts/icsys.htm).

7.5.9.3   Classification: Linear arrangement of items and surrogates

Detailed classification is unlikely to be a satisfactory system for the physical arrangement of visual items. However, the primary characteristic of division is significant in achieving a broad general grouping of items which may

Table 7.9   *Faceted classification scheme for visual items*

	Questions	Facets	Terms
P	Who?	People	Politicians, Famous Personalities
M	What?	Objects	Buildings, Scenery
E	Action?	Activities	Work, Sport, Travel
		Events	Meetings, News, Sport, Performing Arts
S	Where?	Location	Countries, Counties, Cities, Towns, Streets
T	When?	Time	Year, Month, Date, Time, Season, Period

then be browsed. Facet analysis is very applicable, and involves an examination of the relative importance of the aspects: 'What? How?, Where?, etc.', as discussed in Section 7.5.5. A multiplicity of characteristics of division may be applied, including creatorship, subject analysis and physical description. The physical features may dictate the basic arrangement of the items. From the discussion of the use of the facets in classification schemes in Section 5.3.4 it is clear that the latter approach facilitates the description of an item from many different perspectives.

Thus, for visual items in the broadcast news agency described in Section 1.8, it would be appropriate to use a very broad classification scheme, and to supplement it with a post-coordinate system of keywords or phrases assigned to individual still and moving visual images. The general classification scheme might be based on the faceted structure shown in Table 7.9. This sequence would be appropriate for arranging the items in some linear form: for example, for publication in a printed catalogue or text, for placing in a filing cabinet, or for sequential retrieval from a video disk. It is clear that this arrangement, as with all classification schemes, is unsatisfactory from some perspectives, thus supporting the reservations expressed earlier about the limitations of classification. For example, if the facets are combined in the order PMEST, then items dealing with a particular time period will be very scattered, while items dealing with the same Personality facet will be grouped together.

7.5.9.4   Classification in film libraries

UDC is popular in film libraries in many European countries, including the UK, while LC is the predominant scheme in the USA. Harrison (1973) describes how some libraries have to build classification by film format into the system they use. General film libraries may have to allow for different types of film: for example, the British Film Institute expands the UDC number for film (791.4) by the use of auxiliaries to cover non-fiction, news films, documentary, propaganda, compilation, cartoon, experimental, television, etc. The basic number in a classification scheme is not altered by this expansion, and the scheme can be adapted to suit the subject or the medium being classified. Stockshot and newsfilm libraries may classify by the type or angle of shot: for example, the UDC schedules, may be adapted to allow for camera motion.

7.5.10   Conclusions on subject analysis and representation

The conceptual approaches of pre- and post-coordinate retrieval may be applied to collections of non-textual information. The ability to assign multiple access keys and to coordinate these in a post-coordinate way is crucial for precise retrieval of visual items. The physical requirements of the items may make unusual demands for storage; browsing is not as automatic or convenient an option as with most textual items. Post-coordinate retrieval, supported by adequate descriptive keys, is the main mechanism for access. Linear arrangements only become useful when there is some mechanism for scanning or browsing the content of the items. The physical arrangement of items is more likely to be chronological or random, so separate mechanisms are required to allow for specific retrieval and browsing. A very simple linear arrangement, supplemented by post-coordinate retrieval, is likely to work well for browsing and retrieval. The use of Boolean logic in retrieval is valuable in providing for multiple access points and their coordination.

Facet analysis can be applied to the description of both the subject content and the physical medium of visual items. A combination of Ranganathan's PMEST facets, the 'of' and 'about' concepts of Shatford and Panofsky, and facets which are specific to a particular physical medium, gives a flexible and comprehensive approach. It may be used as a consistent method of assigning keywords for subject retrieval, in addition to the more usual applications of a classified arrangement. Facet analysis may be implemented in a computerized environment with a relational database structure. The combination of normalization and powerful query languages enable users to specify their own individual combination of search characteristics. If a linear arrangement is required, this should be by primary characteristic of division. It should be clear that a linear arrangement will not meet all requirements, and should be supported by multiple access points. The relative importance of primary, secondary and tertiary subject matter must be identified, and decisions made on which to use and the need for links between these levels. 'Of' and 'about' concepts are important – it must be decided whether either, or both, are to be described. Guidelines for specificity and depth of indexing are necessary.

There is a need for vocabulary control, particularly for the description of primary subject matter. The subjective nature of secondary subject matter makes control even more important. The AAT and subject-based thesauri are useful models, with modifications for the physical medium. Modified versions of general classification schemes may be used; alternatively, specialized solutions such as ICONCLASS and TELCLASS may be applied. Hierarchical menu indexes have a role to play in steering a user in the right general direction, but are very dependent on the extent to which the primary characteristics of division reflect an individual user's interests, and on the terminology used to describe these categories. If the menu system is constructed cleverly, and allows for multiple routes to the same item, then some of these reservations may be overcome.

7.6   Representation of visual items in computer storage

Handling visual images in a computer system raises questions regarding methods of input, storage and output, and alternative data structures. Alternative input mechanisms are required: for example optical character recognition and raster scanning equipment. ASCII (plain text) character codes no longer apply, and the images are stored as bitmapped or vector graphic data. Digital images can be created to any required degree of resolution, but the size of a digital image grows very quickly when the resolution is increased. An 8.5 inch by 11 inch A4 black-and-white image at 300 DPI (Dots Per Inch) contains almost 8.5 million pixels ($8.5 \times 300 \times 11 \times 300$). Thus over 1 Mb of space is required per black and white image at this level of detail. For this reason, most digital visual images are compressed when stored on magnetic media.

The distinction between analogue and digital data which was identified in Section 6.2.1 applies to visual images. Laservision and CD-I are analogue media, while CD-ROM is digital. The reader is referred to computer texts and articles (e.g. Stern and Stern, 1996) for a full discussion of these two types of image representation; only those aspects which affect subject access are dealt with here:

* digital image input, storage and output;
* image databases;
* image extraction – both human and computer.

7.6.1   Digital image input, storage and output

The term 'digital image' refers to the representation of a picture in the binary 1s and 0s of digital computing. The picture – a photo, printed page, diagram, etc. – becomes a digital image by being digitized into picture elements, or pixels. Another way of describing this process is to visualize a fine grid placed over a picture. Each open space in the grid is a pixel location. During digitization, the brightness of each pixel is sampled, and a numerical value is assigned to the brightness or darkness of the image at that point. When this process has been completed for each pixel, the image is represented by a rectangular array of whole numbers. Each pixel has a location or address, and a brightness measure called the grey level. When output is requested, the computer operates on one or several of these lines of numbers, and generates the image pixel by pixel.

We can distinguish two types of image: the raster or bitmap image, and the line art or vector graphic image. A raster image is a matrix of pixels, quite literally a bitmap. Raster or bit images are simply a dump (usually to disk) of an area of memory containing the image, such as the screen memory. The image is faithfully reproduced when the memory is restored from the dump. A vector graphic image is really a data structure of descriptions of simple geometric objects that make up the image. Such descriptions contain geometric coordinate data that define the shape of the components of the object, object attributes such as line style, colour or surface texture, and connectivity relationships and positioning data that define how components fit together. The drawing objects in a word-processing package provide a simple example of this data structure. Vector graphic images are generally used for drawings, charts and diagrams – pictures that can be de-composed into simpler geometric shapes and descriptions. The computer analyses the vector graphic images, and turns them into raster images for display.

In general, vector representations are more compact than raster representations. They are also easier to edit, but they require more complicated processing to turn them back into raster images for display. Both types have strengths and weaknesses for retrieval, which will be discussed in Section 7.6.3.

7.6.2   Image databases

An image database stores a large amount of image data and related information in an integrated manner with a management system. In spite of rapid developments in storage and display technology, there are problems associated with the development of image databases, which include:

- How does one represent structural information in a database?
- What information is to be retrieved?
- Is the desired output a physical image, descriptive information, or just relevant information?
- What is a unit of an image entity? How is the appropriate level of visual item defined (e.g. 'whole or part', etc., as discussed in Section 2.3)?
- When are derivable image features computed?

Image databases differ from conventional databases in many ways, including: characteristics of the data, acquisition, verification, data models, types of operations performed, hardware, software, communications, legality of data, users, user-friendliness, applications, design complexity and database design tools. Lunin's (1987) review provides a rigorous comparison of these differences.

7.6.3   Image extraction: Both human and computer

It should be clear from the preceding section that it is feasible to store huge amounts of visual images electronically, and the consideration of future developments later in this chapter will reinforce this point. However, the advances in input, storage and output of images have not been paralleled by advances in information retrieval. The majority of methods for retrieval of these images are still based on human descriptions of subject content, and computerized methods of describing image content are still in their infancy. Both approaches are discussed below.

The elements of digital images – such as individual people, or buildings of a particular type, or events of a particular description – are not described by the picture equivalent of the uniquely defined word or sentence; they are built up by numbers. The human brain is able to span all the complications of variations in image orientation, scale, size and quality, and to say of a series of photographs: 'These are pictures of Big Ben, and not a mantel-piece clock' or 'That's the Sydney Opera House, and not the Statue of Liberty.' The abstracting and analysis of information from computer images, which were built from raw data, is done by the human brain. Such abstracting would be greatly assisted if computers could recognize shapes or patterns with the same efficiency with which they recognize letters or numbers.

The brain scans and files information very differently to the computer. The computer's laborious process of dissecting the picture or frame into readings of colour and density of the 100,000 or so pixels which are the basis of the record is slow and uninformative. The image it records fails to distinguish the component sub-images (trees, flowers, people) that our eyes and brains can recognize. Thus the computer cannot easily say 'This image shows a bridge, lots of boats, a river and people', let alone recognize the precise examples of these items. However, if it is told that the items in question are all bridges or people, and it is asked to recognize a specific example of either of these, it can do so. Davies et al. (1990) provide detailed descriptions of the difference between scanning by the human brain and digital computer devices.

There are a range of general approaches, which are based on how the visual image is represented in computer storage:

- if analogue – there is no retrieval based on content;
- if digital and vector-based – retrieval is based on shape-oriented similarity measures;
- if digital and bitmapped – retrieval is based on pattern matching.

7.6.3.1   Human

A very simple level of retrieval, particularly for mixed text and visual mate-rial, is to just include a reference to the fact that a particular item includes a photograph. This approach has been adopted by several commercial on-line database services, including NEXIS on Mead Data Central. Users can search for a specific field name 'graphic', and look for the occurrence of free text terms such as cartoon, caricature, chart, table, graph, map, photo, picture – all with truncation options, plus the ability to link in other search terms, using Boolean logic, in both the 'graphic' field and elsewhere in the record, as in the command:

> graphic (cartoon or caricature and Presley).

This is used to look for cartoons or caricatures of the singer Elvis Presley. The original image is not retrieved or displayed, but a reference is given to where it can be found. A corresponding facility for specifying 'pictures' is provided by the Internet search engine Lycos.[6]

Another similar approach is provided by allowing for manual identifica-tion and indexing of specific objects, shapes, sizes or trademark symbols by the large IMARK database of Italian and international trademarks. There is retrieval by a variety of keywords from the mark, letters of the mark, numbers of letters, words in the mark, colour, figurative elements (pure device mark, combination of words or special script and/or device or word-mark) in addition to various dates and numbers, international classification of goods and services, and designated products and services. But no visual images are stored or retrieved, and the search mechanisms are based on cumbersome word- or code-based descriptions of the marks.

A fourth example of this manual approach has been implemented as a controlled list of terms used to describe the shapes (forms) of graphical symbols used in engineering design. This list takes account of the elemen-tary shapes, general and specific characteristics, the positioning, colouring and orientation of the elements, and also avoids ambiguous or synonymous terms. The lexicon consists of general terms, geometrical terms, positional terms, qualifiers of direction, shape, modifications of aspect, as well as con-ventional signs and colours.

7.6.3.2   Shape-oriented approaches

The core of automatic indexing of visual images should be a system able to analyse an image, to localize the shapes which are possibly associated with structures of interest for the application, and to describe them, evaluating their properties. The DOMINO system directly manages the internal description of images and illustrated texts without using their textual forms.

It assigns keywords to the shapes which are found in the images, and which denote structures of interest in the visual item (Bordogna et al., 1990). Geometric figures such as chromosome images may be stored and retrieved through the use of shape-oriented similarity measures. It is possible to search successfully for chromosomes which are roughly similar to a sample chromosome.

7.6.3.3 Pattern-matching approaches

Mechanical methods based on pattern recognition enable the extraction of unique symbols and images to generate alternative retrieval keys. Query By Image Content (see Section 6.4.6) has been developed most fully for visual items. It enables image databases to be sorted and queried by colour, shape and texture. It also enables searching by keywords, provided these access points have been added manually.

QBIC operates on the principle that the best way to query a database of images is to show the user some likely images. The user can then ask for images which are 'similar' to one of the displayed images. If, when viewing thumbnail images, the user sees one that is very suitable, he or she can click on it to see the full details. Alternatively, more complex shapes can be sketched by the user. QBIC will then bring up all images which are similar to this one.

Similarity is calculated based on numerical values of several image descriptors:

- the average colour of the image;
- the colour distribution;
- the texture, based on coarseness, contrast and directionality;
- the position of the different colours within the image;
- shape parameters.

When responding to a query, QBIC ranks the numerical values of images in the database to indicate their similarity to the query image. QBIC is incorporated into two IBM commercial products: *Ultimedia Manager* and *DB2 Extenders*. Two extenders deal with visual items: *DB2 Image Extender* and *DB2 Video Extender*.[7] The latter can determine where scenes begin and end, and can find one or more representative frames to describe each scene. It can also measure camera movements, such as pans and zooms, and it can delete a moving object from a frame.

Finn (1996) provides a clear, non-technical description of the principles of QBIC, and Holt and Hartwick (1994) describe its use to retrieve art images at UC Davis. Fuller technical details are contained in a range of research papers by the IBM research team, including Barber et al. (1994). Readers may test QBIC interactively via the Internet,[8] a sample search is shown in Figure 7.6.

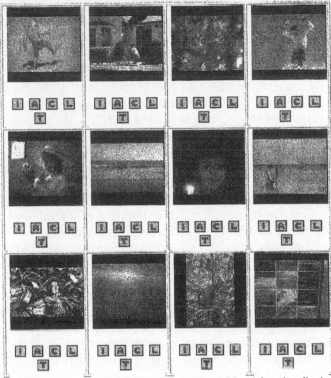

Usage: ▦: Get Info ▦: Find Similar Color ▦: Find Similar Colors
▦: Find Similar Layout ▦: Find Similar Texture

Many images courtesy
of Applied Optical
Media Corp. (now a
part of Rom Tech,
Inc.).

Goto:
Custom Color Query
Custom Color % Query
Custom Paint Query
Random Images

QBIC Home

(Use a Java-capable Web browser to enable additional functionality.)

Query was:
Random

Figure 7.6   *QBIC* search example
Source: Search results: ⟨http://wwwqbic.almaden.ibm.com/cgi-bin/photo-demo⟩.

7.7 Summary

When designing a retrieval system for visual information items, the system
is usually a trade-off between two extremes:

- a database of surrogates based on titles or captions of items, with little intellectual subject analysis;
- a computer-stored file of images with computer analysis of primary meaning, with human-generated links from secondary to primary meaning.

As regards the physical arrangement of the items, a linear approach which allows browsing may not be relevant because of the physical medium, but the ability to retrieve a broad set of items and use visual scanning to refine this selection is of value. If a linear arrangement is required, the primary characteristic of division in classification should be applied. Additional access points provide multi-dimensional access.

It may make sense to group items into batches, as it may be impractical to carry out detailed manual subject analysis of each one, particularly of continuous items such as videos or films. If items are available in computerized form, the data structure will have a significant influence on the extent of automatic retrieval. Ideally, a combination of mechanical extraction of retrieval keys coupled with intelligent subject analysis following strict guidelines is needed. Guidelines could be incorporated into an expert system for description of visual items. Attempts at more sophisticated analysis and representation include pictorial and visual comprehension, cognitive psychology and iconographic analysis.

Concepts such as faceted classification and hypertext play a major role because they cater for the multitude of alternative perspectives from which a visual image may be interpreted and used. User modelling and relevance feedback also allow for the recognition of different user perspectives on the information. Local gateways will play an important role in catering for specific groups of specialists by providing pathways to images which are based on criteria of importance to the local specialists. Lectures, reports, even textbooks, will be based on specialist pathways.

7.8 Notes

[1]   Reel: The Planet's Biggest Movie Store: ⟨http://www.reel.com⟩.

[2]   Library of Congress sample catalogue: ⟨http://lcweb.loc.gov/rr/print/tgm1/sample.html⟩.

[3]   TGM I: ⟨http://lcweb.loc.gov/rr/print/tgm1/⟩. TGM II: ⟨http://lcweb.loc.gov/rr/print/tgm2/⟩. Sample catalogue: ⟨http://lcweb.loc.gov/rr/print/tgm1/sample.html⟩.

[4]   AAT: ⟨http://www.gii.getty.edu/aat_browser⟩.

[5]   Getty Information Institute vocabularies: ⟨http://www.gii.getty.edu/vocabulary/index.html⟩.

[6]   Lycos pictures and sounds: ⟨http://www.lycos.com/picturethis/⟩.

7   *DB2 Image Extender*:
⟨http://www.software.ibm.com/data/db2/extenders/image.htm⟩.
DB2 Video Extender: ⟨http://www.software.ibm.com/data/db2/extenders/video.htm⟩.
8   *IBM QBIC* demo: ⟨http://wwwqbic.almaden.ibm.com/stage/demo.html⟩.

7.9   References and further reading

Armitage, Linda and Enser, Peter (1997) 'Analysis of user need in image archives', *Journal of Information Science*, **23**(4), 287–99.

Barber, R. et al. (1994) 'Ultimedia manager: Query by image content and its applications', *Digest of Papers of the Spring COMPCON '94* (28 February–4 March, San Francisco, CA), 424–9.

Bordogna, G. et al. (1990) 'Pictorial indexing for an integrated pictorial and textual IR environment', *Journal of Information Science*, **16**, 165–73.

Bovey, J.D. (1995) 'Building a thesaurus for a collection of cartoon drawings', *Journal of Information Science*, **21**(2), 115–22.

Bruckmann, Denis (1988) 'Graphic materials and libraries', *International Library Review* **20**(4), 451–8.

Bruckmann, Denis (1990) 'Le vidéodisque images de la Revolution Française', *Bulletin des Bibliothèques de France*, **35**(2), 122–8, 130–5.

Bulick, Stephen (1990) 'Future prospects for network-based multimedia information retrieval', *The Electronic Library*, **8**(2), 88–99.

Cawkell, A.E. (1993a) 'An introduction to image processing and picture management', *Journal of Documentation and Text Management*, **1**(1), 53–63.

Cawkell, A.E. (1993b) *Indexing Collections of Electronic Images: A Review*, British Library Research Review 15, London: British Library.

Cawkell, A.E. (1993c) 'Picture-queries and picture databases', *Journal of Information Science*, **19**(6), 409–23.

Dane, William J. (1968) *The Picture Collection Subject Headings* (6th edn), North Haven, CT: Shoe String Press.

Davies, D. et al. (1990) *The Telling Image: The Changing Balance between Pictures and Words in a Technological Age*, Oxford: Clarendon.

Dwyer, James R. (1986) 'Getting down to the reel thing: improved access to films and videos through subject headings, added entries, and annotations' in Berman, Sanford (ed.) *Cataloguing Special Materials*, Phoenix, AZ: The Oryx Press, 1–12.

Enser, P.E.G. (1993) 'Query analysis in a visual information retrieval context', *Journal of Document and Text Management*, **1**(1), 25–52.

Enser, P.E.G. (1995) 'Pictorial information retrieval (Progress in Documentation)', *Journal of Documentation*, **51**(2), 126–70.

Finn, Robert (1996) 'Query by image content', *IBM Research*, **3**, 22–5.

Foucault, Michel (1972) *The Order of Things*, London: Tavistock Publications.

Getty Art History Information Program (1994) *Art & Architecture Thesaurus* (2nd edn), New York: Oxford University Press. Available on: ⟨http://www.ahip.getty.edu/aat_browser⟩.

Gorman, Michael and Winkler, Paul (eds) (1993) *Anglo-American Cataloguing Rules* (2nd edn), prepared under the direction of the Joint Steering Committee for Revision of AACR, Chicago, Ottawa and London: American Library Association, Canadian Library Association and Library Association. (Note: *The Anglo-American Cataloguing Rules* (2nd edn, 1998 revision) is published jointly by the same publishers in paperback and CD-ROM.)

Harrison, Helen P. (1973) *Film Library Techniques*, London: Focal Press.

Hendley, A.M. (1985) *Videodiscs, Computer Discs and Digital Optical Systems: An Introduction to the Technologies and the Systems and their Potential for Information Storage, Retrieval and Dissemination*, Hatfield: Cimtech.

Holly, Michael Ann (1984) *Panofsky and the Foundations of Art History*, Ithaca, NY: Cornell University Press, 174–93.

Holt, Bonnie and Hartwick, Laura (1994) 'Retrieving art images by image content: The UC Davies QBIC project', *ASLIB Proceedings*, **46**(10), 243–8.

Holton, Gerald (1973) *Thematic Origins of Scientific Thought: Kepler to Einstein*, Cambridge, MA: Harvard University Press.

Knight, R. Cecilia (1986) 'Fine arts' in Berman, Sanford (ed.) *Cataloguing Special Materials*, Phoenix, AZ: The Oryx Press, 115–32.

Krause, Michael (1988) 'Intellectual problems of indexing picture collections', *Audiovisual Librarian*, **14**(2), 73–81.

Library of Congress (1995a) *Thesaurus for Graphic Materials I: Subject Terms (TGM I)*, Washington, DC: Library of Congress. Available on: ⟨http://lcweb.loc.gov/rr/print/tgm2/toc.html⟩.

Library of Congress (1995b) *Thesaurus for Graphic Materials II: Genre and Physical Characteristic Terms (TGM II)*, Washington, DC: Library of Congress. Available on: ⟨http://lcweb.loc.gov/rr/print/tgm2/⟩.

Lunin, Lois (1987) 'Electronic image information', *Annual Review of Information Science and Technology*, 22, 179–224.

Markey, Karen (1983) 'Computer-assisted construction of a thematic catalog of primary and secondary subject matter', *Visual Resources*, **III**, 16–49.

Panofsky, Erwin (1962) *Studies in Iconology: Humanistic Themes in the Art of the Renaissance*, New York: Harper and Row.

Parsons, Michael (1987) *How We Understand Art*, Cambridge: Cambridge University Press.

Peterson, Toni and Barnett, Patricia J. (eds) (1994) *Guide to Indexing and Cataloguing with the Art and Architecture Thesaurus*, New York: Oxford University Press.

Ranganathan, S.R. (1959) *Elements of Library Classification* (2nd edn), London: Association of Assistant Librarians.

Ranganathan, S.R. (1963) *Documentation and its Facets*, London: Asia Publishing House.

Shatford, Sara (1984) 'Describing a picture: A thousand words are seldom cost effective', *Cataloguing and Classification Quarterly*, **4**(4), 13–30.

Shatford, Sara (1986) 'Analyzing the subject of a picture: A theoretical approach', *Cataloguing and Classification Quarterly*, **6**(3), 39–62.

Shatford Layne, Sarah (1994) 'Some issues in the indexing of images', *Journal of the American Society for Information Science*, **45**(8), 583–8.

Stern, Nancy B. and Stern, Robert A. (1996) *Computing and the Information Age* (2nd edn), New York: Wiley.

Svenonius, Elaine (1994) 'Access to non-book materials: The limits of subject indexing for visual and aural languages', *Journal of the American Society for Information Science*, **45**(8), 600–6.

Chapter 8

Audio information

8.1 Introduction

Audio information is all-pervasive, and the quantity and quality of the recording media continue to enhance its attractiveness. The range of subject areas, formats, and levels of detail is wide. The alternative options range from resources as local and personalized as a Walkman CD player to remotely accessible audio databases on the Internet.

The information may be presented in traditional formats, such as cylinder recordings and reel-to-reel tapes, 7 inch and 12 inch single and LP (Long Play) disks, or more current media such as DAT (Digital Audio Tape) and CDs, interactive multimedia products and Internet-searchable resources.

Key issues which arise when organizing audio recordings include:

- responsibility for creatorship, in particular the competing roles of composer and performer;
- multi-level items, for example a series of CDs of the collected works of a number of composers;
- vague titles or subject description, for example for off-air recordings or sound effects;
- the difficulty of automatically assigning keywords for items without words;
- the existence of items in a variety of languages or translations;
- the existence of related manifestations of an original item, for example a musical text or score, one performance, another performance, one recording, another recording, a transcript of an interview, a score or wordsheet for music and song, or a graph of the sound volume;
- different levels of meaning occur, which may be described as objective, subjective and interpretative.

8.2   Features and categorization of audio items

The wide-ranging holdings of the British Library National Sound Archive (NSA) include:

- popular music;
- recordings of festivals, conferences, and seminars;
- jazz from all periods and in all styles;
- Western art and world music;
- oral history;
- drama and literature – non-musical performance;
- wildlife sounds;
- industro-mechanical sound – characteristic sound of work and transport;
- sound effects – for radio and film recordings and live performances.

This gives a good indication of the range of audio material and its information content. Material is drawn from commercial releases, broadcasts, and the NSA's own recordings. The formats include 7 inch and 12 inch singles and LP disks, CDs, cassettes and DAT tapes.

The wide range of audio items may be categorized by the following criteria:

- content (subject/person/audio effect);
- original item, or manifestation;
- discrete item, or part of a series;
- by storage medium;
- analogue or digital;
- contains words, or not;
- contains music, or not;
- broadcast/published/unpublished;
- ratio of physical to logical item(s); an item may be spread over a number of physical entities, or there may be several items on one physical item, or there may be a simple one-to-one relationship.

Table 8.1 shows an appropriate categorization for audio information items. These categories must be reflected in the surrogate, especially in the description. It is necessary to distinguish between an original music score, a recording of the complete work, another recording of a part of a live performance of the work, or a manifestation of the work in a different format, such as opera based on a play. A distinction is made between two types of sounds, called 'sound effects' and 'sounds' in Table 8.1. 'Sound effects' refers to artificially generated sounds, for example the shaking of a hard plastic container filled with small pebbles to create the sound of rain drumming on a roof. 'Sounds' refer to naturally occurring industrial and wildlife

Table 8.1 *Categorization of audio items*

Audio item	Subject content	Original/ manifestation	Words/music/ sounds	Published/ broadcast
Interview	Any	Original	Words	Broadcast
Lecture	Any	Original	Words	Broadcast
Report	Any	Original	Words	Broadcast
Speech	Any	Original	Words	Broadcast
Documentary	Any	Original	Words and music	Broadcast
Radio programme	Any	Original	Words and music	Broadcast
Language lesson	Language	Original	Words and sounds	Published
Sound effects	Any	Original	Sounds	Either
Play	Drama	Manifestation	Words	Broadcast
Poetry reading	Poetry	Manifestation	Words	Either
Book reading	Book	Manifestation	Words	Either
Song	Any	Manifestation	Words and music	Published
Opera	Drama and music	Manifestation	Words and music	Published
Music	Compositions	Manifestation	Music	Published
Sounds	Any	Manifestation	Sounds	Either

Note: This categorization is very general, and the values for each item are not definitive. For example, for the distinction between 'Published' and 'Broadcast', many items may exist as either category.

sounds, such as a motor car's engine starting, an alarm bell ringing, the mating call of a songthrush, a volcano erupting.

The most significant questions for description and access are whether audio items:

- have words, which may be used to generate a text;
- have other components, which may be used automatically to generate keys for retrieval;
- have no easily generated keys, and are dependent on other cues for information retrieval.

If the items contain words, considerable effort is required to listen to recordings and make transcripts. It may be worth listening just to generate keywords, without actually making a transcript. Even if there are words, the transcript itself will not be sufficient for describing subject content, as the bland text may hide aspects of the content such as local accents, emotional delivery, background effects and atmosphere.

8.2.1 Manifested items

A sound recording may be a manifestation of another item: a recording of a book reading, a play, an opera, a concerto, a song, an animal, an environmental happening, naturally occurring noises, artificially or deliberately created sound effects, etc. As a result of the ease with which an original may be reproduced, the concept of a unique original (master copy) with definitive characteristics may be difficult to maintain. The content of a commercial LP, cassette and CD may be identical, or the content may be modified in some way. Similarly, an original radio programme may have snippets extracted and represented in different audio media, or integrated with other media, as in a video recording. These are good examples of the 'manifestation' concept identified in Chapter 2.

For many audio items, there may not be a clear distinction between an original item and its manifestation, depending on the relative importance attached to performance compared with various forms of recording or transcription of the item. In musicology, a recording of a performance of a composition is seen as the definitive version of the original item, and the score as a more subjective view. This is unsatisfactory for retrieval, unless there are guidelines which enable us to identify the definitive performance of a work from a number of recordings. Two suitable criteria for doing this include:

- the earliest form of an item;
- the form which most fully conveys the content of the item.

According to the first criterion, the medium in which the creator worked would determine the original item. Thus if a composer works by committing a masterpiece to paper using musical notation, this score would become the original item. If he or she creates by recording, performing or using a computer synthesizer, then this version would become the original item. All other performances, recordings and conversions to other media would become manifestations. Using the second criterion, the prominence of the live performance is acknowledged as the item which embodies the content of the item to the fullest extent. Thus a reading of a play, with several actors participating, is identified as the original item, with the text as a manifestation.

The purpose of the collection, the type of users and the availability of the technical equipment needed to listen to the item will determine which of these, or other, criteria are used. In any case, it is clear that there may be many different manifestations of an audio item, each of which contains very similar information, but with different styles of presentation and formats.

8.2.2   Logical, physical and multi-part items

What constitutes an item: is it the piece of music, or the volume in which it appears – the artistic unit, or the physical unit? This problem is at its most acute in, for example, a collection of songs by various composers. There may be a hundred in a volume, so to treat each one separately increases the workload considerably. Not to do so, on the other hand, may mean that a specific item will be overlooked by someone who seeks it. The frequency of collections in music publishing and other types of audio recording makes recognition of this level of item crucial. Thomas (1992) at the Rodgers and Hammerstein Archive at New York Public Library has analysed the problems of multi-part collections thoroughly. His solution is described in Section 8.6.1, and shown schematically in Figure 8.1.

However, separate publication of extracts from longer works is very much more common for audio items than for books. The publishing of vocal and musical scores for individual numbers from an opera or a musical is commonplace. The equivalent in the world of literature is an individual poem, which may be published in a volume of the poet's works or in an anthology of verse.

8.3 Surrogates

8.3.1 Introduction

Surrogates of audio items are developed using the same basic principles as surrogates of other types of media, but certain objectives increase in significance. There is a clear need to distinguish between the different formats of audio items, such as the original score, a review by a music critic of a performance, and an audio recording of the item. Traditionally, library catalogues have not been helpful in this role, but many search engines on the Internet do help: for example, Lycos allows searches to be restricted to specific formats, including audio. There is an increased need for uniform titles to bring together different manifestations of an item. There are also additional problems with identification of the main creator, where the audio item may be composed by one person or group, and interpreted by another person or group.

Access by performer and composer are considered very significant, but subject is less important, and other access points arise, such as the title of the item, which is particularly significant for anonymous works. 'Subject' is usually rather objective: names of people, places and events, etc. 'Creator' may be the composer or interpreter, corresponding to creatorship by origination and assumption for visual items in Section 7.4.1. Abstracts are very useful for spoken items, as they assist potential users in deciding whether they would wish to listen to the original or consult a full transcript if available. An abstract for local history, for example, would identify the most important topics discussed, people and places mentioned, etc.

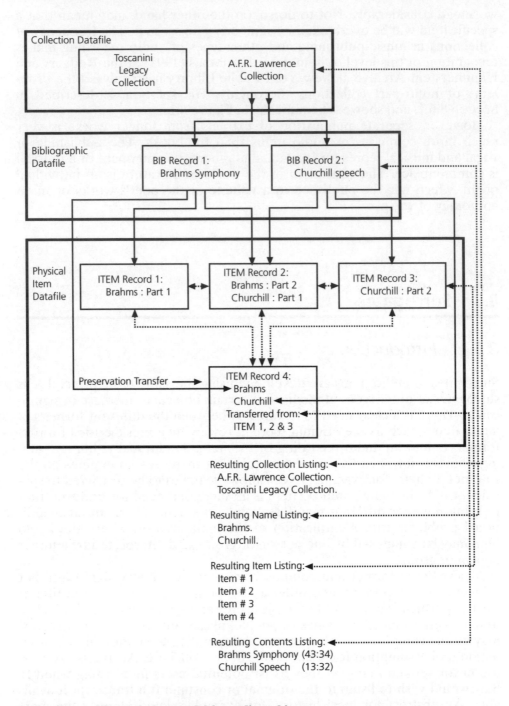

Figure 8.1   Thomas's data model for audio archives
Source: Thomas (1992, pp. 30–1). Reproduced with permission of the Music Library Association.

8.3.2 Standards for surrogates

The standards identified in Chapter 4 are followed widely. In addition, specific standards have been developed for creation of surrogates of audio material. These include:

- the *Manual of Archival Description*, produced in the UK, which contains various special formats, including one for sound archives (Cook and Proctor, 1989, 1990), facilitates multi-level descriptions without the detailed punctuation rules of AACR2;

- for music, the three main authorities are AACR2, the Library of Congress, and the Music Library Association in the USA (MLA). Chapter 5 of AACR2, which deals with description of music, has had the greatest impact (Gorman and Winkler, 1993). The *New Grove Dictionary of Music and Musicians* (Sadie, 1980) is a useful authority reference for names of composers, performers, terms and definitions.

8.3.3 Examples of surrogates

Figure 8.2 shows a sample catalogue entry for the National Sound Archive (UK) general catalogue, based on the following surrogate components:

- composer;
- genre (e.g. cradle song, dances – piano);
- performer(s) and their roles (e.g. piano, speaker, male/female, tenor);
- accession number and accession date (if possible);
- date of recording;
- relationship to another item (e.g. 'contains', 'contained in ...', 'continued on', 'talks about his poems', 're-issue of...');
- physical description (medium, specific location on medium, size, playback speed, mono/stereo, publisher/distributor);
- other contributors (e.g. sleeve notes);
- place;
- subject;
- location/shelf mark.

These surrogate examples illustrate a rigorous structure of three interlocking files:

- the works file, which contains authorized names for various types of creators, a uniform title and alternative titles;
- the recordings file, which contains entries for the unique entry which is a recording, for example the capture on a recording medium of a performance of a work by one or more agents at a specific place and time;
- the products file, which contains information about the particular physical medium on which a recording has been made.

Example A

```
XX(2184717.1)

            Work title: Cradle song
       Author/Composer: Bridge, Frank, 1879-1941 (composer)
            Work notes: 1902. For violin or cello and piano
           Short title: Cradle song/Bridge

    WORKS-FILE CALL NUMBER                  COPY MATERIAL   LOCATION
    1) LINK TO RECORDINGS                    1 WORK         ON-PRODUCT
```

```
1LP0111290 S1 BD5 PEARL

          Short title: Cradle song/Bridge
            Performer: Welsh, Moray, 1947- (cello)
            Performer: Vignoles, Roger, 1945- (piano)
       Recording date: 1982.06.04

    RECORDING CALL NUMBER                   COPY MATERIAL   LOCATION
    1) 1LP0111290 S1 BD5 PEARL               1 RECORDING   ON-PRODUCT
```

```
1LP0111290

         Accession no.: 1LP0111290
         Accession no.: 2LP0078173
         Product title: British music for cello and piano
                 Label: PEARL SHE 571
           Label match: PEARLSHE571
              (P) date: 1982
               Carrier: disc 2 s 30 cm 33 rpm stereo
    Copy condition code: B (2LP0078173)

    PRODUCT CALL NUMBER                     COPY MATERIAL   LOCATION
    1) 1LP0111290                            1 DISC         MIC
    2) 2LP0078173                            1 DISC         BSP
```

Example B
```
M84W C1

        Broadcast title: New comment: a weekly review of the arts
        Performer name: Kavanagh, Patrick, 1904-1967 (speaker, male)
        Performer name: Smith, Peter Duval (speaker, male; interviewer)
            Item notes: Peter Duval Smith talks to Patrick Kavanagh about his
                        recently published Collected poems
       Name as subject: Kavanagh, Patrick, 1904-1967

    RECORDING CALL NUMBER                   COPY MATERIAL   LOCATION
    1) M84W C1                               1 RECORDING   ON-PRODUCT
```

```
M84W

           Broadcaster: BBC TP 19640818
       Broadcast title: New comment: a weekly review of the arts
   Carrier description: tape 1 reel mono

    PRODUCT CALL NUMBER                     COPY MATERIAL   LOCATION
    1) M84W                                  1 TAPE         STP
```

Figure 8.2   Sample entries from the National Sound Archive general catalogue
Source: Reproduced with permission of the National Sound Archive.

Example C
XX(1732468.1)

```
            Work title: Dances, piano
     Alternative title: Three dances
      Author/Composer: Ireland, John, 1879-1962 (composer)
            Work notes: 1. Gypsy dance; 2. Country dance; 3. Reaper's dance
           Short title: Dances, piano/Ireland
```

WORKS-FILE CALL NUMBER	COPY MATERIAL	LOCATION
1) LINK TO RECORDINGS	1 WORK	ON-PRODUCT

1LP0144160 S2 BD4-6 EMI

```
           Short title: Dances, piano/Ireland
             Performer: Adni, Daniel, 1951- (piano)
        Recording date: 1978
```

RECORDING CALL NUMBER	COPY MATERIAL	LOCATION
1) 1LP0144160 S2 BD4-6 EMI	1 RECORDING	ON-PRODUCT
2) 2LP0071518 S2 BD4-6 EMI	1 RECORDING	ON-PRODUCT

1LP0144160

```
         Accession no.: 1LP0144160
         Accession no.: 2LP0071518
         Accession no.: 1LP0034546
         Accession no.: 2LP0078238
         Product title: Daniel Adni plays piano music by John Ireland
      Published series: HMV virtuoso series
                 Label: HMV HQS 1414
           Label match: HMVHQS1414
           Label match: GRAMOPHONEHQS1414
              (P) date: 1979
         Pressing code: uk
               Carrier: disc 2 sides 30 cm 33 rpm stereo
         Documentation: sleeve notes by Ernest Chapman
   Copy condition code: B (1LP0034546)
   Copy condition code: B (2LP0078238)
```

PRODUCT CALL NUMBER	COPY MATERIAL	LOCATION
1) 1LP0034546	1 DISC	MIC
2) 1LP0144160	1 DISC	STP
3) 2LP0071518	1 DISC	BSP
4) 2LP0078238	1 DISC	BSP

Example C.1
XX(1762233.1)

```
            Work title: Songs (1925). Weathers
     Alternative title: Weathers
      Author/Composer: Ireland, John, 1879-1962 (composer)
           Short title: Songs (1925). Weathers/Ireland
```

WORKS-FILE CALL NUMBER	COPY MATERIAL	LOCATION
1) LINK TO RECORDINGS	1 WORK	ON-PRODUCT

Figure 8.2   **continued**

Example D
NP995W+R TR1-2

```
        Broadcast title: Old Ireland free: the story of the Easter rising in
                         1916
        Performer name: Rodgers, William Robert (speaker, male)
            Item notes: Compiled and introduced by W. R. Rodgers
               Subject: Ireland - History - Sinn Fein Rebellion, 1916
       Recording notes: Broadcast on the 50th anniversary of the start of the
                         Easter rising in Dublin (24th April 1916). The story
                         is told by participants and witnesses of the week of
                         rebellion
```

```
     RECORDING CALL NUMBER                 COPY MATERIAL    LOCATION
     1) NP995W+R TR1-2                     1 RECORDING      ON-PRODUCT
```

NP995W+R

```
           Broadcaster: BBC TP 19660424
       Broadcast title: Old Ireland free: the story of the Easter rising in
                        1916
   Carrier description: tape 1 reel mono
```

```
     PRODUCT CALL NUMBER                   COPY MATERIAL    LOCATION
     1) NP995W+R                           1 TAPE           STP
```

Example E
P594R C1

```
        Performer name: MacLiammhóir, Micheál, 1899- (speaker, male)
        Performer name: Mason, Ronald (speaker, male; interviewer)
        Recording date: 1968
            Item notes: The distinguished Irish actor discusses his own career
                        and the Irish theatre
               Subject: Theatre - Ireland
       Name as subject: MacLiammhóir, Micheál, 1899-
```

```
     RECORDING CALL NUMBER                 COPY MATERIAL    LOCATION
     1) P594R C1                           1 RECORDING      ON-PRODUCT
```

P594R

```
           Broadcaster: BBC R3 19710114
   Carrier description: tape 1 reel mono
```

```
     PRODUCT CALL NUMBER                   COPY MATERIAL    LOCATION
     1) P594R                              1 TAPE           STP
```

Figure 8.2   continued

Example F
XX(2335470.1)

```
         Work title: Ireland, Mother Ireland
     Author/Composer: Loughborough, Raymond (composer)
     Author/Composer: O'Reilly P. J. (author)
           Publisher: Boosey & Hawkes Music Publ. Ltd.
         Work notes: Loughborough died in 1967, O'Reilly in 1924
         Short title: Ireland, Mother Ireland/Loughborou
```

```
   WORKS-FILE CALL NUMBER                 COPY MATERIAL   LOCATION
   1) LINK TO RECORDINGS                  1 WORK          ON-PRODUCT
```

1LP0111207 S11 BD8 PEARL

```
         Short title: Ireland, Mother Ireland/Loughborou
           Performer: McCormack, John, 1884-1945 (tenor)
     Original issue no.: Re-issue of 78 rpm disc Victor mx BVE 56192-4.
         Item notes: Label: Loughborough
```

```
   RECORDING CALL NUMBER                  COPY MATERIAL   LOCATION
   1) 1LP0111207 S11 BD8 PEARL            1 RECORDING     ON-PRODUCT
```

1LP0111207

```
         Accession no.: 1LP0111207
         Product title: The voice that calls across the years
                 Label: PEARL GEMM 240/5
           Label match: PEARLGEMM2405
               (P) date: 1982
               Carrier: 6 discs 12 s 30 cm 33 rpm mono
           Copy notes: NSA hist. 250548
```

```
   PRODUCT CALL NUMBER                    COPY MATERIAL   LOCATION
   1) 1LP0111207                          1 DISC          MIC
```

Figure 8.2   continued

Tables 8.2–8.4 and Figures 8.3 and 8.4 give additional examples of surrogate structures used in a variety of collections of audio information items, showing the variation in surrogate structure. The following points emerge from these surrogates:

- All have the following components:
  - creator (except BBC Sound Effects);
  - subject;
  - duration;
  - location indicator.
- The role of creator/performer is indicated.
- The NSA example includes items which contain words only, music only, and combinations of both, within one structure (see Figure 8.2).
- The NSA example goes to considerable lengths to indicate multi-part items and links between logical items, as in the 'Ireland, Mother Ireland' example and the cross-reference in the NSA 'Ireland, John,

Table 8.2   *BBC Sound Archive: Record structure*

CLA	Classification, from a controlled list
STT	Series title
HED	Heading (this may be more precise than title)
SBH	Subheading
CON	List of participants, their role, and their affiliation in some cases
PNN	Specific subject headings, again from the in-house Subject Authority List
PRE	Précis (summary) of item
DTF	States if a script is available
. . .	
SAN	Accession number
MED	Medium (e.g. tape)
FRO	Format (mono/stereo)
SPD	Recording/playback speed
MIN	Minutes
SSC	Seconds
TDT	Transmission date
RCD	Recording date

Source: Reproduced with permission of the BBC Sound Archive.

Table 8.3   *Imperial War Museum Sound Archive: Record structure*

AC	accession number	DU	duration in minutes
SE	series/project	AD	acquisition date
FN	brief description of contents	PR	date processing completed
NA	name of informant (or performer)	OR	original format
RK	rank or title of informant	TR	typescript available
NAT	nationality	SU	detailed reel-by-reel summary
GE	gender	IP	index: people
BO	date of birth	IU	index: units/organizations
DD	date of death	IS	index: sites/locations
PD	recording date	IE	index: events
PC	production company	BEG	start date (of contents)
FR	donor	FIN	finish date
ME	method of acquisition	NT	notes
TY	type of acquisition	IC	index: concepts
R	name of interviewer	IO	index: objects
CH	copyright holder	RI	related items, e.g. photographs
RES	access restrictions	CAT	cataloguer's initials and date
LA	language	IN	computer inputter's initials and date
IT	number of 30-minute reels	FO	informant's birthplace

Source: Reproduced with permission of the Imperial War Museum Sound Archive.

Table 8.4   *BBC Sound Effects catalogue of compact disks: Record structure*

The entry for each sound effect contains the following:

1. As precise a description as possible, e.g.
    - indoor market, chatter and footsteps, distant traffic (Devon);
    - applause, cheers and stamping after work, stamping and slow hand-clapping;
    - near miss and applause (Wembley Cup Final, 1989);
    - Hampstead Heath winter afternoon with coal tit, long-tailed tit, nuthatch, robin, goldcrest, crow, distant dogs, children and traffic skyline.

2. The duration in minutes and seconds.

3. The location indicator (the number of the appropriate CD).

4. On occasions, links to other CDs (e.g. CD number; whether reprocessed).

Source: Reproduced with permission of the BBC Sound Archive.

A: Brief display

Author:	Beethoven, Ludwig van, 1770-1827.
	Fidelio (1814)
Title:	Fidelio [sound recording]
Published:	New York, NY : RCA Victor Gold Seal, 1991.
Publisher no.:	09026-60273-2 RCA Victor Gold Seal
Description:	2 sound discs : digital.
Other authors:	Toscanini, Arturo, 1867-1957.
Notes:	Compact disc.
Location:	Music Sound Recordings
Call number:	CD1098
Status:	Not checked out

B: Long display

Author:	Beethoven, Ludwig van, 1770-1827.
	Missa solemnis. Latin
Title:	Missa solemnis : op. 123 / [sound recording].
Published:	New York, NY : RCA Victor Red Seal, p1990.
Publisher no.:	60272-2-RG RCA Victor Gold Seal
Description:	2 sound discs : digital, mono. ; 4 3/4 in.
Subjects:	Masses
	Requiems.
Other authors:	Marshall, Lois.
	Merriman, Nan.
	Conley, Eugene, 1908-1981.
	Hines, Jerome, 1921-
	Toscanini, Arturo, 1867-1957.
	Cherubini, Luigi, 1760-1842. Requiems, no. 1, C minor. Latin. 1990.
	NBC Symphony Orchestra.
	Robert Shaw Chorale.
Notes:	Sung in Latin.
	Durations: 74:42 (1st work); 48:04 (2nd work).
	Compact discs.
	Program notes in English with French, German and Italian translations, and Latin text with English translation (35 p.: ill.) in container.
	Lois Marshall, soprano, Nan Merriman, mezzo-soprano, Eugene Conley, tenor, Jerome Hines, bass (in the 1st work) ; Robert Shaw Chorale ; NBC Symphony Orchestra ; Arturo Toscanini, conductor.
	Recorded: March 30, 31 & April 2, 1953 in Carnegie Hall (1st work); NBC broadcast of February 18, 1950, in Studio 8-H, New York City (2nd work).
Series:	Arturo Toscanini collection , v. 61
Location:	Music Sound Recordings
Call Number:	CD613
Status:	Overdue as of dd/mm/yy

Figure 8.3   Sample catalogue records from the Gabe M. Wiener Music & Arts Library at Columbia University

Source: Reproduced with permission of the Gabe M. Wiener Music & Arts Library at Columbia University.

The American Variety Stage, 1870 - 1920

AMERICAN VARIETY STAGE AUDIO SAMPLER

Variety entertainment dominated the popular recording industry's acoustic era (pre -1925), from its beginnings in the 1890s, when records were made on wax cylinders, right up to the beginning of the jazz age in the mid-1920s. From slapstick vaudeville routines and ethnic dialect skits to romantic ballads and dramatic recitations, sound recordings brought variety entertainment into the homes of millions of Americans. The following ten sample recordings are representative of the variety acts captured on 78 rpm disc by the Edison Company.

The Arkansas Traveler (Descriptive Scene), performed by Steve Porter and Ernest Hare
Edison 51010-R, recorded 1922
RealAudio version of this recording.
WAV version of this recording.

This is a classic "rube" sketch that has its origins in an 1852 lithograph by Currier & Ives depicting a wise-cracking, fiddle-playing hillbilly's encounter with a sophisticated city-slicker. Originally released on a wax cylinder in the 1890s, The Arkansas Traveler was probably the best-selling example of the popular genre "descriptive scene" (also called "descriptive specialty"), a humorous dramatic sketch that often included sound effects and music. Steve Porter was a versatile vaudeville comedian who wrote and performed many comedy routines on early sound recordings. Ernest Hare teamed with Billy Jones in 1920 to form Jones & Hare, "The Happiness Boys" of radio fame, and the most popular singing comedians of the 1920s.

Desperate Desmond - Drama, written and performed by Fred Duprez
Edison 50254-L, recorded 1915
RealAudio version of this recording.
WAV version of this recording.

Fred Duprez was a vaudeville comedian and was famous for his comic monologues. An Edison record catalog, circa 1927, had this to say about the Desperate Desmond bit: "Duprez invented all this himself and has given it before many audiences. It is really very cleverly worked out; some of the incidental music fits the characters with a burlesque fashion, and some of it, apparently to Duprez's intense disgust, is wildly inappropriate. To quote a popular advertisement If you can't laugh at this, see a doctor.'"

Figure 8.4   Surrogate from the American Variety Stage Audio Sampler
Source: American Variety Stage: ⟨http://lcweb2.loc.gov/ammen/vshtml/vssnde.html⟩. Reproduced with permission of the Library of Congress.

1879–1962 (composer) Her song' example to the general heading of 'Songs (1925)' (see Figure 8.2, examples F, C and C1 respectively).

- The BBC Sound Archive structure is specially developed for recordings of radio broadcasts (see Table 8.2). General information on the BBC Sound Effects CD may be found in Hine's (1992) article.
- The Imperial War Museum Sound Archive structure provides an excellent framework for describing and indexing the subject content of interviews (see Table 8.3).
- The BBC Sound Effects structure is very simple. It is appropriate for a

commercial product with limited subject content and no acknowledged creator (see Table 8.4).

- The Gabe M. Wiener Music & Arts Library at Columbia University uses a typical library AACR2 structure for recorded music. The brief display provides the key surrogate components in a concise form for an example of a performance of Fidelio by Toscanini. The long display example illustrates the potential of AACR2 to provide access points and description for a multi-part item (see Figure 8.3).
- The American Variety Stage example is typical of an Internet surrogate, with full subject description, very brief physical description, and the option to play the original recording in two alternative formats (see Figure 8.4).

8.3.4 Access points

It is essential that access points to audio items be standardized. Names of performers, authors, composers and titles of works, should be consistent in order that they may be retrieved from a printed index or computerized search. Ward (1990) identifies the difficulties which this may pose for music collections, where names have variant spellings, and titles may appear in an original language and in a variety of translations. The recommended solution is to use an authority file of standard spellings, which incorporates cross-references to variants. The *New Grove Dictionary of Music and Musicians* provides a good basis for standard titles for music names and titles (Sadie, 1980).

The alternative approach is a free-text vocabulary, with a facility to bring together variant spellings if they have word roots in common. This system is used, for example, by the Mechanical Copyright Protection Society for searching their massive files of works, composers, etc. Filing under composer is common in both practices, and raises a few problems with music, such as form of foreign names, dates of birth and death, and transliteration of names.

The uniform-title concept of AACR2 draws together translations or other closely related manifestations of an item. The language in which the title has been printed becomes of limited importance, while excerpts, arrangements and other related versions are brought together under a standard title in one language. If an item is written in a standard musical form or one which has an internationally accepted meaning, such as a symphony or a nocturne, then the uniform title is presented in English, or the local language where this is not English. If, on the other hand, a composition has an individual and distinctive title – for example, an opera or a well-known orchestral work – then the uniform title is that given by the composer to the item.

The uniform title is an important part of the heading for music. Since many classical composers were prolific, the number of entries filed under one heading can be very large, even in the catalogue of a small collection, and if the order within each heading is determined by the first words of the title as given in the description, an unhelpful sequence will result. Provision has to be made for all entries relating to the same piece of music, whatever the language of the title page, to be retrievable together or, at worst, to be linked in some way. One may therefore decide to classify items under types of work, relying on this to bring together groups of items small enough for one to be found.

A musical work may be available in several different manifestations: the collection could well contain a miniature score of a Beethoven symphony, an edition of the same work arranged for solo piano, another for a piano duet, and a fourth for violin and piano. The music collection could also contain simplified versions of compositions, modified to suit children or adult performers of limited technical accomplishment. There should be an individual entry for each item, but the different versions should be filed in immediate proximity in a pre-coordinate sequence, or be retrievable together in a post-coordinate system.

8.3.5   Description and location indicators

The significant standards for description include both AACR2 and the *International Standard Bibliographic Description for Printed Music* (IFLA, 1991), which is a specific ISBD for printed music (ISBD (PM)). Descriptive cataloguing has always been dependent on the title page, which is an unsatisfactory source for music, but ISBD recognizes various levels of sources, which assists in cataloguing music.

A useful element in the description is the musical incipit: the introductory bars of a musical piece. Incipits usually comprise three or four measures of the leading voice, and ideally include the clef, key signature, metre, any written indication of style or tempo, and where relevant, the instrument on which the piece is played. The idea of incipits has tremendous scope in a multimedia environment, where the system could play the first few notes of the item to assist the user in its recognition.

The function of location indicators for published recordings is fulfilled by Record Label Issue Numbers – unique identifiers akin to ISBNs – which have been assigned consistently since the inception of the record industry. For location of audio items in a specific institution, there will usually be some hierarchical system which is linked to the storage medium. Table 8.5 highlights the location indicators for the surrogate examples cited in Section 8.3.3.

Table 8.5   *Location indicators for the surrogate examples in Section 8.3.3*

Example	Location indicator
Figure 8.2	Product call number and location
Table 8.2	Accession number and medium
Table 8.3	Accession number
Table 8.4	Number of appropriate CD
Figure 8.3A	Music sound recordings CD 1098
Figure 8.3B	Music sound recordings CD 613
Figure 8.4	Edison 51010-R (original recording)
	RealAudio version of this recording .
	WAV version of this recording

8.4   Creatorship

The responsibility for creation of audio items is often confused; the key issues are:

- How much credit is given to the person(s) who made the recording?
- How much credit is given to the performer, compared with the composer of the original item – the reader of a poem, compared with the author of the original; the performers of music, compared with the original composers, or the adapters of a play for a radio broadcast?
- Recordings and re-recordings increase the number of creators, and generate doubt about chief responsibility.
- There are also problems relating to form of name.

8.5   Subject content analysis and representation

In general, the level of subject analysis and representation in audio collections is very basic. Sound archives and music libraries place heavy dependence on keyword searching of LCSH; music collections may use Dewey or LC classification. Yet there is considerable scope for subjective interpretation of audio sounds, and technological developments such as digital recording provide potential to exploit the digitized audio data.

Table 8.6   *Levels of meaning*

	Primary	Secondary	Tertiary
Words	Words	Words in context	Why was this recorded?
Music	Technical description of the score	What musicians will learn by looking at a score, e.g. loud, restless, slow, peaceful, melodic	Overall theme, e.g. 'The Four Seasons'
Sounds	Technical description of sounds	What they represent	Wider message

8.5.1   Subject analysis

The subject content of audio material is fairly objective, but local history may be subjective, as it is likely to be interpreted in different ways by different people. Sound effects or the mood of music also present problems for description of content.

The concepts of primary and secondary meaning, and 'of' and 'about', can be applied to audio material, as shown in Table 8.6. A recording is of a person, an event, a place, a performance, a composition, etc. It may be about more subjective concepts, such as happiness. The extent to which this is analysed and described will vary between applications, and may be unimportant in many operational environments.

Facet analysis is also appropriate:

- What is recorded?
- Who has been recorded?
- What is happening?
- Why is it happening?
- When?
- Where?

It may also be feasible to link subject analysis to the needs of specific user groups. Initial research at the Belfer Audio Archive and the School of Information Studies in Syracuse University in this area showed hopeful results in the mid-1980s, but has not been implemented in any retrieval system (Beth Oddy, personal communication, 1986).

8.5.1.1   Subject content: Words

The subject content of audio recordings may cover any of the following topics:

- local history (interviews with senior citizens talking about the 'good old days');
- recording of speeches at local elections;
- speeches at an opening of a new shopping centre/factory/housing estate;
- speeches at a sporting event, for example by the captain of a winning FA Cup Final or Superbowl team;
- an entire radio programme, for example *Lake Woebegone* (PBS) or *The Archers* (BBC);
- lectures by experts;
- a lecture/talk/interview from specific programmes, on specific themes by specific people, by people with specific characteristics (e.g. who play a sport, live in a particular place, are from a particular era or place); these are all original items;
- recording of specific events for their intrinsic interest;
- recording of specific events for the sounds they contain;
- a performance of a play;
- a reading of poetry;
- a serialized reading of a book.

For literature and the spoken word, author, title and performer are the most important access points; subject access may be useful for speech. It becomes more important for oral history, wildlife sound, and industrial and mechanical sound. For oral history, different interpretations are subjective, and may be influenced by the background and perspective of the listener.

The analysis of subject content corresponds to that of a written transcript of the item, with additional clues for 'about' in each facet, plus overall 'aboutness', which are established by the atmospheric tone of the piece: for example, the emotion conveyed by the human voice. Descriptions of oral history interviews should include an abstract and index entries from a variety of perspectives. Ward warns of the danger of neglecting 'aboutness' concepts such as 'racial discrimination', 'household budgeting', 'marriage customs', 'adolescence', etc. which are unlikely to appear in ordinary speech or in written transcripts (Ward, 1990).

8.5.1.2 Subject content: Music

In a collection where the music is of interest for its own sake, for its musical characteristics, then access by composer, performer and title is sufficient. Subject analysis becomes important when there is a need to retrieve musical items for specific purposes: for example background music which engenders a mood of 'relaxing on a tropical beach', or 'city sounds'.

Subject content analysis of music is complicated by the fact that the music may be:

- by a specific composer;
- with many interpreters;
- by a specific interpreter, from many composers;
- of a specific composition, with one or many interpreters;
- at a specific festival or conference.

It is also very subjective, in that the composer, performer and various listeners may associate different meanings with a musical item. The composer will frequently intend subject meaning which will be known to the subject expert and will become clear to the amateur who explores documentary texts about the music. In some cases, the music may not be 'about' anything, yet it may engender a certain mood in the listener, such as terror, happiness, romance or optimism: for example, Mussorgsky's *A Night on the Bare Mountain*. To interpret this meaning, the indexer can:

- research the intentions of the creator;
- read reviews;
- listen attentively to the items.

Thus we see the equivalent of Panofsky's (1962) three levels of meaning for musical items, where the primary subject meaning corresponds to a layperson's reaction to an item, the secondary meaning corresponds to the interpretation by a musical expert, based on his knowledge of the composer's intentions, and the third level of meaning corresponds to an advanced level of analysis, as practised by musicologists.

8.5.1.3   Subject content: Sounds

Sound effects may be created in order to provide reusable sounds, or they may be a by-product of some other recording. They may be described from the point of view of the person who created the recording, or from the point of view of possible users of the collection. The name of the creator may also give clues to subject content. While the number of sound files on the Internet is growing rapidly, the level of subject content analysis is very basic. The best options include the Lycos search engine and the *DB2 Audio Extender*.[1] When a user selects the 'Sounds' option on Lycos, he or she can then search on specific words or phrases which occur in the titles of sound files. For sample searches on topics such as 'sea' or 'happy', this gives very variable results, as items are retrieved just because the search word occurs in their titles. An improvement is the menu option, which allows one to select either 'Sound Effects' or 'Music Clips', which will be discussed in Section 8.5.3. *DB2 Audio Extender* will be described in Section 8.6.1.

8.5.2 Subject representation and controlled vocabularies: Thesauri and alphabetical subject terms

Thesauri for audio media should have three components:

1. a list of terms which deal with a very wide range of subject areas, including music and current affairs, as appropriate;
2. a list of terms which relate specifically to the physical medium, such as a discography;
3. a list of atmospheric terms which are specific to the medium, for example type of sounds for audio items.

The subject authority list at the BBC Sound Archive, which is based on the collections, includes:

- subjects;
- geographical names;
- names of organizations;
- musical forms;
- commemorative days;
- names of people;
- subdivisions which are used with each country;
- index terms which have the name of a country or nationality as subdivisions.

Where there is local atmosphere, the term 'Atmosphere' is used with an appropriate subdivision. A sample section of the subject authority list is shown in Figure 8.5. In reality, this is a mixture of a thesaurus, a subject headings list, a classification scheme and a rotated index. The BBC Sound Effects catalogue of compact disks uses similar subject headings:

- Crowds: Interior: Boos;
- Crowds: Interior: Chatter;
- Crowds: Interior: Cheering;
- Crowds: Interior: Laughter;
- Crowds: Interior: Sympathetic 'Aaahs';
- Crowds: Public House: *See* Public houses, crowds;
- Crowds reaction: Exterior;
- Crowds: Spain;
- Crows;
- Crying: *See* Babies;
- Cuckoos.

Dossers   USE - Tramps
Dotterels
       BT Birds/Natural History: Birds
Double Basses
       BT Musical Instruments
       NT Occupations: Instrumentalist: Double Bass
Double Summer Time   USE - Time
Down and Out
       RT Beggars/Homeless People/Tramps/Vagrancy
Down, Co.
       BT Ireland, Northern
Down's Syndrome
       BT Mental Health
       RT Children: Handicapped/Disabled
Dowsing
       RT Water
Dr. Barnardo's   USE - Barnardos
Drag Artists   USE - Imitations/Occupations: Actor
Drama SEE - subdivisions listed below
       BT Arts, (The)
       RT Entertainment/Mummers' Play
Drama: Actors and Playwrights
        <u>Scope</u> For talks by a second party
        NT . . .
        RT . . .
Drama: Amateur
       . . .
Drama: Community
       . . .
Drama: Experimental
Drama: Farce
Drama: Historical
Drama: History and Criticism
       . . .
Subdivisions for Countries:
Actuality (atmosphere)
Agriculture
Customs
Defence
Economy
Education
Elections
Foreign Policy and Relations
History
Immigration and Emigration
National Anthems
Nationals Abroad
Parliament
Politics and Government
Security
Social Conditions
Space

Figure 8.5   Sample subject authority list used at the BBC Sound Archive

Terms with Country/Nationality as Subdivisions:
Arts national
Asian community
Black community
Broadcasting
Carols national
Choirs
Cinema national
Communism
Community singing
Dances: folk and national
Drama national
Exhibitions
Festivals
Folk customs
Funeral rites and ceremonies
Hymns national
Industry
Jews
Literature national
Music national
National characteristics
Orchestras
Police
Race relations
Railways
Religion
Republican Party
Roads
Royal Family
Royal Tours
Schools
Television
World War I
World War II
Musical instruments:
Accordions
Bagpipes
Bells
Castanets
Clarinets
Drums
Flutes
Guitars
Harps
Horns
Lutes
Oboes
Pipes
Rattles
Tamburas
Trumpets
Violins
Xylophones
Zithers

Figure 8.5   continued

8.5.3   Subject representation and controlled vocabularies: Classification

Many alternative approaches are used to arrange collections of audio recordings in libraries and music centres. The most common arrangement seems to be by accession number, with various subject-based arrangements, including modifications of Dewey, also quite popular. It is generally accepted that no single arrangement will meet the needs of all users.

For music, the usual question is whether the primary arrangement should be by form or medium. The major classification schemes have chosen the latter, and so have brought together all works for the voice, those for individual instruments, for orchestra, etc. If there was a division by form, all sonatas would be brought together, be they for piano, organ, unaccompanied violin, two clarinets, or whatever. Significant music classification schemes include the Dewey Decimal Classification (Class 780), the Library of Congress – Classification (Class M – Music) (1978), the Dickinson Classification (Bradley, 1968), and the *British Catalogue of Music Classification* (Coates, 1960). Further details of these schemes may be found in textbooks on music librarianship, such as Bryant (1985). The British Classification of Music (BCM) is particularly interesting, as it is a faceted scheme, where the main facets for instrumental music are performer, form of composition, and character of composition. It arranges material primarily by medium. For books on music, there are more facets to be considered. Here, the order in which the facets are listed is composer, performer, form, elements of music, character, technique, and common subdivision. As the composer facet takes priority, any volume dealing with any aspect of the music of a single composer will be classed under that composer. Scattering will increase as one moves through the list of facets, so it will be difficult to retrieve material dealing with a common subdivision, for example a particular country.

Many music collections tend to develop their own local classified arrangements, generally under such broad headings as 'orchestral', 'chamber', 'instrumental', and 'vocal' works, subdivided again as far as is considered necessary according to the size of the stock. Orchestral music will need special subsections for symphonies and concertos, and ballet music and overtures may be separated from the general sequence. Vocal and choral music will also need a number of subdivisions.

The anthology type of disk which includes works by more than one composer presents problems. One may file these miscellanies under a heading such as 'collections', or under the highest common factor – the artist (particularly if a singer), the instrument (organ, guitar), the country from which the music originated (England, Germany), or even the title given to the collection by the issuing company. Although this type of arrangement separates a collection's symphonies and other genres from one another, the plan may suit the majority of users. The Alpha-Numeric System for Classification of Recordings (ANSCR) is based on whether the first item on a disk occupies more than a third of the side; if so, the class mark is decided by that work. The ANSCR class mark comprises four lines: the first of the four terms shows the musical genre. There are 23 main classes for orchestral music, solo instrumental music, popular music, etc.

Another helpful arrangement for music is by alphabetical sequence of composers' names, although it isn't true classification. Under such a scheme, virtually all records of a composer's music, be they orchestral, chamber music, piano pieces or songs, etc., will be found together on the shelves, as will most works by other composers in their appropriate places. Another option is chronological arrangement by period, with further subdivision as needed.

Langridge (1970) has proposed two schemes for a collection of jazz disks. One arrangement uses style as its basis, with such headings as traditional, mainstream, avant-garde, blues and the like. There are some subdivisions for period. The second scheme is basically chronological, with further subdivisions into different types of music.

When a user of the Lycos search directory selects the 'Sound Effects' or 'Music Clips' option, he or she is presented with a menu of further choices, based on the following simple classification:

1. 'Sound Effects' is subdivided into 'Animals, House, Instruments, Nature, People, Phrases, SFX Misc, Short FX, Special FX, Transportation, and Voices'.
2. Each of these is further subdivided by file type, for example .RA, .MAC and .WAV.
3. There is further subject subdivision, for example the Instruments category is subdivided into 'Electric, Horns, Misc, Bells, Cymbals, Strings, Drums, Perc-Misc, Winds'.

A similar hierarchy results for 'Music Clips', as follows:

1. The first level of division gives 'Ambient, Blues, Businessy, Classical, Contemporary, Electronic, Hawaiian, Instrumental, Jazz, Latin, Mystic, Natural, New Age, Pop, Rhythm, Rock, Symphonic, Techno, Traditional, Urban Contemporary, Vocal Stylings'.
2. Each of these is divided by format into .RA, .MAC, and .WAV.
3. Once the user selects a category, for example 'Urban WAV files', he or she is given a choice of alphanumeric and meaningless file names, such as ny0004.

These examples show a rudimentary but effective classification scheme which has good potential for future development.

8.6   Representation of audio items in computer storage

8.6.1   Sounds

Sound is an inherently analogue medium: the human ear responds to a moving column of air that vibrates the ear drum. Most modern recording media transform the analogue signal into a digital signal, which can then be handled like any other piece of data. The basis of digitization is that the continuously varying sound waveform – the electrical version of the vibrating microphone diaphragm – is sampled. Texts on producing multimedia, such as England and Finney (1996), provide good technical background on these characteristics of audio files. Digitization also enables analysis and retrieval of the audio items based on their technical characteristics, such as length, loudness and pitch.

Relational datafiles and object-oriented databases are widely used for managing surrogates and original audio files on computer. Thomas (1992) has devoted considerable effort to the development of a complex relational database structure using *Advanced Revelation* (A-REV) for the catalogue of holdings at the Rodgers and Hammerstein Archives at New York Public Library. His system provides for cataloguing, searching and retrieval of information about the special collection portion of the archives (approximately 30 000 of the archive's 500 000 recordings, which are in a wide range of formats). Thomas's (1992) data model, which is shown in Figure 8.1, distinguishes between surrogates of the physical item, the logical item, and the various collections in the archives. His excellent analysis shows the limitations of a simple file structure for representing the complex structure of audio archives, where there is a need for printed lists, and online searching for complex audio items. Options considered by Thomas include surrogates in non-relational files, based on the 'work' (e.g. a number in a concert, say Brahms Symphony No. 1), on the physical item (e.g. the reel of tape) or on the event (e.g. the concert programme or the published CD). None of these met all the requirements satisfactorily, until the relational database was developed, with the following structure:

> The relational database ... was one in which collection-level data would be stored in a collection file, discographic data would be stored in another file, and physical item data would be stored in a third file ... Links would be maintained between the levels to identify which records in each data file belong to one another. These links would be reciprocal, so that, for example, the collection ID would be stored in each discographic item record while the discographic ID would be stored in a collection list. (Thomas, 1992, p. 27).

The CADENSA catalogue at the National Sound Archive, which is shown in Figure 8.2, is also based on a relational structure: the Short Title field links the works and recordings files; the accession number links the recordings and the products file.

There are a number of significant commercial developments for retrieval of audio data from computer databases, of which IBM's *QBIC* and *DB2 Audio Extender* are the most significant.[2] The latter enables users to:

- import and export audio clips and their attributes to and from a *DB2* database;
- select and update audio clips based on audio attributes such as number of channels, length and sampling rate;
- query audio clips based on audio attributes or other added data; the former include the format of the audio and the date or time it was last updated; the latter might be name, number or description;
- play audio clips.

The *Audio Extender* supports a variety of files formats, such as .WAV and MIDI, and enables retrieval based on the technical characteristics inherent in the file format in question. It does not provide any 'intelligent' analysis of the audio content of the file.

SoundWorks is an object-oriented database which enables users to manipulate sound interactively through a graphical user interface. The developers' primary goal is to provide standard sound editing features like splicing, looping and mixing. In so doing, they provide operations to modify the amplitude, pitch and duration of sounds. To assist in modifying sounds and creating new ones, they predefine sounds which may also be used as a basis for retrieval. Another experimental system for retrieving speech documents uses an indexing vocabulary which consists of features that are easily recognizable by speech recognition methods. Philip et al. (1987a, 1987b, 1988, 1991) and Peters et al. (1989) have reported successful experiments in speech interfaces to online databases; the same technology could be applied to the content of audio databases.

There have been some interesting experiments providing remote access to digitized holdings of European sound archives for users in various public and academic libraries in Europe, with funding from the EU. These include the Jukebox and Paragon projects, with the latter being particularly ambitious. Both projects involved co-operation between three partner archives, the National Sound Archive (UK), Discoteca di Stato (Italy) and the State and Media Archive (Denmark). Jukebox offered online access to 600 compressed and digitized tracks selected from the holdings of the three participating archives. Paragon extended this to the complete catalogues of the three institutions, with a wider user base. The related HARMONICA project, which deals with music, will be described in Section 8.6.2. Details of these projects are available on the National Sound Archive Web page.[3]

8.6.2 Music

There seems to be considerable potential for the exploitation of the retrieval capability of the symbol for sharp (#) in music notation which occur in the uniform title portions of bibliographic and authority records. In particular, the sharp symbol possesses retrieval capability, as it exists in the MARC character set as the pound sign (£). The flat symbol, however, has virtually no retrieval capability, because it does not have an ASCII value of its own, and must be converted in order to exist as another type of character.

Many schemes have been developed which do not use traditional music notation. These systems assign symbols, such as letters of the alphabet, to represent each note. All of these schemes have built into their systems a means of telling the exact pitch of a note and its relationship to middle C. The LaRue system is based solely on typewriter symbols. It assigns numbers to pitches (but not to each half-step) so that the pitches of the middle octave are represented by the numbers 1–7, and other octaves are shown by placing an appropriate number of apostrophes or commas before the numeral. It is weak in its indication of rhythm. A representation of music may involve the storage of some or all of either its noted score or its recorded performance, and includes the possibility of a completely electronic generation of a musical item, which may therefore be recorded without the benefit of either score or performance.

The most widespread system for representing written music is the Common-Practice Music Notation (CMN). It has both iconic and symbolic characteristics, in that many of its elements are images that are analogous to an audible representation of a piece, yet at the same time these may have symbolic meanings which require translation. The relative height of a note on the musical staff reflects the pitch level, while the horizontal position reflects the order in which the notes are read. These are both iconic. However, there are many additional ambiguities and structural relationships within the notation which determine the ultimate musical work. A major limitation of CMN is the near absence of any notation for the quality of sounds – their timbre – beyond verbal instructions placed directly in the score, for example the Italian words *forte* and *piano*.

McLane's (1996) article reviews systems for computer coding of music, which are known as Music Representation Languages (MRLs). They include:

- alphanumeric music representations, such as the 'Plaine and Easie Code System for Musicke', which is the basis for the RISM database, including musical incipits;
- structured music representation;
- representations for the composition of music, for example MIDI, which is used in many commercial applications;
- Standard Music Description Language (SMDL/Hytime).

All these representations provide at some level for information retrieval in response to specific user needs, but none provides a complete music information system. They are all incomplete because either acoustic or notated information is sacrificed as a result of the difficulty of representing them together. The problem of representing structure and hierarchical relationships in the item – relationships necessary to search for musical meaning – is an additional factor. McLane also makes some interesting suggestions about the possibility of applying text-based techniques such as frequency of word occurrence, distance between words, and the relationships of frequency to rank, to musical analysis (McLane, 1996).

The EU-funded HARMONICA (Harmonised Access and Retrieval for Music-Oriented Networked Information – Concerted Action) programme extends the scope of Jukebox and Paragon as described in Section 8.6.1. It seeks to develop networked music services for libraries across Europe, focusing on the following issues: cataloguing standards, copyright, networking specifications, standards for encoding scores and for digital compression, user interfaces and the fostering of co-operation. It is expected to result in more effective and better-integrated public access to digital music for users in all libraries. Details of HARMONICA are available on the National Sound Archive Web page.[4]

8.7 Summary

The development of audio retrieval systems lags behind those for visual information for a number of reasons:

* the time required to listen to the material in order to make decisions on subject content;
* the availability of words in many audio items enables text-based solutions to be used;
* the extreme difficulty of analysing and representing subject content consistently for items which don't contain words;
* the variations in surrogate structure between items which contain words, music and sounds;
* the lower public profile of the audio medium.

It is anticipated that this area will develop dramatically in the next decade. Research on computer analysis and representation of speech and music will make a major contribution. Increased availability of audio collections on the Internet will encourage the development of retrieval procedures. Commitment to access to information for the visually impaired will require fuller exploitation of audio resources.

For the broadcast news agency described in Section 1.8, the following approach is recommended:

- consistent creation of surrogates based on existing items in various formats;
- conversion of stock to digitized form on a planned basis;
- active monitoring of technological developments resulting from research on analysis and retrieval of digitized audio.

8.8   Notes

1   Lycos pictures and sounds: ⟨http://www.lycos.com/picturethis.html⟩. *DB2 Audio Extender*: ⟨http://www.software.ibm.com/data/db2/extenders/audio.htm⟩.

2   *DB2 Audio Extender*: ⟨http://www.software.ibm.com/data/db2/extenders/audio.htm⟩. *IBM QBIC*: ⟨http://wwwqbic.almaden.ibm.com/stage/index.html⟩.

3   NSA online services: ⟨http://www.bl.uk/collections/sound-archive/cadensa.html⟩.

4   NSA online services: ⟨http://www.bl.uk/collections/sound-archive/cadensa.html⟩.

8.9   References and further reading

Bradley, Carol June (1968), *The Dickinson Classification: A Cataloguing and Classification Manual for Music*, Carlisle, PA: Carlisle Books.

Bradley, Carol June (ed.) (1973) *Reader in Music Librarianship*, Washington, DC: Indian Head Editions.

Bryant, Eric Thomas (1985) *Music Librarianship: A Practical Guide* (2nd edn), London: The Scarecrow Press.

Coates, E.J. (ed.) (1960) *The British Catalogue of Music Classification*, London: British National Bibliography.

Cook, Michael and Proctor, Margaret (1989) *A MAD User Guide: How to Set About Listing Archives – A Short Explanatory Guide to the Rules and Recommendations of the Manual of Archival Description*, Aldershot: Gower.

Cook, Michael and Proctor, Margaret (1990) *A Manual of Archival Description* (2nd edn), Aldershot: Gower.

England, Elaine and Finney, Andy (1996) *Managing Multimedia*, Harlow, UK: Addison-Wesley.

Gorman, Michael and Winkler, Paul (eds) (1993) *Anglo-American Cataloguing Rules* (2nd edn), prepared under the direction of the Joint Steering Committee for Revision of AACR, Chicago, Ottawa and London: American Library Association, Canadian Library Association and Library Association. (Note: *The Anglo-American Catalogu-*

ing Rules (2nd edn, 1998 revision) is published jointly by the same publishers in paperback and CD-ROM.)

Hine, Sally K. (1992) 'Sound effects on compact disc', *Audiovisual Librarian*, **18**(1), 39–41.

Holzberlein, Deanne (1988) *Cataloging Sound Recordings: A Manual with Examples*, New York: Haworth Press.

IFLA (1991) *ISBD (PM): International Standard Bibliographic Description for Printed Music* (2nd edn), Munich: Saur.

Jones, Malcolm (1979) *Music Librarianship*, London: Bingley.

Langridge, Derek (1970) *Your Jazz Collection*, London: Bingley.

Library of Congress. Subject Cataloguing Division (1978), *Classification: Class M – Music and Books on Music* (3rd edn), Washington, DC: Library of Congress.

McLane, Alexander (1996) 'Music as information', *Annual Review of Information Science and Technology*, 31, 225–62.

Panofsky, Erwin (1962) *Studies in Iconology: Humanistic Themes in the Art of the Renaissance*, New York: Harper and Row.

Peters, B.F. et al. (1989), 'Online searching using speech as a man/machine interface', *Information Processing and Management*, **25**(4), 391–406.

Philip, George and Young, E.S. (1987a), 'Man–machine interaction by voice: Developments in speech technology. Part I: The state-of-the-art', *Journal of Information Science*, **13**(1), 3–14.

Philip, George and Young, E.S. (1987b), 'Man–machine interaction by voice: Developments in speech technology. Part II: General applications, and potential applications in libraries and information services', *Journal of Information Science*, **13**(1), 15–23.

Philip, George, Smith, F.J. and Crookes, D. (1988), 'Voice input/output interface for online searching: Some design and human factor considerations', *Journal of Information Science*, **14**(2), 93–8.

Philip, George et al. (1991), 'Design and evaluation of a speech interface for remote database searching', *Journal of Information Science*, **17**(1), 21–36.

Sadie, Stanley (ed.) (1980) *The New Grove Dictionary of Music and Musicians*, London: Macmillan.

Seibert, Don C. and Herrold Jr, Charles M. (1986) 'Uniform titles for music under AACR2 and its predecessors: The problems and possibilities of developing a user-friendly repertoire' in Berman, Sanford (ed.) *Cataloguing Special Materials*, Phoenix, AZ: The Oryz Press, 133–58.

Thomas, David H. (1992) *Archival Information Processing for Sound Technology: The Design of a Database for the Rodgers and Hammerstein Archives of Recorded Sound*, Technical Report 21, Canton, MA: MLA.

Ward, Alan (1990) *A Manual of Sound Archive Administration*, Aldershot: Gower.

Wursten, Richard B. (ed.) (1990) *In Celebration of Revised 780: Music in the Dewey Decimal Classification, Edition 20*, Technical Report 19, Canton, MA: MLA.

Chapter 9

The future

9.1   Introduction

This chapter discusses likely future developments in hardware, software and networking for multimedia databases. Multimedia computers, which allow users to access multimedia presentations and, with a few additional peripherals, to create their own presentations, are now commonplace. In the future, the expectation is that microprocessor power and storage capacity will increase, while costs remain static or drop. In parallel, communications costs will fall, or the transmission capacity provided for a fixed cost will grow dramatically. It will become technically and financially realistic to create and use many local and remote multimedia systems. However, various non-technical issues will grow in complexity in the future, including subject retrieval, copyright clearance, user profiling and information overload.

The ability to create multimedia presentations also generates a demand for sources of components, or assets, which make up the presentations. These may be created from scratch for certain purposes, but there will be many circumstances where a multimedia creator will lack either the time, the talent or the motivation to create an item from scratch. The creator may already possess the asset in his or her own collection, or may decide to obtain it from a media library. Clip art, backgrounds, stock photos, music libraries, sound effects, animations and so on are publicly available, for a fee which compensates the copyright holder. It is crucial that potential users can identify appropriate sources and use them in their own work.

There will also be considerable convergence of technologies: for example, television and radio broadcasting, digital storage media and International Standard Digital Network (ISDN) for communications. The distinctions between television and computers will continue to blur until we have generic media. However, in practical terms, it is still likely that workstations will be targeted at particular types of use, such as entertainment, education or work, otherwise family fights over the remote control for the television would extend into whether the multi-purpose box should be used as a television, a computer, a telephone, a fax machine or a science fiction 'dream machine' for the evening!

9.2   Networked access

Multimedia came into existence as a stand-alone system, with a culture of purpose-built workstations, some of which had analogue components. As the transition to digital multimedia occurred, it became easier to retrieve and use multimedia via networks. A search may be executed simultaneously on multiple databases on different servers using a protocol known as Z39.50: for example, a search engine can scan a whole range of different sites, and return consolidated results. The Z39.50 protocol overcomes the difficulties of different search procedures on the different sites. This enables simultaneous searching of multimedia products, but with the lowest common denominator of search facilities.

Most readers will be familiar with the Internet as an international computer network based on client–server architecture which enables users who make a connection to the Internet to access any other registered computer on the Internet. The World Wide Web is a by-product of the Internet which enables browser access via hypertext links.

The term 'intranet' evolved to describe networked systems within an organization which use Internet technology. Interesting issues arise regarding how information resources are distributed and accessed within an organization. Clearly, one major advantage is that within many organizations' structures, media formats have created boundaries, with individual departments corresponding to media such as sound, still images, moving images and text. Intranets facilitate access to these media regardless of their physical departmental location.

Client–server architecture is the basis of much computer-to-computer communication, including both the Internet and intranets. The local workstation is considered a client; the remote computer system is considered a server; software and processing are distributed as appropriate between the client and the server. The client and the server may be at opposite sides of the globe, or they may be on different logical partitions of one workstation. The client may play a very minor role, leaving most of the work to the server (corresponding to a very centralized system), or it may take on a lot of activities (corresponding to a very distributed system). For the Internet, the client is usually the user's workstation with browser software (e.g. *Netscape*); the server is the Internet site accessed. In the client–server setting, the user may need special viewing/listening software on the local workstation for audio or image files, but it is usually possible to download this for local installation. In this situation, the search engine and the database still reside on the remote server.

Increasing network bandwidth facilitates transmission of multimedia data. The data storage problems caused particularly by moving image, and to a lesser extent by still image and audio, also apply to transmission. The need for synchronization of components also becomes a problem for multimedia, especially for live television broadcasts. ISDN, which is rapidly achieving international acceptance and implementation, brings a range of data sources into each home using one high-capacity cable. This channel handles voice, data, television, radio and multimedia. At present, we have high-speed connections for the central hubs of networks, with the quality and speed decreasing as one moves to more local applications, such as a campus Local Area Network (LAN) or phone lines to an individual's home.

9.3　Subject retrieval on the Internet

The variety and quality of search tools on the Internet is growing almost as rapidly as the number of sites and users. These search tools are described in detail in various print and electronic sources (e.g. Winship and McNab, 1996).

The current level of enthusiasm for the Internet is based on the many strengths associated with the new medium. These include the range and diversity of information resources, media formats and search facilities, and the retrieval of source information, not just references to it. The availability of search engines with sophisticated facilities (e.g. ranked output, proximity searching, etc.) and the multiplicity of hypertext links present the user with a superb range of alternative approaches to searching. The accessibility of items once they are added to a site as a result of automatic scanning by search engines ensures an extremely up-to-date information source.

Unfortunately, the enthusiasm often ignores many of the associated weaknesses. These include the poor quality control for information resources, and the huge volumes of information, which cause information overload. Access and retrieval is mainly based on automatic analysis of content, so it is very dependent on quality and quantity of the creators' descriptions, many of whom are not concerned with consistent and thorough subject analysis and representation. The different levels of depth of analysis result in inappropriate treatment of some resources: the home pages of the Library of Congress, of a refereed full-text electronic journal and of an individual first-year student all have the same status. There are problems with large items which consist of many separate parts, for example the Library of Congress American Variety Stage Audio Sampler page shown in Figure 8.4. Transcripts of many totally unconnected sound recordings on the same Web page will result in retrieval of irrelevant items: for example, searching on 'Desmond' and 'Arkansas' will find the page in Figure 8.4. The AltaVista 'near' search facility overcomes this, by only retrieving items if specified terms are adjacent in the text. The predominance of the English language restricts access to text and other resources in other languages, in spite of the translation facility on AltaVista.[1] The poorly defined and geographically scattered potential user populations for a resource make it difficult to link retrieval to user needs.

A key aspect of the development of the Internet as a successful commercial enterprise is access to its resources. There is no point creating pages which have no links to related pages, have no subject index terms assigned, are not scanned by search engines, and even if they are, have such meaningless titles and source information that they cannot be found. Having a Web page is an essential marketing and promotional tool – if it can be found. Otherwise, it is useless. At the time of writing, it is not possible to find home pages of individuals or institutions by name or location with any degree of confidence, let alone carry out more semantically challenging searches.

Subject retrieval is achieved in three ways. Pre-coordinated retrieval is provided by the hierarchical structures created by individuals and organizations (e.g. BUBL or Yahoo! directories). Post-coordinate retrieval corresponds to automatic extraction of words and other retrieval keys from information items. Originally, these systems were word-based, with associated limitations, but developments such as IBM's *DB2 Extenders* and *Ultimedia* have extended the applications to a wider range of media (images, audio, video, etc.). Multi-coordinate retrieval occurs through the hypertext links, created on an individual, unstructured basis.

The difficulties of analysing and representing subject are exacerbated for the Internet, for the following reasons:

- The information is internationalized, so that local and national preconceptions and intuitive understanding of meaning and context no longer apply.
- The information is presented independently of a hierarchical classification structure, such as that imposed by Dewey classification, or a faculty system in a university.
- It is more difficult to analyse and represent the subject content of visual, audio and integrated multimedia items.
- Since the potential user population corresponds to anyone with access to a Web browser, the information retrieval tools are no longer the property of a local user group.

Enhancement of subject retrieval on the Internet will continue to be an active area of research in the future. Some of the significant themes which have been identified earlier in this book include:

- the development of new metadata standards such as Dublin Core, which facilitate automatic indexing of Web pages based on high-quality human analysis of content, including assignment of controlled vocabulary terms from classification schemes, subject headings lists and thesauri (see Section 4.7.4) (Weibel, 1997);
- initiatives to standardize resource names and to manage changes in locations of Internet-based resources, such as Uniform Resource Names (URNs) and Persistent Uniform Resource Locators (PURLs) (see Section 4.7.4) (Schwartz, R., 1997);
- exploitation of traditional subject content tools in the use of filtering gateways and pathways, such as OCLC's NetFirst database (see Section 5.3.4) (Vizine-Goetz, 1997); ultimately this should result in the ability to individualize the description and organization of information items at local level, and to provide automatic filtering from newsgroups (e.g. the Borges project);
- increased sophistication of systems for automatic content analysis (e.g. QBIC – see Section 6.4.6).

9.4 User profiling

It is clear that deciding on meaning for visual, audio and multimedia information items is even more subjective and open to interpretation than for textual items. This subjectively may be linked to various characteristics of the users of these items. Possibly relevant user characteristics include personality types, gender, cultural experiences, education, hobbies and interests. There is a need for filtering gateways tailored to the needs of specific groups of users, which subdivide search results based on item criteria such as novice/expert, theoretical/experimental, quantitative/qualitative, survey research/case studies. The effect would be similar to that on the Northern Light search engine, where the results may be subdivided into Custom Search Folders by criteria such as type of site, location, language, etc.[2]

The use of psychological testing methods, such as personal construct theory and semantic differential, also enable user criteria for assessing retrieved items to be identified. They could be useful as an additional filtering level applied to search results for multimedia information. Relevance feedback may be used in conjunction with some form of user modelling to improve search performance. Probabilistic retrieval facilitates this interaction, and users must be willing to view, or listen to, retrieved items in order to assess their usefulness and provide feedback. Spink and Losee (1996) identify two types of feedback models:

- cybernetic (traditional, automatic, mechanical);

- social (subjective, situational, cognitive, interactive).

One of the biggest frustrations of the multimedia and Internet revolution is the deluge of information which is available and which is retrieved in response to a request. The problem is not finding some information; the real challenge is filtering out the small amount of gold from the buckets of dross. User profiling and relevance feedback should help the system match user interests more closely.

A futuristic scenario envisages an electronic multimedia assistant which manages internal and external information in a completely intelligent way for the busy executive. Not only does this system respond to questions posed by its user, it also anticipates his or her needs by providing a current awareness service based on earlier expressions of interest. It provides an intelligent interface between diary, e-mail and telephone systems, electronic conferencing and multimedia item review, local and remote information sources (intranet and Internet). For this adviser to operate, it requires user needs to be defined at two levels:

1. very formal, based on keywords, names, dates, etc.;
2. more flexible, based on a comprehensive user profile.

In each mode, it should be capable of learning based on experience, and applying this learning subsequently. For these systems to work sufficiently, it must be possible to articulate the information needs of the user following standard formulae, and to apply sophisticated search procedures, such as have been described in earlier chapters, to the multimedia items. The access points would be those discussed in earlier chapters, with additions such as date information (date added, date required), links to names of specific projects, and calendar and personal information management data. What results is a much more intelligent version of the current generation of personal information advisers – *Sidekick* or *LotusNotes*, or their equivalent – with links to associated files. The apparent intelligence is founded in the principles of organization of information and data structures outlined in this book.

9.5   Data issues

A key issue in the development of multimedia is the digitization of older material. Problems of cost, storage capacity and quality arise when converting to digital form. Data compression algorithms save storage capacity and transmission time, but may have a negative effect on the quality and speed of retrieval. Many significant standards have developed for specific media – communications, compression, etc. – but there is no unique standard for digital multimedia data. Copyright of multimedia items continues to be a problem, especially in a networked environment. Conversion of material from one form to another, and incorporation in more complex products, present legal difficulties for intellectual property which are outside the scope of this book.

9.6 Information-seeking in the future

Candy Schwartz, in her contribution to a panel discussion at the 1996 American Society for Information Science Conference (Schwartz, C. et al., 1997), identifies the recent and expected future changes in three simple information-seeking activities:

- when the next episode of a favourite television programme will be screened;
- planning a trip overseas;
- researching a topic thoroughly for a paper in Library and Information Science.

A modified version of Schwartz's scenario for the year 2010 will now be presented.

The television programme, or its equivalent, will be distributed digitally. The television scheduler will recommend a viewing sequence which recognizes the viewers' commitments for the week, and preferences for particular types of programme at particular times. It will also identify other similar programmes which may be of interest, and build these into a planned personalized viewing menu. There may be use of a gateway which contains television and other media reviews, and comments by other viewers.

The planning of the trip will be facilitated by online booking and payment systems, and by access to hotel information. This would include visual and audio data about buildings, facilities, locations etc. It would also link to maps of locations, which would link in turn to local transport information. Of course, one could question whether the trip would really be necessary at all, given virtual reality travel, electronic conferencing, etc. Let's hope it is!

For the formal research topic, a user would access the digital gateways which specialize in this subject area and which reflect his or her perspective. The user would set up electronic conferences, which would be integrated into a local, flexible database on his or her own workstation. Schwartz also identifies the continuing need for standards for surrogates:

> Surrogation will still be needed and, perhaps, more so both for speed of analysis, for browsing, for selection purposes and also, of course, for non-digitizable objects. (Schwartz, C. et al., 1997, p. 17)

9.7 Virtual reality

The concept of virtual reality has been implemented successfully in video arcade games and in specialized applications like training systems for learner drivers, doctors or astronauts. The user interacts with the computer system in a multi-sensory way as he or she is seated in a purpose-built chair with sensors in various strategic positions. He or she wears special headphones, goggles, and gloves that sense motions and gestures so that he or she can move about and manipulate virtual objects. The user participates in the multimedia presentation very fully, gaining the impression that he or she is part of the experience rather, than a mere spectator or listener. Any actions the user takes have an immediate effect: if the user moves as if to walk uphill to the left, the view he or she sees changes accordingly. If the user flinches in response to the music, either the volume is lowered, or an option to change the disk is presented.

Spring (1992) discusses alternative models for virtual reality. He suggests that virtual reality may be seen as one of four things: tool, art, interface or environment. Two different levels of organization of information arise for virtual reality systems. All of these systems will draw on multiple databases of source data, including geometric and spatial coordinates. This data has to be organized in an appropriate way using the criteria presented earlier in this book. This corresponds to the tool model of virtual reality. If virtual reality is considered as an interface, it may incorporate a formal information retrieval metaphor: a book, filing cabinet or library. The system will then allow users to browse, retrieve and use the information items. Virtual reality has some role in multimedia information retrieval, but it will always be 'virtual', and will never be a complete solution to the organization of information. The reality of the complexity of human communication systems is not susceptible to virtualization.[3]

However, aspects of virtual reality have tremendous potential in facilitating access to information resources by the disabled. The ability to convert from one digital form to another is of tremendous benefit to users with a visual or aural impairment. Clearly, this conversion must be possible for the operating systems, search and ancillary software and surrogates, as well as the data itself. Thus digital conversion between media is required for each of the following:

* access points – multi-sensory thesauri which links icons, words and sounds;
* search mechanisms and options;
* presentation of search results;
* retrieval of original items.

9.8   Summary

There will be scope for three levels of organization of multimedia information items in the future:

- greater emphasis on quality surrogate creation by the user, with a possible slogan, 'Best described, first found';
- automatic processing of multimedia items and surrogates, with automatic content analysis based on pattern recognition;
- human content analysis, especially more interpretative levels of analysis for specialist subject areas.

The following research areas will also have a significant effect on future multimedia information systems:

- psychological experiments which group users into categories based on the characteristics which they use to assign subject meaning;
- reflection of these categories in gateway systems and local browsers;
- incorporation of user feedback into search facilities;
- enhancement of the surrogate components or the content of information resources.

9.9   Notes

[1]   AltaVista: main page: ⟨http://www.altavista.digital.com/⟩.
[2]   Northern Light search: ⟨http://www.northernlight.com⟩.
[3]   Weiser, Mark, *The computer for the 21st century: Scientific American* Ubicomp Paper after editing: ⟨http://www.ubiq.com/hypertext/weiser/SciAmDraft3.html⟩.

9.10   References and further reading

Burke, Mary A. (1997) 'Meaning, multimedia and the Internet: Subject retrieval challenges and solutions', in Beaulieu, Micheline et al. (eds) *Library and Information Studies: Research and Professional Practice: Proceedings of the Second British Nordic Conference on Library and Information Studies, Queen Margaret College, Edinburgh, 1997*, London: Taylor Graham, 61–78.

Efthimiadis, Efthimis N. (1996) 'Query expansion', in Williams, Martha E. (ed.) *Annual Review of Information Science and Technology*, 31, Medford, NJ: Information Today, 121–87.

Ellis, David (1996) *New Horizons in Information Retrieval* (2nd edn), London: Library Association.

Oddy, Pat (1996) *Future Libraries, Future Catalogues*, London: Library Association.

Schwartz, Candy et al. (1997) 'Reflections on our future', *Bulletin of the American Society for Information Science*, December/January, 16–23.

Schwartz, Ray (1997) 'Uniform Resource Identifiers and the effort to bring "bibliographic control" to the web: An overview of current progress', *Bulletin of the American Society for Information Science*, **24**(1), 12–14.

Spink, Amanda and Losee, Robert (1996) 'Feedback in information retrieval' in Williams, Martha E. (ed.) *Annual Review of Information Science and Technology*, 31, Medford, NJ: Information Today, 33–81.

Spring, Michael (1992) ' "Being there", or models for virtual reality', in Stone, Susan and Buckland, Michael (eds) *Studies in Multimedia State-of-the-art Solutions in Multimedia and Hypertext: Proceedings of the 1991 Mid-Year Meeting of the American Society for Information Science, San Jose, CA, April 1991*, Medford, NJ: Learned Information, 237–53.

Stone, Susan and Buckland, Michael (eds) (1992) *Studies in Multimedia State-of-the-art Solutions in Multimedia and Hypertext: Proceedings of the 1991 Mid-Year Meeting of the American Society for Information Science, San Jose, CA, April 1991*, Medford, NJ: Learned Information.

Vizine-Goetz, Diane (1997) 'From book classification to knowledge organization: Improving Internet resource description and discovery', *Bulletin of the American Society for Information Science*, **24**(1), 24–7.

Weibel, Stuart (1997) 'The Dublin Core: A simple content description model for electronic resources', *Bulletin of the American Society for Information Science*, **24**(1), 9–11.

Winship, Ian and McNab, Alison (1996) *The Student's Guide to the Internet*, London: Library Association.

Woodward, Jeanette (1996) 'Cataloguing and classifying information resources on the Internet', in Williams, Martha E. (ed.) *Annual Review of Information Science and Technology*, 31, Medford, NJ: Information Today, 189–223.

Index